Rilke's *Duino Elegies*

Rilke's *Duino Elegies*

Cambridge Readings

edited by
Roger Paulin
and
Peter Hutchinson

Duckworth & Ariadne Press

First published in the UK in 1996 by
Gerald Duckworth & Co. Ltd.
The Old Piano Factory
48 Hoxton Square, London N1 6PB

First published in the USA in 1996 by
Ariadne Press
270 Goins Court
Riverside, CA 92507

A catalogue record for this book is available
from the British Library

ISBN 0 7156 2729 5 (Europe)
ISBN 1 57241 032 9 (USA)

Typeset by Peter Hutchinson
Printed in Great Britain by
Antony Rowe Ltd, Chippenham, Wiltshire

CONTENTS

LIST OF PLATES

PREFACE

Rainer Maria Rilke is usually claimed as the greatest poet writing in the German language in the twentieth century. His famous *Duino Elegies* were begun in 1912, while he was a guest at the castle of Duino, near Trieste, but war, turmoil, and uncertainty interrupted his original vision, and it was not until 1922 that the sequence was completed (in Muzot, Switzerland). It was first published in 1923.

The *Elegies* are Rilke's crowning achievement as a poet, and the last great poetic cycle of their kind in the German language. Their proximity to *The Waste Land* can be see in the message of crisis and cultural alienation that pervades both; as poetry, however, Rilke's hymnic verse draws creatively on a tradition of elegiac utterance in German while radically extending that language to the limits of its expressive powers in image and allusion.

The *Elegies* have a reputation for being 'difficult' — and rightly so. These ten introductory readings, given before general audiences by members, and former members, of the Faculty of Modern and Medieval Languages in Cambridge, seek both to come to terms with the problems of Rilke's language and imagery, and to bring out their poetic qualities. Commentary and text are interwoven in such a way that the reader is taken step by step into Rilke's world, while fresh English translations, inspired by the interpretative slant of the respective commentators, are provided for those unable to read the original. As close readings, the interpretations confront the reader with the great themes of Rilke's oeuvre — the existential loneliness of modern existence, the loss of the old religious congruities and certitudes — as they are revealed in the poetic evocation of angels, lovers, children, animals, heroes, the gamut of human emotions, in a cycle that moves gradually, but with growing confidence, to an acceptance of the limitations of human life and death. Above all, it is Rilke's poetic voice that is heard, and the volume concludes with the Elegies and translations in uninterrupted sequence.

Roger Paulin　　　　Peter Hutchinson

NOTES ON CONTRIBUTORS

The late PETER STERN was Professor of German at University College, London and Honorary Fellow of St John's College, Cambridge. His reading, revised for publication by Sheila Stern, reflects a lifelong interest in modern thought and poetry.

MICHAEL MINDEN is University Lecturer in German in the University of Cambridge and a Fellow of Jesus College. He has written extensively on twentieth-century German literature.

EDWARD TIMMS is Professor of German at the University of Sussex and a Life Fellow of Gonville and Caius College, Cambridge. He is an expert on modern Austrian literature.

PATRICK BOYDE is Serena Professor of Italian in the University of Cambridge and a Fellow of St John's College. An internationally known Dante scholar, he has never lost his early enthusiasm for Rilke.

NAOMI SEGAL, formerly College Lecturer at St John's College, Cambridge, is Professor of French at the University of Reading. She is author of the study *The Banal Object: Theme and Thematics in Proust, Rilke, Hofmannsthal and Sartre.*

PETER HUTCHINSON is University Lecturer in German in the University of Cambridge and a Fellow of Trinity Hall. He is a specialist in German post-war literature.

DAVID MIDGLEY is University Lecturer in German in the University of Cambridge and a Fellow of St John's College. He has published especially on European modernism.

TERRY LLEWELLYN is University Lecturer in German in the University of Cambridge and a Fellow of Christ's College. His interests in poetry extend from the Baroque to the twentieth century.

KAREN LEEDER, formerly University Assistant Lecturer in the University of Cambridge and Fellow of Emmanuel College, is Faculty Lecturer in German in the University of Oxford and a Fellow of New College. Her special field of interest is contemporary German poetry.

ROGER PAULIN is Schröder Professor of German in the University of Cambridge and a Fellow of Trinity College. He has written widely on German poetry of the eighteenth and nineteenth centuries.

WORKS OF REFERENCE, COMMON ABBREVIATIONS

The following list is not intended as a bibliography, but contains standard items that are referred to by at least one of the contributors. Publication details of these are not repeated within the notes. Two key abbreviations are used throughout. 'SW' for Rilke's *Sämtliche Werke*, edited in six volumes by Ernst Zinn; and 'DE' for the three volumes of "Materialien' collected by Ulrich Fülleborn and Manfred Engel. Roman and arabic numerals following these abbreviations refer to volume and page number respectively.

Bassermann, Dieter, *Der späte Rilke*, Essen and Freiburg im Br., 1948

Buddeberg, Else, *Rainer Marie Rilke. Eine innere Biographie*, Stuttgart, 1955

Butler, E. M., *Rainer Maria Rilke*, Cambridge, 1941

Cohn, Stephen, *Duino Elegies*, Manchester, 1989

De Man, Paul, *Allegories of Reading*, New Haven and London, 1979

Faber, Marion, *Angels of Daring: Tightrope Walker and Acrobat in Nietzsche, Kafka, Rilke and Thomas Mann*, Stuttgart, 1979

Fülleborn, Ulrich and Manfred Engel, *Materialien zu Rilkes* ***Duineser Elegien***, 3 vols, Frankfurt/Main, 1980-82

Görner, Rüdiger, (ed.), *Rainer Maria Rilke*, Darmstadt, 1987

Guardini, Romano, *Rainer Maria Rilkes Deutung des Daseins. Eine Interpretation der* ***Duineser Elegien***, Munich, 1953; also in English translation, *Rilke's Duino Elegies*, tr. K. G. Knight, London, 1961

Hamburger, Käte, *Rilke. Eine Einführung*, Stuttgart, 1976

Kippenberg, Katharina, *Rainer Maria Rilkes* ***Duineser Elegien*** *und* ***Sonette an Orpheus***, Frankfurt/Main, 1946

Komar, Kathleen L., *Transcending Angels. Rainer Maria Rilke's Duino Elegies*, Lincoln and London, 1987

Kreutz, Heinrich, *Rilkes* ***Duineser Elegien***, Munich, 1950

Leishman J. B. and Spender, Stephen, *Rainer Maria Rilke: Duino Elegies*, London, 1939

Meyer, Herman, 'Die Verwandlung des Sichtbaren', in Rüdiger Görner (ed.), *Rainer Maria Rilke*, Darmstadt, 1987, pp. 131-84

Rilke, Rainer Maria, *Sämtliche Werke*, ed. Ernst Zinn, 5 vols, Frankfurt/Main, 1955-66

___________, *Gesammelte Briefe in 6 Bänden*, ed. Ruth Sieber-Rilke and Carl Sieber, Leipig, 1938

___________, *Briefe aus Muzot 1921 bis 1926*, ed. Ruth Sieber-Rilke and Carl Sieber, Leipzig, 1937

___________—Lou Andreas-Salomé, *Briefwechsel*, Zurich and Wiesbaden, 1952

Schnack, Ingeborg, (ed.), *Rainer Maria Rilke. Leben und Werk im Bild*, Frankfurt/Main, 1973

Steiner, Jacob, *Rilkes* ***Duineser Elegien***, Berne and Munich, 1962, 1969

Subramanian, B., *Engel und Mensch*, Berne, Frankfurt/Main, New York, 1986

Ziolkowski, Theodore, *The Classical German Elegy 1795-1950*, Princeton, N. J., 1980

ELEGY ONE

The late Peter Stern, revised by Sheila Stern

In January 1912, Rainer Maria Rilke, then 36 years old, was staying as the guest of Marie, Princess Thurn und Taxis, in the castle of Duino, which stands on a rock above the Adriatic not far from Trieste. There he wrote down, in hours of strenuous, concentrated inspiration, the first of the ten elegies which form the summit of his life's work; it was a life wholly devoted to poetry. The cycle was completed exactly ten years later, in February 1922, in the little castle of Muzot in the Swiss Valais.

Elegies, traditionally composed in alternating hexameters and pentameters known as elegiac couplets or distichs, are poems expressing regret, usually for the loss of a loved one. Rilke's elegies are written for the most part in *vers libérés* — that is, verse which alludes to but has also liberated itself from a pre-existent form, here the elegiac distich.

This combination of allusion and liberation evokes in the German reader memories of a whole elegiac tradition, from Klopstock through Goethe[1] to Hölderlin and August von Platen. The double device of allusion and liberation is characteristic not only of the rhythmic scheme, but also of other important aspects of this cycle of poems. These are modern poems, poems concerned to describe, evaluate and perhaps overcome the condition of modernity. As such they proceed, as the rhythmic scheme proceeds, by a combination of allusions and liberations — allusions to what has gone before, liberations from it — indeed one might say that this double device provides one of the ways of defining modern poetry; it is in the nature of these elegies that they make a special issue of a common poetic practice.

There are ten of them, perhaps like arrows centripetally arranged, or like the landscapes and portraits of a family album, combining differences and overlapping family resemblances, or again like a collection of episodes from an anthropology or mythology of a new time. They all present different balances between descriptive detail, regret, criticism and jubilant affirmation, though on the whole the poignancy of regret prevails. For the modern age which is here evoked elegiacally is characterized by a pervading sense of deprivation, a lack of existential assurance, or again a lack of the certainty of faith. Hence the First Elegy begins, emphatically enough, not with an assertion, but in the conditional mode:

WER, wenn ich schriee, hörte mich denn aus der Engel
Ordnungen?

WHO, were I to call, would hear me from among the ranks
of angels?

We are apt to think of the anguish expressed in this first line and those that follow as resulting from a spiritual deprivation. That would be wrong. Rilke is highly critical of such contrasting distinctions as that between spiritual and material implied in such an interpretation. The deprivation he has in mind is similar to the kind expressed triumphantly in Friedrich Nietzsche's rhetoric of the death of God and the desuetude of faith, its discontinuance (the consequences of which Nietzsche foresaw as affecting every aspect of the age that was to follow on his own, the age of modernity).

WER, wenn ich schriee, hörte mich denn aus der Engel
Ordnungen? und gesetzt selbst, es nähme
einer mich plötzlich ans Herz : ich verginge von seinem
stärkeren Dasein. Denn das Schöne ist nichts
als des Schrecklichen Anfang, den wir noch grade ertragen,
und wir bewundern es so, weil es gelassen verschmäht,
uns zu zerstören. Ein jeder Engel ist schrecklich.
  Und so verhalt ich mich denn und verschlucke den Lockruf
dunkelen Schluchzens.

WHO, if I cried out, would hear me among the ranks
of the angels? and even if one of them suddenly
clasped me to his heart, I should die of his
stronger being. For beauty is nothing
but the very beginning of terror we're only just able to bear,
and its wonder for us is that it casually spares us
instead of destroying. Each one of the angels is terrible.
  And so I hold back, stifle the luring-call
of my dark sobbing.

The first thought in the poem is an appeal for help to 'the Angels.' All that we are told about them at this point is that they are, or have, a being stronger than ours — you notice a comparative, 'stärkeres Dasein', 'stronger being', which leaves us to add the other term of the comparison (as in some of Hölderlin's poems); but we also know that they, the Angels, represent supreme beauty, a perfection which is greater than we can bear, so that beauty becomes 'nothing but' ('nichts als') a form and 'the beginning' of terror; and though no poetry could be less political than Rilke's, we are reminded of W.B. Yeats's phrase from his poem on the Easter rising of 1916, 'a terrible beauty is born', if for no other reason than that it points to the continuity between 'beauty' and 'terror'.

Thus in the first line we have the first of those numerous images which derive their context-determined meaning in Rilke's poem from the double process I have mentioned. The allusion which the word 'Angels' carries for us, pointing to both the Old and the New Testaments, seems inescapable, these assuredly are the only angels we are bound to know something about. Even though Rilke himself, in his own numerous, indeed all-too-numerous comments on the cycle, goes out of his way to disclaim any Christian allusions, saying at one point that if anything we should be reminded of the angels of Islam, it is to the familiar scenes of the angelic salutation of Mary (Luke 1: 28, where the angel says 'Fear not, Mary'), and again of the shepherd's visitation by the angels (Luke 2: 9), ending with the words 'and the glory of the Lord shone around them, and they were sore afraid' — it is to these scenes that we are bound to turn in trying to understand this image of the Angels as bearers of the continuity between perfection and terror, reinforced in line 7, by 'Each one of the angels is terrible.' And our feeling that there isn't all that much difference between the Hebrew, the Christian and the Islamic conceptions of the angels (to which the Hellenistic may be added) — this feeling is confirmed in Peter Lamborn Wilson's magnificent book, *Angels*, which, without ever mentioning Rilke, greatly helps us to understand their function in Rilke's poetry (as when Wilson says that 'the Islamic version of the Annunciation differs from the Christian one only in dress'[2)]. But there is no ignoring Rilke's disclaimer, that we are not to think of a Christian symbolism and imagery, to think rather of his partial liberation from them (and thus from his own past, including his earlier poems to the Virgin). This disclaimer is no mere rhetoric: he completes (in lines 5 and 6) the thought of the deprivation and the terror it entails with an astonishingly concise and entirely pagan, Olympian turn: our survival (in the face of that angelic strength) is made to depend on the mere disdain of Beauty for what we are, filling us with amazement that (in a borrowing the present version makes from Stephen Cohn's) 'it casually spares us'. And so (lines 8-9) I had better stifle the lure, the call to the Angel to come to my succour. '*Der Lockruf*' is the luring call to bring a bird to the hand; it makes explicit the physical quality of the winged being.

Ach, wen vermögen
wir denn zu brauchen? Engel nicht, Menschen nicht,
und die findigen Tiere merken es schon,
daß wir nicht sehr verläßlich zu Haus sind
in der gedeuteten Welt. Es bleibt uns vielleicht
irgend ein Baum an dem Abhang, daß wir ihn täglich
wiedersähen; es bleibt uns die Straße von gestern
und das verzogene Treusein einer Gewohnheit,
der es bei uns gefiel, und so blieb sie und ging nicht.
O und die Nacht, die Nacht, wenn der Wind voller Weltraum
uns am Angesicht zehrt —, wem bliebe sie nicht, die ersehnte,
sanft enttäuschende, welche dem einzelnen Herzen
mühsam bevorsteht. Ist sie den Liebenden leichter?
ach, sie verdecken sich nur mit einander ihr Los.
Weißt du's noch nicht? Wirf aus den Armen die Leere
zu den Räumen hinzu, die wir atmen; vielleicht daß die Vögel
die erweiterte Luft fühlen mit innigerm Flug.

Alas, who then is left
we can ask for help? not angels, not people,
and the quick-witted animals knew long ago
that we are not quite securely at home
in the interpreted world. Perhaps all we have
is some tree on a slope, one that we see every day,
or yesterday's street where we walked,
and the spoilt faithfulness of a habit
that liked being with us, stayed on and never left.
O and the night, the night, when the wind, swelled with cosmic space,
comes to devour our faces — , night is there for us all, longed for
and gently disappointing, and for the lonely heart
a travail always in prospect. Is night easier for lovers?
each is only a shield for the other to hide from their fate.
Haven't you, even yet, learned this? Throw that emptiness out of your arms
out to the spaces we breathe; it may be the birds
will feel the air widened, and fly with more grace.

We need help — but who is there that will help us, that we can make use of? Not, as we have seen, the angels — but why not other people? Rilke doesn't think there is any need to explain why not. It seems obvious to him (as it seemed obvious to Nietzsche) that the sphere of association, where we come together for mutual aid, is the sphere of inauthenticity, is the very last source from which men and women can draw strength (and this repudiation of the social represents the most important difference between Rilke's Elegies and Eliot's *Four Quartets*, a cycle, or a family album of scenes in some ways closely related).

Even (line 11) the dumb yet canny animals notice our weakness and unease — even they know, instinctively, without the need of ratiocination, without the alienation that thinking brings into being — even they 'know' (if you can call it 'knowing') that we are indifferently and unreliably at home... in the world? No, not even in the world, but 'in the interpreted world.'

As in a lot of modern poetry, these lines lie on the very boundary of philosophy, they allude to philosophical reflection and its vocabulary, yet they retain the freedom to use it poetically. The very concision and thrust of these lines disclose one of the central données of our existence. The world we live in, unlike the world of our ancestors, is an interpreted world, a world in which what we (but not Rilke) call 'the media', the agents of interpretation, play an incomparably greater part than they have ever played before. Poets from Shakespeare to Hofmannsthal have told us that 'all the world's a stage / and all the men and women merely players...' Rilke's image of 'die gedeutete Welt' tells us that what was once an enchanting metaphor has come to function as a mere prosy perspective on our entire lives, encompassing our cultural pursuits, our sciences and our emotions, and yet here, for all its philosophical prosiness, it has been transmuted into the memorable image of 'the interpreted world'. It is a complex image. The more we think of it, the more it disquiets us by implying that where 'interpretation' is at issue, there is an allusion entailed to something not interpreted, the presence of some sort of absolute text. So that this image of the interpreted world, too, implies the deprivation already spoken of, on which this entire poem is built.

And still we go on asking what it is that could supply our existential want, whence we might draw strength for the attainment of that 'stronger being' which we lack. Might it not (ll. 13-17) be something quite inconspicuous, some indeterminate, contingent thing — 'irgendein Baum', 'some tree on a slope that we see every day,' or maybe 'yesterday's street', or again — you will note the extraordinary reification and personification in this utterly personal poetic practice — might it not be a habit ('eine

Gewohnheit') which 'has grown fond of us' and sticks to us, consoles us, offers us reassurance?

With the invocation of 'the night' the tone changes from that of a complex personification to a purely lyrical mode, expressing night's consoling mystery, connecting us with 'the vacant interstellar spaces' of which Eliot speaks. Again and again the poem resorts to questions: take 'the night', perhaps a first intimation of death — isn't that something which 'remains', or rather ('bliebe') 'might remain' valid as a source of succour we can use? Yet it too is 'gently disappointing' ('sanft enttäuschend'). And now the thought turns again, and what looked like sources of help we could call on turn out to be tasks imposed upon us.

Imposed by whom? We don't know. (We recall: interpretation — of what?) Other ages had a God who set men and women their destination, their destiny. But just as the angels will turn out to be messengers 'moving between heaven and earth with a lightly rushing motion' (as Plato says) messengers with we don't know what message from we don't know whom, so we have tasks set on we don't know whose authority. This sounds like a difficult metaphysical or perhaps mystical speculation, but is arguably something much simpler and less recondite: the mention of tasks imposed on us is this poet's way of conveying something we know only too well: it is the intimate search for meaning, a search that is always on, a search for something elusive and always in the moment to come; and this search for a meaning in experience, which may or may not have been familiar to mankind at other times, is assuredly central to our modern condition. It is an arduous task that faces us, challenging us as the night challenges the lonely heart ('welche dem einzelnen Herzen / mühsam...'), and if the single individual cannot accomplish what he or she has been set, and people in mutual association with each other also fail (as Rilke expects them to fail), why then can the task (whatever it is) not be accomplished by the lovers, their strength combining toward the fulfilment of that given task?

At this point the reader ought to become aware of the variety of the personal pronouns that are being used, as if offered as alternatives. The first person singular is essential to the heartfelt private experience of the first four lines, but is repeated only once or twice after this opening section; it gives way, at the mention of 'beauty', to the plural 'we', and here, at line 23, to the intimate second person, 'du', 'thou'. This 'you' predominates through the rest of the poem, with an exceptional first person at line 66, then yields to 'we' again in the last ten lines. The changes from one pronoun to another arise very naturally and easily, but a reader may feel faintly misled by the 'you' — as in its first appearance (line 23) where, if the effect is almost of an admonition to the reader, it is not what the poet intends here, though it will come to that as the poem proceeds. The poet is speaking to himself, using either the first or the second person, as we do when we speak to ourselves. In the Duino Elegies as a whole it is, no doubt, the inclusive assertion of 'we' that is most often heard, but in this first one what seems to introduce dialogue is often an overheard communing with the self, a self that is treated with the utmost concern and attention. Perhaps this is what is referred to towards the end of this Elegy, line 78, in the words

in unendlich ängstlichen Händen
(in tirelessly careful hands).

To return to the place we had reached in the text, line 21, it is here, with the mention of the lovers, that most hostile criticism of Rilke's picture of the world and thus of his poetry sets in. Again and again the Elegies have been criticized for apparently disdaining love when it is seen as the emotion shared by two people, for apparently condemning love as a distraction and a drain on a man's or woman's inward intensity, for perversely glorifying unrequited love and the self-contained ardour of undistracted because un-shared feeling. This is explicit in that injunction which uses 'you' for the first time (line 23) — to cast out the emptiness of shared love as if it were a useless burden, and a pretence to mask the truth of loneliness. A Cambridge poet, now neglected, expressed a similar thought at very much the same time:

[...]— such are but taking
Their own poor dreams within their arms, and lying
Each in his lonely night, each with a ghost.
Some share that night. But they know, love grows colder,
Grows false and dull, that was sweet lies at most.[3]

It is a sign of the times, but in this case the idea remains profoundly sad, unredeemed.

A space separates this from the next section of the poem, in which memory summons moments that are evidently felt as possible themes for poetry.

Ja, die Frühlinge brauchten dich wohl. Es muteten manche
Sterne dir zu, daß du sie spürtest. Es hob
sich eine Woge heran im Vergangenen, oder
da du vorüberkamst am geöffneten Fenster,
gab eine Geige sich hin. Das alles war Auftrag.
Aber bewältigtest du's? Warst du nicht immer
noch von Erwartung zerstreut, als kündigte alles
eine Geliebte dir an? (Wo willst du sie bergen,
da doch die großen fremden Gedanken bei dir
aus und ein gehn und öfters bleiben bei Nacht.)

Yes, Spring has needed you. And many a star
meant you to notice its presence. Towards you
a wave rose up from a long-ago sea, or
out of an open window as you went by
a violin made its surrender. All this was a task laid upon you.
But did you perform it? Were you not always
distracted, expecting it all to announce
new love, a new sweetheart ? (And where could you keep her,
when you know you have all those great strange thoughts
constantly coming and going and quite often staying the night.)

As a kind of consolation for the harshness of that command to cast out shared love, which as I said seemed addressed to the poet's self, there follows this delicately assembled short catalogue of things and moments in the world that might be called epiphanies, things that could not have existed without his receptive consciousness — the Spring, the stars that needed human eyes to watch them, a wave of the sea, the sound of a violin. Then again the note almost of upbraiding, now clearly directed to the self (line 31), reminds him that all these were part of a task, and that he has taken such epiphanies to be the announcements of love, which distracted him from their true meaning. The interplay between the material and the immaterial is underlined here by a parenthesis (lines 33 to 35) that has its humour, rare but by no means absent in Rilke.

Sehnt es dich aber, so singe die Liebenden; lange
noch nicht unsterblich genug ist ihr berühmtes Gefühl.
Jene, du neidest sie fast, Verlassenen, die du
so viel liebender fandst als die Gestillten. Beginn
immer von neuem die nie zu erreichende Preisung;
denk: es erhält sich der Held, selbst der Untergang war ihm
nur ein Vorwand, zu sein: seine letzte Geburt.

Aber die Liebenden nimmt die erschöpfte Natur
in sich zurück, als wären nicht zweimal die Kräfte,
dieses zu leisten. Hast du der Gaspara Stampa
denn genügend gedacht, daß irgend ein Mädchen,
dem der Geliebte entging, am gesteigerten Beispiel
dieser Liebenden fühlt: daß ich würde wie sie?
Sollen nicht endlich uns diese ältesten Schmerzen
fruchtbarer werden? Ist es nicht Zeit, daß wir liebend
uns vom Geliebten befrein und es bebend bestehn:
wie der Pfeil die Sehne besteht, um gesammelt im Absprung
mehr zu sein als er selbst. Denn Bleiben ist nirgends.

But, if this is your longing, then sing of the lovers; there's need
to make the fame of their feeling much more undying.
Those you have envied, or almost; the forsaken, those
you thought had so much more love than the happy. Begin
again and again the praise that can never be perfect;
think: the hero lives on, even his death was for him
only a pretext for life: his last birth.
But Nature, exhausted, takes lovers back into herself
as if she hadn't the strength to bring forth more than once
that creation. Have you given your thoughts
to Gaspara Stampa enough — and how any young girl
who is left by her lover, may think of that grander example
and say: let me be as she was?
Shouldn't these oldest of sufferings
be more of use to us now? Isn't it time that in love
we learned to be free of our lover and, trembling, endure it,
as the arrow endures the bowstring, and then, centred for flight
becomes more than itself. For there's no standing still.

Line 36 ... 'so singe die Liebenden' — no doubt here that the poet addresses himself. He is to celebrate the abandoned, the unsuccessful lovers, their intense, as it were unconditioned emotion. This becomes the occasion for invoking the name of Gaspara Stampa of Padua (line 45), a poetess of the mid-sixteenth-century who was deserted by her lover, and who transmuted that suffering into poetry. In some of these poems she expresses the confidence that her grief has its own greatness, its ardour equal to the joy of love. The mention of this lady is only one among the many scenes and episodes and images suggesting, often merely hinting at, the uses of deprivation which Rilke enumerates. Another (lines 51-53) is provided by the image (familiar to us from Zen Buddhism and the art of archery) of the arrow that 'quiveringly endures' or 'stands on' (Rilke creates his own pun on 'besteht') the bowstring and takes the energy of its flight from it in the same way as we, freeing ourselves from the loved one, become more than ourselves.

These then are images embodying a central concern of the Elegies, which is at the same time a central theme of modern poetry, or at least of modern German poetry: I mean the theme of the gain that is entailed by loss, the validation (or, as they used to say: the bonification) of suffering, the heroism of sacrifice, the purchase of value and meaning at the highest conceivable price, and perhaps even beyond the price that the imaged agents of the poem can pay. And this, a central issue of the cycle, is summed up for the first time in lines 49-50 :

> *Sollen nicht endlich uns diese ältesten Schmerzen*
> *fruchtbarer werden?*

The operas of Hofmannsthal and Richard Strauss should remind us how, in the culture of early German and Austrian modernism, it is the male partner in love who is the source of inauthenticity and distraction, while the female partner, in her suffering, is the source of trust, authenticity and spiritual strength.

But how do we answer the criticism I have mentioned, levelled against this Rilkean vision of inward-turned, unshared, non-transcendent love? The critics' objection is not far to seek. To place this strange validation of strenuous, unrequited love above the comfort and ease of love that is fulfilled and requited in the history of literature (or for that matter in modern opera) is one thing; to defend that vision against the charge of perversity and excessive sophistication is surely quite another. Nevertheless, this is what the poem demands. Let me, then, return to lines 21-23: If the single heart cannot face the night, and the arduous task each of us has been set, the poem then asks, 'is that task lighter for lovers?' Not at all, it answers, for

> *Ach, sie verdecken sich nur miteinander ihr Los.*

> *Alas, they can only hide from their fate, each shielding their eyes with the other*

(— to translate inelegantly for clarity's sake).

I would remind you here of those two interludes in John Osborne's *Look Back in Anger*[4] when the two disenchanted main characters try to avert the quarrel that is about to erupt between them by 'playing bear and squirrel', blocking out the world in their tight embrace, burying their heads each in the other's shoulder, in order to draw strength, 'stärkeres Dasein', from the other; but the ritual doesn't work, it cannot work because all they can do is try to draw strength from their weaknesses and by using one another as cover, hide from what awaits them. This is the kind of love — not a conjoining of strong, mature emotions, but (as Rilke puts it in the 'Letter to a Young Poet') of things incomplete and blurred, mere rudiments of feeling leaning against each other — this is the kind of love that he regards as characteristic of the contemporary condition; so that, compared with that defective emotion — a sort of 'loving and partly loving', to misquote T.S. Eliot[5] — those who were betrayed and forsaken, and whose love remained unrequited (l. 38) are seen to be 'more loving', capable of greater love, greater strength of being.

These (and not those two who are playing bear and squirrel) are the proper objects of praise; 'the hero' does not need our praise, since his very destruction ('sein Untergang') is a pretext for being, is what creates him, another, last birth. The year, let us remember, is 1912 — in another two years' time poets everywhere, in England no less than in Germany, including very briefly Rilke himself, will be politicising and mythologising the greater strength of being in military heroism, will be celebrating the rebirth of mankind in 'the supreme sacrifice'.

The third section begins with voices, perhaps those of the lovers in grief:

Stimmen, Stimmen. Höre, mein Herz, wie sonst nur
Heilige hörten: daß sie der riesige Ruf
aufhob vom Boden; sie aber knieten,
Unmögliche, weiter und achtetens nicht:
So waren sie hörend. Nicht, das du Gottes ertrügest
die Stimme, bei weitem. Aber das Wehende höre,
die ununterbrochene Nachricht, die aus Stille sich bildet.
Es rauscht jetzt von jenen jungen Toten zu dir.
Wo immer du eintratst, redete nicht in Kirchen
zu Rom und Neapel ruhig ihr Schicksal dich an?
Oder es trug eine Inschrift sich erhaben dir auf,
wie neulich die Tafel in Santa Maria Formosa.
Was sie mir wollen? leise soll ich des Unrechts
Anschein abtun, der ihrer Geister
reine Bewegung manchmal ein wenig behindert.

Voices, voices. Listen, my heart, as, till now,
only saints listened: so that the thundering summons
raised them up from the ground; but they stayed in their kneeling position
impossibly, kneeling in air, and oblivious:

that's how they listened. Not that you would be able to bear
the voice of God. But hear on the whispering air
the news that the silence creates, never ceasing.
Now the faint sound comes from the young dead to your ears.
Wherever you entered a church, did you not hear
in Rome or in Naples, the soft voice of their destiny speaking to you?
Or an inscription stood proud in your sight
like that tablet just lately in Santa Maria Formosa.
What do they want of me? That I should efface the seeming injustice
Whose traces make heavy, at times,
their spirits' lightness of movement.

The exhortation (addressed to '*mein Herz*') is to hear, to listen to the voices. It thus introduces 'the saints' (line 55): those who could be so completely lost in their act of prayer, their listening to the voice of God, that they became oblivious of their surroundings; even, it is said, when a miracle had raised them, kneeling, into the air — 'sie... achteten's nicht' — 'they did not notice it'. For the poet, not a saint, God's call would be beyond enduring, as the Lord who addressed Moses from the burning bush was beyond human enduring (Exodus iii : 6). Voices he can hear, and should endure, are those of 'the young dead' (lines 61-65), such as (for instance) those commemorated on an inscription (solemn and 'in high relief': 'erhaben') in the Venetian church of Santa Maria Formosa — Rilke loves inscriptions, as you will see in the Fifth Elegy. At this point the second person pronoun gives way to the first (line 66), with the question 'Was sie mir wollen? leise soll ich des Unrechts / Anschein abtun...' It is as if the effort fully to understand the whispered message ('das Wehende') recalls to the poet's mind his listening audience, the audience that poetry must have, and their need to understand the message with him. It is, for a moment, no longer in dialogue with himself that he can make this most clear — he must step forward, turn to his readers to claim his role as mediator.

Perhaps as you put together this interpretive pattern you will begin to think of the poem in distinctly philosophical terms. It is to be hoped that you won't. Rilke does not say (as some of his critics have suggested), 'Intensity is all.' We must not lumber him with this, or indeed with any other philosophical or ideological maxim. An important aspect of Rilke's poetic activity is (as we may see in a moment) the endeavour to shape the poems from the implications not of any ideas but of the very shapes and sounds that figure in the poems, the shapes and sounds that determine their structures. He shows us scenes — including these scenes of the young dead — each of which (line 64) 'offered itself', 'imposed itself on you' ('trug sich dir auf ') as an example of the strength of that 'stronger existence' which other ages possessed, but which we in our own age lack. But again, this is not, either here or elsewhere in the Elegies, a historicist perception: Rilke has no philosophy of history, the past, for him, is not a series of causally or teleologically connected events, but a series of *scenes* -- beautiful or moving or in some other way powerful and thus aesthetically significant.

In its last two sections the poem homes in on those young dead. Slowly, line by line, the poet's praise of them emerges as the task he has been set; it is praise which should 'gently remove the semblance of injustice' (line 64: 'des Unrechts / Anschein') implied in our lament for their early death. Here at last is the task we have been given: praise, which (in the elegiac context) is lament without rebellion. And this praise is both the object and the source of our inward intensity.

Enumeration, unless it is deliberately chosen, is a weakness in lyrical poetry. There are three moments in this poem where the enumerative mode is cut short and the poem recovers under the impact of lyrical affirmation: first in line 18, 'O und die Nacht...', the paean to the night and the contact with the cosmos that it vouchsafes us; then in line 54 (the opening of a new section) with the invocation of the voices that came to the praying saints, that come to us from the cosmic spaces, indeed from everywhere as long as we are undistracted enough to attend to them; and thirdly, at line 69, the next section, turning as it were to another aspect of dying, youthful or prematurely, 'Freilich ist es seltsam, die Erde nicht mehr zu bewohnen...'.

Freilich ist es seltsam, die Erde nicht mehr zu bewohnen,
kaum erlernte Gebräuche nicht mehr zu üben,
Rosen, und andern eigens versprechenden Dingen
nicht die Bedeutung menschlicher Zukunft zu geben;
das, was man war in unendlich ängstlichen Händen,
nicht mehr zu sein, und selbst den eigenen Namen
wegzulassen wie ein zerbrochenes Spielzeug.
Seltsam, die Wünsche nicht weiterzuwünschen. Seltsam,
alles, was sich bezog, so lose im Raume
flattern zu sehen. Und das Totsein ist mühsam
und voller Nachholn, daß man allmählich ein wenig
Ewigkeit spürt. — Aber Lebendige machen
alle den Fehler, daß sie zu stark unterscheiden.
Engel (sagt man) wüßten oft nicht, ob sie unter

Lebenden gehn oder Toten. Die ewige Strömung
reißt durch beide Bereiche alle Alter
immer mit sich und übertönt sie in beiden.

True, it is strange not to inhabit the earth any more
no longer to practise the customs so lately acquired,
not to perceive, in roses and other things laden with promise
a meaning for what is to come, for a human future;
no longer to be the self that we were, in tirelessly
careful hands, and even abandon
our own given names as if they were toys that are broken.
Strange, not to desire our desires any more. Strange
to see all the pattern of things blown about in space
fluttering, separate. It's hard work, being dead,
and having to try to collect, to catch up, until very slowly
a little eternity dawns. — But the living all make
the same error, they draw lines too hard and fast.
Angels, (it's said) are often unable to tell
if they move among living or dead. The eternal river
swiftly carries all the ages through the two kingdoms
for ever, and outroars their voices in both.

What this section does, so clearly that it needs no detailed comment, is something Rilke is supremely good at. I mean this: time and again the line opens on a scene, or even on a mere sentence or phrase of the utmost succinctness, as in 'to inhabit the earth no longer', and then the poem proceeds to draw out the imaginative implications from that scene or phrase; though to speak of 'implications' is to fail to convey the fully concrete, sensuous character of what follows — material and sensuous even though, here, it is the implications not of being but of not being, of death, that the poetry celebrates. Death, then, consists in no longer dwelling on the Earth, in not following the habits we have scarcely had time to acquire, in not welcoming, in roses or other things we loved, their symbolical meaning and promise and (line 74-75) 'in laying aside / even one's own proper name, like a broken toy.'

Of course, when you come to think of it, the only at all convincing things we can say by way of describing that state, the state of death, are, or seem to be, of two kinds. Either we can use the language of transcendence, speaking perhaps of the future clarity, of seeing 'face to face' all that here and now we can only see as in a glass darkly; in doing this we draw on or appeal to a Christian orthodoxy which Rilke regarded as not open to him. The alternative seems to be to insist that the 'here' and the 'there' aren't perhaps so very different after all. But, when you come to think of it again, as far as language is concerned there really is no difference. Leaving aside any special, as it were technical, terms of orthodoxy, we do indeed have only one language, the language of the worldly 'here', and how can Rilke proceed on any other assumption? I am not sure whether we are justified in ascribing to him the language of mysticism. But either way that language too, however hermetic or esoteric its lexis, and however distant from our prosy discourse it may be, still proceeds by drawing on meanings which allude to our common usage, to what Wordsworth calls 'the world of common indication.'[6]

I mention this inclusion of the metaphysical lexis in the singleness or unitary nature of our language because it offers (as it seems to me) the key to the penultimate section of the poem. If the state of the young dead is 'strange' (as the opening line of the section has it) this must be because we, the living (line 81) 'make the mistake of drawing distinctions too sharply', of allowing distinctions to sharpen into differences — when the poet knows better, reporting (for instance) that 'Angels... are often unable to tell / whether they move among the living or the dead'; or, the poet adds, 'so it is said...'. But the poet is not alone in this. Plato in the *Symposium* (211 b, c) speaks in very similar terms of the gradual unfolding of the mystery of love, and (as Peter Lamborn Wilson writes in *Angels*, apparently without any knowledge of Rilke's poetry) 'it can never be said for certain if the "beloved" being addressed [in Persian poetry] is human or divine... Surely such a figure, which thus mediates for the lover between this world and heaven, deserves above all others to be called an Angel.'[7]

It might be shown how the endeavour to avoid the either/or of 'too sharp distinctions', and the seeking out of images of transition, constitute the strength of the language and imagery which is Rilke's poetry; and how this is connected with the language game of allusions and liberations to which we have been attending; how in particular the image of 'the eternal current' ('die ewige Strömung' of line 83) is designed to whirl all the ages, the scenes of history, 'through both realms', the 'here' and the 'there', immanence and transcendence, 'drowning out the human voices in both'; though this journey through history is for Rilke a journey through scenes which are aesthetically significant.

But again it is important to recall that Rilke's undertaking is poetic; to recall (to misquote T.S. Eliot once more) that the poetry does matter; that it matters, not to the exclusion of meanings (as

Paul de Man argues in the second chapter of *Allegories of Reading* — as though poetry could ever do that), but to the celebration of meanings everywhere, even, or perhaps especially, where they hurt. But just as we should not reduce Rilke's album of family resemblances to the blunt statement of a philosophical maxim, so we must beware of casting him in the role of the founder of a '*religio intransitiva*' (as some critics have done). His poetry is neither that nor its opposite. The unitary nature of worldly and metaphysical experience which he praises and ascribes to the angels is not a creed but a series of images, most of them of unparalleled subtlety and designed to respond to our hopes and fears, our expectations. He shares some of the flaws of the age he is describing, flaws he is seeking to overcome; the presumption of a religious prophet is not one of them.

Schließlich brauchen sie uns nicht mehr, die Früheentrückten,
man entwöhnt sich des Irdischen sanft, wie man den Brüsten
milde der Mutter entwächst. Aber wir, die so große
Geheimnisse brauchen, denen aus Trauer so oft
seliger Fortschritt entspringt —: ***könnten*** *wir sein ohne sie?*
Ist die Sage umsonst, daß einst in der Klage um Linos
wagende erste Musik dürre Erstarrung durchdrang;
daß erst im erschrockenen Raum, dem ein beinah göttlicher Jüngling
plötzlich für immer enttrat, das Leere in jene
Schwingung geriet, die uns jetzt hinreißt und tröstet und hilft.

They who have died too soon, in the end they don't need us,
they are weaned from the Earth as we gently
are weaned from the breasts of our mother. But for us,
whose need is for greatness and mystery, whose mourning so often
brings blessing and progress—; how ***could*** *we exist without them?*
It can't be in vain that the legend of mourning for Linus
tells how music first dared then to steal through bleak numbness,
so that in the shocked space he, almost godlike,
had left so abruptly for ever, the void
first quivered with sound that now enchants and consoles us und helps.

The last section demonstrates what I mean by the subtlety and responsiveness of Rilke's images. The First Elegy comes back at its end to the question of who there is that can be of help to us; and it answers, first, by pointing once again to 'the early departed' and the sustainment we receive from them, and then, more specifically, to a myth, the myth of Linus; and in its fragmentariness this myth offers a particularly striking example of Rilke's poetic procedure. For all that we know of the young demigod

Linus is that he, son of the Muse Urania, was killed by Apollo whom he challenged to a singing contest; yet Rilke suggests that Linus's sudden death became the source from which music itself was born. In the empty space which Linus left behind, music was born: that music which 'now enchants and consoles us and helps' (like the poetry of Gaspara Stampa that was born out of her suffering).

This, finally, may be the occasion for emphasizing Rilke's use of motifs from the three sources that mattered to him in the writings of his maturity. You may think they form an incongruous group, but then they figure here not as in a history of ideas, but as the sources of poetry. They are Nietzsche, the Old Testament and the New, and classical mythology. It is the use of these sources which, in the *Elegies*, in the *Sonnets to Orpheus* and in countless other poems demonstrates with great poignancy and clarity that combination of allusion to the scenes and personages that were there long before the poem was ever conceived, *and* the liberation from those pre-existent données, for the sake of the new thing that is his, the poet's, own accomplished task.

---

1 Goethe used the designation 'Elegie' primarily as referring to the metrical pattern; some of the poems he calls elegies are indeed laments, others, particularly *Römische Elegien*, are joyful celebrations of experience.

2 *Angels* (London, 1980), p. 61.

3 Rupert Brooke, 'Love', *Complete Poems* (London, 1932), p. 108.

4 *Look back in Anger* (London, 1957), p. 34.

5 *Murder in the Cathedral* (London, 1935), p. 19.

6 'Residence in London', *The Prelude* (1850), vii, 636.

7 op. cit., p. 193, footnote 2.

ELEGY TWO

Michael Minden

The Second Elegy was written immediately after the First at the castle of Duino at the end of January and beginning of February 1912. It is part of the original inspiration of the cycle as a whole, and in some ways is a continuation of the First. But it also has its own independent character as a poem within the cycle.

It is about the angels — as we already know, Rilke insisted his angels were not Christian angels but peculiar to his own poetry — and it is about the transience of human experience, about ordinary lovers, and about Greeks who had a different attitude to each other and to the gods than early-twentieth-century man. Angels, lovers, Greeks, these are really the landmarks in a journey of exploration in language and of language, but also of what lies beyond it. If I was asked to say what this Elegy really seemed to me to be about, rather than what was named in it, I should say that it was about the relations amongst men and women, the relation of man to himself, the relation of human beings to God, and therefore also the relation of language and poetry to what it cannot say or be. But more than that I should say that it was about the abstract concept of relation itself. 'Bezug ist alles': 'relation is everything'. Here, as everywhere, Rilke is obsessively interested not only in things in and for themselves, but in the relation between them. It is into the spaces between things and between words or into their invisible places of connection that Rilke directs his poetic quest for the true spiritual dimension of the world.

JEDER Engel ist schrecklich. Und dennoch, weh mir,
ansing ich euch, fast tödliche Vögel der Seele,
wissend um euch. Wohin sind die Tage Tobiae,
da der Strahlendsten einer stand an der einfachen Haustür,
zur Reise ein wenig verkleidet und schon nicht mehr furchtbar;
(Jüngling dem Jüngling, wie er neugierig hinaussah).
Träte der Erzengel jetzt, der gefährliche, hinter den Sternen
eines Schrittes nur nieder und herwärts: hochauf–
schlagend erschlüg uns das eigene Herz. Wer seid ihr?

EVERY angel is terrible. And still, alas,
I sing to you, near-deadly birds of the soul,
In knowledge of you. Where have they gone, the days of Tobias,
When one of those radiant beings stood at a simple threshold,
A little disguised for the journey and no longer terrifying
(a youth to the youth, as he peered out inquisitively).
Should now the archangel, full of danger, step from behind the stars
Just one pace downwards and toward us: outbeating
itself our own heart would destroy us. Who are you?

'Every angel is terrible': continuing from (and varying slightly) a sentence in the First Elegy, Rilke takes up the question of the angels. The first section thus addresses head-on the key question of the relation of the poet to the unsayable — for this is what I take 'the angels' to indicate — and of the ambivalent status of a poetry which does this. This poetry is referred to in the phrase 'ansing ich euch'. In translating I put 'I sing to you'. But in a way I should have written 'I sing *at* you'. This song, in other words, does nothing to give life to or celebrate the relation of man and angels. It is only a signal of their near complete distance from each other. Ordinary German would be 'sing ich euch an', but this would be to embrace the angels within the activity, to surround the angels in the verb describing the poet's activity. That would be misleading.

But relationship there is, however fraught. The interconnection of man with the unsayable is manifest in the phrase 'near-deadly birds of the soul'. Whose soul? Presumably our own, hence they are within us, yet they are deadly, and being within us they destroy us, thus cancelling out all possibility of relation. But the poetic formulation does not say deadly; it says 'near-deadly'. Logically this is a barely permissible usage like saying 'nearly perfect' or 'practically unique'. But in committing this violence upon logic, that is, in being poetry, the formulation *produces* a relation between men and angels, albeit an unhappy one.

We come now to Tobias and the angel. In the apocryphal Book of Tobit ('Buch Tobiae'), angels and men do meet and connect. The angel Raphael accompanies the youthful Tobias on a quest and sees that it comes to a successful conclusion. Presumably it is not only the religious and spiritual contrast which attracts Rilke's mind here, but the artistic or cultural one too. This meeting of Tobias and the angel is a marvellous topic for visual artistic representation because sacred and secular meet in the same space. Rilke now turns to it for some relief from the opening mood of the poem. It is precisely its pictorial quality which redeems and animates abstraction: the curiously abstract juxtaposition 'Jüngling dem Jüngling', 'youth to the youth', is brilliantly made specific by the detail of Tobias peering out inquisitively to look at the stranger, and a near rhyme (hinaussah/furchtbar) softens the implacable 'furchtbar'. Of course it is easier in poetry than in painting to convey the lovely idea of the angel being only 'slightly' disguised. Man and angel meet in these lines on a threshold at once symbolic and real, and it is this 'at once' that is important.

These times are past, however. This beautiful cultural reminiscence of another time and another spiritual state does not overcome the present impasse. In the Elegy, now, the happy reconciliation between concrete and abstract is violently burst asunder. Just one *pace* out from behind the stars on the part of the archangel, and our hearts would beat so strongly as to destroy us. The apparently harmless, and very concrete, gesture of the single pace modulates alarmingly into cataclysm. This is the first rhythmic and thematic climax of the poem. In the words 'Hochauf/schlagend erschlüg uns...' , 'Schlagen' is set against 'schlagen', the language of the poem turns upon itself, and figures, in its climactic intensity, the destruction of the heart that outbeats itself, and thus of all relation between man and angel and thus of poetry too. Time to pause; time to take stock: the completely unpoetic 'wer seid ihr?' helps us recover, and return to the philosophical itinerary upon which the poem has set out, the reflection on what the angels are, upon their ontological status.

I hesitate to say too much about the next section (lines 10-17). It has its own sort of visual authority, so clear is its shape and direction and movement:

Frühe Geglückte, ihr Verwöhnten der Schöpfung,
Höhenzüge, morgenrötliche Grate
aller Erschaffung, — Pollen der blühenden Gottheit,
Gelenke des Lichtes, Gänge, Treppen, Throne,
Räume aus Wesen, Schilde aus Wonne, Tumulte
stürmisch entzückten Gefühls und plötzlich, einzeln,
***Spiegel:** die die entströmte eigene Schönheit*
wiederschöpfen zurück in das eigene Antlitz.

Early-happy ones, the world's fond favourites,
Majestic heights, ridges of all creation
touched by the dawn, pollen of blossoming Godhead,
junctures of light, passages, stairways, thrones,
spaces of being, shields of bliss, tumults
of feeling in storms of delight and suddenly, singly,

> ***mirrors**, each pouring its own beauty*
> *back into its own countenance.*

This passage is so white hot with poetic ardour, that to comment upon it seems impertinent. Its rhythmic power is self-evident. It is a progression of restraint and release building up to an explosive turn which I think must be called orgasmic. Its metaphorical richness is remarkable, the very urgent succession of formulations suggests some inexhaustible linguistic source from which they stream, and which is infinitely productive. Creations' early successes, become the world's cherished favourites; the dawn of creation becomes a mountain landscape touched by that dawn; the Godhead becomes a blossoming flower. And then: 'Gelenke des Lichts': 'Gelenk' means 'joint', or 'hinge', and thus, generally, 'point of articulation', point, precisely of relation. It is, in this heightened poetic context, in itself, a perfect fusion of abstract and concrete, it is a word for where two things join, defined by them, defining them, yet not those things, indeed not anything but their relation; and then on top of that, 'Gelenke des *Lichts*', junctures of light, light which is both visible and disembodied, making of this phrase the most stunning realisation of the concept of pure relation, the joining of two things with no origin other than their junction. By the operation of an invisible genitive, a palace of light now appears in metaphorical fragments; corridors, stairways, thrones, only, then, to tip over into 'Räume aus Wesen'. 'Räume' is both a continuation of this visionary light-architecture, 'chambers', 'rooms', and also an abstraction, but not just any abstraction: the most abstract thing there is: space, yet, space*s* full of being: poetry's disregard of logic here is absolutely imperious. The dominant alliterations in this linguistic tour de force are on 'l' ('Gelenke des Lichts') and 't' ('Treppen', 'Throne'): the two sounds, the lateral 'l' and the stop 't' contrast with each other like flow against resistance. The phrase 'Schilde aus Wonne', shields of delight, expresses the same contrast. Shields: blocks, objective surfaces, and the fluency and release of subjective delight. This interaction of sounds is concentrated in the word 'Tumulte' which has them both, and which just precedes now the climax of the section, which comes in the word 'plötzlich', also including the two sounds, and which bends the dimension of time into the space of the angels. Apparent division, the word 'einzeln' upon which the stanza turns, simply prepares the way for the startling release of the word 'mirrors' which lifts all division for ever. Mirrors in real life separate the face which consults them from the image they return to it, they establish identity in the very act of separating the subject from its image of itself. Not so these mystical mirrors. The angels are their *own* mirrors, they are subject and object at the same time, they are consciousness folded back upon itself, and thus relation so pure as to abolish the very concept, discovering at the impossible point of connection, undivided continuous cosmic unity. Finally the word 'Antlitz', a poetic word for face, i.e. 'countenance', combines and consolidates 't' and 'l', and clinches the absolute plenitude of angelic being.

I hesitated to say much about this section, but I have said rather a lot. I fear I may have got carried away. But the point is, so has the poet. What business has he describing the angels? He knows and has told us that they are immeasurably far away and beyond us. The more magnificent the evocation or invocation, the more miserable the absence of what is being invoked. The stronger the sun the deeper the shadow. This utterly memorable, brilliant section is illicit. Guardini may have seen in it 'one of the great achievements of visionary writing',[1] and I am persuaded that it may well be. But it is also — there is a double movement in the elegy — blankly narcissistic. In narcissicism too the mirror answers all the longings of the one who consults it, but to the exclusion of the rest of the world. It is therefore the *antithesis* of relation rather than its transformation. It is to be locked up in subjectivity, in the subject, and find no link at all either to the angels or to anything outside the self. The poet has succumbed to the seduction of poetry, and in dreaming of self-fertilization has spent his power in a transitory euphoria, upon which sadness must inevitably follow.

This sadness is now the subject of the next section (lines 18-36), which is about the transience of human experience:

Denn wir, wo wir fühlen, verflüchtigen; ach wir
atmen uns aus und dahin; von Holzglut zu Holzglut
geben wir schwächern Geruch. Da sagt uns wohl einer:
ja, du gehst mir ins Blut, dieses Zimmer, der Frühling
füllt sich mit dir... Was hilfts, er kann uns nicht halten,
wir schwinden in ihm und um ihn. Und jene, die schön sind,
o wer hält sie zurück? Unaufhörlich steht Anschein
auf in ihrem Gesicht und geht fort. Wie Tau von dem Frühgras
hebt sich das Unsre von uns, wie Hitze von einem
heißen Gericht. O Lächeln, wohin? O Aufschaun:
neue, warme, entgehende Welle des Herzens —;
weh mir: wir ***sinds*** *doch. Schmeckt denn der Weltraum,*
in den wir uns lösen, nach uns? Fangen die Engel
wirklich nur Ihriges auf, ihnen Entströmtes,

oder ist manchmal, wie aus Versehen, ein wenig
unseres Wesens dabei? Sind wir in ihre
Züge soviel nur gemischt wie das Vage in die Gesichter
schwangerer Frauen? Sie merken es nicht in dem Wirbel
ihrer Rückkehr zu sich. (Wie sollten sie's merken.)

For we, in our feelings, evaporate; alas we
breathe ourselves out and away; from ember to ember
yielding a fainter tang. Someone, it is true, may say:
yes, you are in my blood, this room, this springtime
is full of you... What's the use? He cannot hold us,
we vanish within him and around him. And those who have beauty,
who can restrain them? Ceaselessly appearance
begins in their faces and goes forth. Like dew from the morning grass
what's ours leaves us, like the heat rising
from a hot dish. O what becomes of a smile? Of a gaze:
new, warm, ephemeral wave of the heart —;
Woe is me: this is *what we are. Does the cosmic space*
into which we dissolve, perhaps bear our taste? Do the angels really
only gather in what is theirs, what they give off,
or is there sometimes, as if by mistake, a little
of our own being there too? Are we mixed in with their
features, like the vagueness into the faces
of pregnant women? They do not notice it in the whirlwind
of their return to themselves. (How could they notice it.)

Poetry, real poetry, must apply its resources to the resistances of real experience, and find the moments within them, hidden at the points of juncture between the things and between the words of the normal world, at which a spiritual dimension is genuinely glimpsed and a genuine relation to the angels established. The word 'fühlen' (feel), is physically dissolved into the word 'verflüchtigen' (evaporate), which contains and disperses all its letters. The words 'Anschein' and 'Aufschaun', both nouns close to verbs, and nouns with prepositions embedded in them, seek to find and fix the interface between state and motion. These are the deeply characteristic linguistic devices Rilke uses to express the difficult idea of the dispersal and loss, the evaporation, of human consciousness: the nullity of what passes for relationship in normal usage, and the difficulty for poetry to 'hold' any of this, to focus upon the direction of a smile, or the life of the 'appearance' in a face, a face not vouchsafed the miracle of being also its own mirror.

Two general points can be made: first, note how poetry can exploit its own limitations. Having evoked a fulness it can never deliver, and thus increased the misery of isolation, it can nevertheless use that evocation to establish a context for the partialness of human experience, of which it has become so intensely aware. *We* are not like that, the faces of the beautiful amongst us transmit beauty into the void, we are all self-loss, etc. And in the second movement of the section, the notion of plenitude can again be used: are we somehow taken up in its perfect circularity? Does the worldspace taste of us, and finally, do the faces of pregnant women perhaps have something of the self-possession of the angels?

Second, the marvellous return of the mundane cannot pass unremarked, the heat rising from the uncovered dish of food is a very daring image to use after the sublimity of the angels. But it is just this proximity of concrete physical images and lofty abstraction, which is characteristic of the poetry of the Elegies. Note too the curious way that the smell of cooking lingers on in this stanza: does the cosmos taste of us, are we ingredients in it, mixed into it, like the vagueness is mixed into (note the accusative case) the faces of pregnant women? Furthermore, it is not just on the level of imagery that sublime and everyday mix: this stanza sees the introduction of ordinary speech: 'you are in my blood'; 'what's the use' etc., thus posing the vital issue of the relation between language used as communication and language as poetry. Poetry strives to transcend those short circuits of superficial communication to achieve something more permanent and real.

Finally, there is a syntactical ambiguity at the end of the section which is important for the movement of the poem as a whole. 'They do not notice it in the whirlwind/ of their return to themselves (how could they notice it)', must refer to the angels, but grammatically refers to the pregnant women. The two are thus identified or superimposed within the poetic operation of Rilke's language so as to say: yes, here is a moment in our ordinary lives where the quality of the angels can be fleetingly discerned, and, here, fleetingly held, in poetry. Behind the throwaway resignation of 'how could they notice it', poetically there is therefore a touch of optimism.

The next section (lines 37-43) comprises seven lines and is, I think, one of the most resistant and difficult parts of this Elegy to understand.

Liebende könnten, verstünden sie's, in der Nachtluft
wunderlich reden. Denn es scheint, daß uns alles
verheimlicht. Siehe, die Bäume **sind**; *die Häuser,*
die wir bewohnen, bestehn noch. Wir nur

ziehen allem vorbei wie ein luftiger Austausch.
Und alles ist einig, uns zu verschweigen, halb als
Schande vielleicht und halb als unsägliche Hoffnung.

Lovers, if they only knew how, might speak wondrously
in the night air. For it seems that everything
conceals us. See, the trees **are***; the houses*
in whicn we live still stand where they were. We alone
pass by all this like air changing places with air.
And all things conspire to silence us, half
in shame and half in inexpressible hope.

Although it starts with the lovers, and thus with a topic already familiar to us from the previous Elegy, it rapidly dismisses them to turn instead to a sentence which, while appearing simple, is actually a startling inversion of normal expectations. 'For it seems that everything conceals us'. Whereas we would normally expect to be the ones who conceal things, here it is the things that conceal us. Very simple language turns out to be doing something very basic and subversive: displacing us from our assured position in it. After another reminiscence of the First Elegy — the notion of the 'things' of the world, more real than human beings who are ephemeral — this surprising and mysterious turn recurs in the line 'alles ist einig, uns zu verschweigen'; 'everything conspires to keep us a secret'. This time it is explicitly a linguistic form of hiding: a keeping silent. We are here, even more clearly, in some sense being kept out of language.

I do not intend to attempt to gloss the meaning of this here, but to seek instead to make sense of it by pointing to another, not immediately apparent, but actually very important aspect of these seven lines, namely their symmetry. In the middle of the stanza the formulation of 'sein', the ontological theme which runs through the poem, confronts the emptiness of human experience, in a fresh arresting formulation — air changing places with air. On either side of this, enclosing it, are formulations of this transposition of subject and object to which I referred, which balance each other. The beginning and the end of the section tell of secret meanings. This sense of symmetry is increased when one realises that the fourth line of this section, i.e. its middle line, is also the actual centre of the whole poem: 39 lines before and 39 lines after.

This is thus the secret turning point of the poem. And what happens here? Around a statement of the central problem of relation, that of the relation between evaporating human beings and substantial enduring being, something vital occurs: a transposition of the relation between, on the one hand, our experience and, on the other, language (and thus poetry too). A further symmetry: the word 'reden' balances its opposite the word 'verschweigen'. We — the readers and the poet, indeed the lovers themselves, whose language it would be if only they were capable of it — are *outside* this discourse, this 'reden'. But, and here is the point, *we* are *within* the 'verschweigen': it is we who are being kept silent, waiting to be spoken. And this imagined language, unlike the empty exchange of air characterising ordinary human speech, *can* encompass the truth of the human condition rather than miss it completely and continually: namely, that it is both a shameful one and the ground for — precisely — *in*expressible hope.

The first section of the poem, this one, and the final one, all in some way refer to the role of poetry (a further manifestation of the poem's symmetry). The difference is that whilst the initial reference is a hopeless one: I sing at you angels, and the final one, as we shall see, a muted but marvellously successful elegiac one, here the ambivalence, which is the very life of the poem, is for once explicit: a point of balance; one might say a 'Gelenk' or point of relation.

Strange how, in so tightly constructed a poem, the impression of hesitancy should be intentionally enhanced as Rilke now repeats his reference to the lovers. Perhaps not so strange, on second thoughts, since this symmetry cannot be a rigid or static one, but a structure through which different intensities of passion and reflection move. At all events, the poem now (lines 44-65) seems to resume its course after the still point of the previous section: pregnant women might perhaps have some affinity with the angels, maybe lovers do too, in their self-sufficiency.

Liebende, euch , ihr ineinander Genügten,
frag ich nach uns. Ihr greift euch. Habt Ihr Beweise?
Seht, mir geschiehts, daß meine Hände einander
inne werden oder daß mein gebrauchtes
Gesicht in ihnen sich schont. Das giebt mir ein wenig
Empfindung. Doch wer wagte darum schon zu ***sein****?*
Ihr aber, die ihr im Entzücken des anderen
zunehmt, bis er euch überwältigt
anfleht: nicht ***mehr*** *—; die ihr unter den Händen*
euch reichlicher werdet wie Traubenjahre;
die ihr manchmal vergeht, nur weil der andre
ganz überhandnimmt: euch frage ich nach uns. Ich weiß,
ihr berührt euch so selig, weil die Liebkosung verhält,
weil die Stelle nicht schwindet, die ihr, Zärtliche,

zudeckt; weil ihr darunter das reine
Dauern verspürt. So versprecht ihr euch Ewigkeit fast
von der Umarmung. Und doch, wenn ihr der ersten
Blicke Schrecken besteht und die Sehnsucht am Fenster
und den ersten gemeinsamen Gang, ***ein*** *mal durch den Garten:*
Liebende, ***seid*** *ihrs dann noch? Wenn ihr einer dem andern*
euch an den Mund hebt und ansetzt —: Getränk an Getränk:
o wie entgeht dann der Trinkende seltsam der Handlung.

Lovers, you who are satisfied in one another,
I ask about us. You hold each other. But do you have proof?
See, sometimes it happens to me that my hands
grow aware of each other, or that my used-up face
finds refuge in them. This gives me a little
sensation. But who from this alone would presume to ***be****?*
You, though, increasing in the other's rapture
till he, overwhelmed, implores you:
no ***more*** *—; in each other's hands*
growing more abundant for one another like vintage years,
perishing sometimes, only because the other
flourished too vigorously: you I ask about us. I know
why there is such bliss in your touch: because your caress is sustaining,
because the place does not vanish which, so gently,
you cover; because beneath it you sense
pure permanence. And so you promise each other eternity, almost,
from an embrace. And yet, if you endure
those first frightened glances and the longing at the window,
and the first walk, ***once*** *through the garden together:*
Lovers, ***are*** *you still lovers? When you*
raise each other to your lips —: drink against drink:
O how strangely the drinker eludes the drinking.

But first there is another digression, as the poet turns in upon himself. This self-reference takes up and develops strands in the Elegy in two ways. First, it resumes the idea of faces which has been important in the poem so far. The angels' faces (although the word is 'Antlitz', countenance) are guarantees of fulness. The faces ('Gesichter') of the beautiful, on the other hand, are the departure point for an unbearable loss of beauty, evaporating into indifferent empty space. The faces (again, 'Gesicht') of pregnant women then perhaps have something of the secretive ability to withold themselves from the promiscuous world. Now the poet can momentarily hold his face ('Gesicht') in his hands and perhaps interrupt the process of living which uses it up. I stress the German word 'Gesicht', because it expresses more clearly than the word face how mysteriously ambiguous the human face is. It is that by which we are known and universally identified, but it is invisible to us, except via the detour of the mirror. It is a place to see and be seen, and these two — different — functions are clearer in the German than in the English. The face is a strange threshold where subject and object meet, only to miss each other completely. That is why the mirror-faces of the angels are so miraculous.

The second way in which the reference of the poet to himself adds to the organisation of the poem is in the reference to hands. His hands protect his face: there is a sort of intensity about this protective gesture, even the hands are returned to themselves, not dirtied by the business of the world, not sullied with instrumentality. Hands and holding, and the related 'verhalten', which has meanings to do with control and restraint, are key terms in the poem: they are part of the concrete poetic representation of the idea of relation, in the sense of human handling of the network of relations in which he finds himself. The face is passive, the hands active, and these two functions must find a balance.

The poet's gesture of self-gathering, however, is only a passing moment of 'feeling'; it does nothing to transform the state of subjectivity into a state of grace; nothing to release the subject from his subjugation into the liberation of 'der andere Bezug'. So, and this was the point, back to the lovers. There now follows the second intense poetic excavation of the notion of relation in the poem: the fusion of erotic love. To illustrate, these lines:

> *Ihr aber, die ihr im Entzücken des andern*
> *zunehmt, bis er euch überwältigt*
> *anfleht: nicht* ***mehr*** *—*

They are a triumph of linguistic conflation: giver and taker, self and other, cease to be distinguishable. 'You' ('Ihr') is plural, but within that plural entity there is mixed in a quality called 'the other'; so that both are at once self and other, growing in each others rapture, until 'he', that 'other', overcome, pleads 'no more'. But you could read 'überwältigt' as a verb rather than an adverb, so that the other overcomes you ('you' is again plural in the German), and that overcoming itself melts into an entreaty, as part of a continuum of experience, in which two subjects are rearranged into a series of points of sensation.

Prepared in the first half of the poem, the imagery of hands and touching reaches its first climax here. The poet cannot defend his face in his hands: lovers, in their touch, sense 'being' beneath that spot where they touch one another, that point where two 'surfaces' meet to become a new essence. In his reflections upon Rodin's sculptures, Rilke stresses how they address not the individual isolated classical integrity of the human body, but seek a new artistic focus in the points of contact *between* bodies.

'And so you promise each other eternity, almost, from an embrace'. 'Ewigkeit, fast' is another of those impossible phrases, like 'fast tödlich', which Rilke uses to exploit the limits of ordinary language. These lines superimpose the sublime poetic image of the rapture of erotic love onto mundane experience. 'Eternity' belongs to the almost angelic intensity of the lovers' deepest fusion, but at the same time we have arrived back at ordinary speech: 'I promise to love you for ever' the most banal of sincere lies. It is this compression of the registers, poetic and everyday, that is a measure of Rilke's extraordinary virtuousity. 'Versprechen' also has more connotations in German than promise in English, because 'sich versprechen' ('so versprecht ihr euch ...') can mean 'slip of the tongue', and suggest how these lovers fail to 'speak wondrously', 'wunderlich reden', from within their union.

This marvellously 'double' sentence is the turning point in this transport of bliss. There may be a hint of the angels, we now read, in the first moments of love — the word 'Schrecken' suggests this — but love inevitably becomes just another love story. It is extraordinary how Rilke here imbues the stock images of the love story, the first look, the first walk, the longing, with the quality of cliché, but clichés still resonant with the passion that has just departed from them.

The poetry now goes beyond any narrative or argument to resolve this line of thought in an image — an image notable for its refusal to be visualised; to be a visual image at all. The two lovers raise each other to each others lips, to find they have lost each other in the ambiguity of faces.

Those with an interest in symmetry will have noticed that this figure, if we arrange the poem into a mirror-image sequence, A B C D C B A, corresponds to the other immediately post-climactic image of the poem, that, precisely, of the mirror faces of the angels. (Note how '**ein** Mal' echoes 'einzeln' in the earlier passage, note too how both transports are sexual in rhythm and implication). But this image is the *mirror* image of the mirror *image*, if I may express myself thus. Both poetic figures confront face with face, but the first expresses fulness, and this one contrives to lend poetic formulation to the moment of vanishing. We look forward to a climactic clinching picture, to find: nothing: the actor deserts the action. We are left at the impossible threshold between them.

The point of this repetition and variation is surely as follows: where the evocation of the angels was poetically magnificent but existentially unsound, and had to be revoked, this poetic realisation of loss is poetically equally magnificent, but remains an existential gain. It does not have to be revoked. Since it is real and not imaginary, there is no price to pay for it. It is 'lament without rebellion', to pick up that memorable phrase from the first reading. The quality of the angels, one might say, has been transformed into the poetic realisation of something that *is* inalienably our own: our partialness.

The final section of the poem completes its symmetrical form, by, first, taking up another moment of the past which has been captured in art, relief sculptures on Greek grave monuments rather than Tobias and the angel, and then balancing the initial despondency with a cautious optimism:

Erstaunte euch nicht auf attischen Stelen die Vorsicht
menschlicher Geste? war nicht Liebe und Abschied
so leicht auf die Schultern gelegt, als wär es aus anderm
Stoffe gemacht als bei uns? Gedenkt euch der Hände,
wie sie drucklos beruhen, obwohl in den Torsen die Kraft steht.
Diese Beherrschten wußten damit: so weit sind wirs,
***dieses** ist unser, uns **so** zu berühren; stärker*
stemmen die Götter uns an. Doch dies ist Sache der Götter.

Fänden auch wir ein reines, verhaltenes, schmales
Menschliches, einen unseren Streifen Fruchtlands
zwischen Strom und Gestein. Denn das eigene Herz übersteigt uns
noch immer wie jene. Und wir können ihm nicht mehr
nachschaun in Bilder, die es besänftigen, noch in
göttliche Körper, in denen es größer sich mäßigt.

Did not the circumspection of human gestures on Attic stelae
surprise you? Were not love and parting
laid so gently upon their shoulders, as if made
of different stuff than with us? Remember the hands,
how they rest without pressure, though there is strength in the torsos.
Thus controlled, they knew: this is what we are,
***this** much is ours, to touch each other **thus**; the gods*
bear upon us more fiercely. But that is the concern of the gods.

Could we but find a simple, sheltered, small
human place, a strip of land, fertile of our own.
between river and rock. For our own heart exceeds us
as theirs did of old. And we can no longer gaze
after it, forming images in which it is calmed, or
godlike bodies in which it finds a larger restraint.

The reference to the angels at the beginning corresponds to the reference to the Greek gods at the end; the unhappy song of the beginning, meeting angelic indifference, is answered by the success of Greek art, 'Bilder', in responding aesthetically to human need. Where, at the beginning, the beat of the heart is fatal, beyond the power of song to fulfil and contain it, here the heart finds its restraint in an art and a theology which are commensurate with it. Moreover the rhetorical situation implied by this section is not the hopeless one of an address to the angels, but one in which experience is shared between the poet and his readers.

The Attic stelae to which Rilke refers are Greek grave monuments which often depicted scenes of leave-taking from the beloved departed. Humans take leave of those they have loved, knowing that death is stronger than their particular attachment, but not despairing for that. Here the theme of death from the First Elegy returns. They touch each other, not with delusions of eternity, but with a proper restraint, beautifully expressed here, and beautifully expressed by Shakespeare in the 94th sonnet: 'They that have power to hurt and will do none... They rightly do inherit heaven's graces'. This last section of the Elegy has certain qualities of a sonnet, it comprises fourteen lines, and although it doesn't rhyme, it does divide into an octave and a sestet. Interestingly, Shakespeare's sonnet also has the line: 'They are the lords and owners of their faces'; which must be allowed to suggest here, that however specific to the early twentieth-century Rilke's poetic concerns are, they are not discontinuous with those of the sixteenth.

In the context of our master-theme of relation, the relation between men, and their relation to the gods are here in order. Active and passive, hands and faces, are balanced. 'Remember the *hands*, these controlled ones knew...'. I translated 'Thus controlled', because, again, I see here a significant double meaning: they are self-controlled, *and* controlled by the gods, without these functions interfering with each other, as they do in the first section of the Elegy. The functions are joined in one word.

The final lines, the sestet of this sonnet within an elegy, like the first lines of the elegy are of lament, but the lament is far more restrained, 'verhalten', here, far more rhythmically focused and poetically productive. What is produced is a memorable passage evoking a desirable place for the habitation of human beings. Note how the quality of being 'ours' almost vanishes amongst the other qualities of this utopian dream, 'fertile', 'narrow', 'human' etc. Subjectivity ceases here to be such intractable isolation, becoming instead one quality among others of a human country. And finally, the proper relation of poetry — that is 'Bilder', realised images — to these conditions of a wise life is explained: images which have the power to soothe the unhappy circumstances which they cannot change materially, except to give them form. Although this status and power of poetry is attributed to Greek culture, and although its lack in early twentieth-century European civilisation is lamented, if my reading of this poem is valid, then, in lamenting what it cannot do, it does it, or nearly.

---

[1] *Rilkes Deutung des Daseins*, from the translation by K.G.Knight, p. 54.

ELEGY THREE

Poetry as Self-Therapy

Edward Timms

The Third Elegy explores the realm of night ('Nacht-Raum', line 33). It thus forms a stark contrast to the first two Elegies, which are irradiated by angels. And yet these three Elegies, taken together, form a coherent sequence. The Third takes up two of the most fundamental themes introduced in Elegies One and Two. On an existential plane it explores the theme of 'terror' ('das Schreckliche'), identified in the earlier Elegies with the inaccessibility of the angelic realm, but here displaced into the all too physical dimension of sexuality. At a more personal level the Third Elegy develops the theme of the lovers, of what they experience at night, and whether the language of love might suffice to explain the mystery of existence. 'Night, is she gentler to lovers?', asks the First Elegy ('Ist sie den Liebenden leichter?', line 21). The Second hints more hopefully that 'lovers, if they knew how, might speak wondrously / under the night's silent air' ('Liebende könnten, verstünden sie's, in der Nachtluft wunderlich reden', lines 37-8). But the Second Elegy ends with an acknowledgement that it is no longer possible to capture the feelings of the heart 'in images that soothe it' ('in Bildern, die es besänftigen', line 78).

The opening lines of the Third Elegy form a direct response to the final lines of the Second. This uncharacteristic continuity reflects the fact that it was not only the first two Elegies that were written at Duino in January and February 1912. For at that date Rilke also wrote the first two lines (but only the first two lines) of the Third. In place of images that soothe, however, we are now confronted by images that threaten: 'that hidden, guilty river-god of the blood' ('jenen verborgenen schuldigen Fluß-Gott des Bluts'). It was thus clear from the start that the theme of the Third Elegy would be the tension between love and sex. Why did Rilke break off at this point? Why was it only eighteen months later, in autumn 1913, that the Third Elegy was completed? To suggest an answer, that is, to provide a framework within which this Elegy may be interpreted, we may begin by considering factors which first inhibited his creativity, and finally released it.

Poetry as Self-Therapy

One of the questions preying on Rilke's mind while he was staying at Duino was whether to undergo psychotherapy. This question is debated in his correspondence with Lou Andreas-Salomé, a close friend who was also a member of Freud's circle. Writing to Lou from Duino on 28 December 1911, just a few days before the Elegies were begun, Rilke mentions the idea of therapy, only to discount it as 'too radical a remedy' ('eine zu gründliche Hülfe').[1] The analyst he had in mind was an acquaintance of Lou's whom he had first met in Paris, Emil von Gebsattel. To Gebsattel he wrote on 14 January 1912, again from Duino: 'Es ist klar, daß diese Stille hier eine Art von Entscheidung mit sich bringen muß, unter allem, was mir so durch den Kopf geht, ist natürlich auch die Analyse' ('It is clear that the tranquillity here must bring about some kind of decision; the various things that are going through my head naturally include having myself analysed'). It was Rilke's wife Clara, who was in the process of divorcing him, who was urging him to have himself analysed. The situation sounds familiar: the wife who welcomes marriage guidance counselling, while the husband resists it. Clara evidently believed that her husband's reluctance to undergo therapy was due to 'cowardice' ('Feigheit'); Rilke, however, in his letter to Gebsattel, associates his reticence with 'piety' ('Frömmigkeit', DE, I, 47).

On 20 January, the day before he completed the First Elegy, Rilke again wrote to Lou about psychoanalysis. What he knows of Freud's writings, he observes, is by no means congenial to him, and yet his personal malaise is so profound that he hardly has the right to refuse the psychoanalytic assistance offered by Gebsattel. At the same time he fears that being 'tidied up' or 'cleared out' ('Aufgeräumtwerden') by means of psychotherapy would leave him spiritually impoverished. It might leave him with something like a 'disinfected soul' ('eine desinfizierte Seele', DE, I, 48).

It was the completion of the First Elegy that finally settled the matter. On 24 January 1912 Rilke wrote to Gebsattel that he had decided not to proceed with the proposed treatment. That same day he clarified his position in a letter to Lou: 'Ich weiß jetzt, daß die Analyse für mich nur Sinn hätte, wenn der merkwürdige Hintergedanke, *nicht mehr zu schreiben,* [...] mir wirklich ernst wäre. Dann dürfte man sich die Teufel austreiben lassen, da sie ja im Bürgerlichen wirklich nur störend und peinlich sind, und gehen die Engel möglicherweise mit aus, so müßte man auch das als Vereinfachung auffassen' ('Now I know that for me analysis would only be meaningful if I was really serious about that strange idea I have at the back of my mind: *to give up writing* [...] In that case one would be entitled to have one's devils expelled, since in ordinary life they are really only disturbing and embarrassing, and if by chance the angels as well should disappear, one would have to regard that too as a simplification', DE, I, 54). The inspirational moment provided by the first Elegy thus led Rilke to abandon thoughts of therapy for fear of forfeiting his poetic vision. The angels of his poetic vision might be lost if he succeeded in exorcising the devils of his personal distress.

Rather than have himself analysed, Rilke set out again on his travels, which took him first to Venice and finally to Spain. In a letter of February 1914 to Magda von Hattingberg (Benvenuta) he describes this journey as an alternative to having himself analysed, either by his friend Gebsattel or indeed by Freud himself: 'Während der letzten schweren Jahre stand ich dann wirklich zwei oder dreimal vor dem Entschlusse einer Analyse, sei es durch diesen Freund, sei es durch Prof. Freud selbst; zuletzt im Herbst 1912 wars fast eine Wahl: Analyse oder Reise nach Spanien. Du weißt, ich wählte die Reise' ('During the last difficult years there really were two or three occasions when I was on the verge of deciding to have myself analysed, either by that friend or by Professor Freud himself, the last time being in autumn 1912, when the choice was in effect: analysis or journey to Spain. As you know, I chose the journey').[2]

The evidence suggests that Rilke felt psychotherapy and poetic creativity to be mutually exclusive. This is the view adopted by the majority of critics, especially those who (like Jacob Steiner) repudiate psychoanalytic readings of the Third Elegy as reductive.[3] Against this, however, we surely need to bear in mind a number of counter-arguments. First, the burst of inspiration which led to the writing of the first Elegies occurred at the very moment when Rilke was agonizing about psychoanalysis. Thus the two impulses cannot be entirely unrelated; indeed, the Elegies seem in some sense to be the poetic correlative of that inner crisis that led Rilke to contemplate analysis.

Moreover Rilke himself, in that letter to Lou Andreas-Salomé of 20 January 1912, suggests that his own activity as a poet may be seen as a form of 'self-treatment' or 'self-therapy' ('Selbstbehandlung'). Whereas his wife Clara lacks the sustenance provided by creative work, and is thus dependent on the support provided by Gebsattel as her analyst, Rilke's creative powers make him more self-sufficient. But in the same sentence in which he defines his own work as 'self-therapy', he goes on to add: 'admittedly, to the same degree that it developed and became something autonomous, it increasingly loses its therapeutic and conciliatory quality and makes demands' ('allerdings in demselben Maaße, als sie sich entwickelte und etwas Selbständiges wurde, verliert sie immer mehr das Therapeutische und Rücksichtsvolle und stellt Forderungen', DE, I, 49). Thus we may expect to find in the poetry, and in the Third Elegy in particular, a tension between residual elements of 'self-therapy' and the impulse towards 'autonomous' poetic creation.

Thirdly, the depressions from which Rilke suffered involved a malaise which is one of the classical subjects of psychoanalysis: a revulsion with his own body. In his letter to Lou he lists a series of somatic symptoms, emphasizing 'the fact that I am pretty unbearable to myself in a purely physical sense' ('die Thatsache, daß ich mir rein körperlich recht unerträglich bin'). He even suggests that his bodily self is in danger of becoming 'the caricature of his spiritual self' ('Mein Körperliches läuft Gefahr, die Karrikatur meiner Geistigkeit zu werden.' DE, I, 48-9). This formulation (as we shall see) has some bearing on the themes of the Third Elegy.

Finally, to round off this account of Rilke's early encounters with psychoanalysis, we may note that Rilke did not completely turn his back on Freud and his followers. His journey to Spain merely brought him back to psychoanalysis by a circuitous route. Early in September 1913, during the Munich Psychoanalytic Congress, Rilke was actually introduced to Freud by Lou Andreas-Salomé. And this was not simply a casual personal encounter. Rilke records that on 8 September he spent most of the day at the Psychoanalytic Congress, listening to various papers and meeting leading analysts, including Gebsattel, Eitington and Ferenczi, Frederik van Eeden and Poul Bjerre.[4] Among the papers presented were Freud's 'The Problem of Choice of Neurosis' and Jung's 'The Question of Psychological Types'. This was the period when both Freud and Jung were extending their psychological inquiries into the realm of the 'archaic heritage'. And it is possible that their ideas helped to stimulate Rilke's own interest in the genetic determinants of human experience. Describing his impressions of the Munich Congress in a letter of February 1914 to Benvenuta, he concludes that to have undergone analysis would have been catastrophic for a poet whose inspiration derived precisely from the fact '*that it did not know itself*' ('*daß es sich nicht kannte*'). At the same time he emphasizes that the meeting with Freud and his followers was 'important and memorable' for him ('mir wichtig und merkwürdig'): 'their whole tendency and application is certainly one of the most essential movements in medical science, indeed in that *human* science which actually does not yet exist' ('ihre ganze Richtung und Anwendung gehört sicher zu den wesentlichsten Bewegungen der ärztlichen, ja jener *menschlichen* Wissenschaft, die es eigentlich noch gar nicht giebt').[5] The excitement caused by this renewed encounter with psychoanalysis almost certainly restimulated Rilke's creativity. For it was approximately a month later that he finally succeeded in completing the Third Duino Elegy.

The Drama of Individuation

Seen from a psychoanalytic perspective, the Elegies may be read as a journey towards individuation. The working-through of existential and emotional dilemmas is not, however, structured by the benign attentiveness of a therapist who, if we were to cry out, could be counted upon to 'hear' (opening line of Elegy One). The journey towards individuation unfolds through a landscape bereft of metaphysical reassurances. There is no great psychotherapist up in the sky. The angels preside over an existential wasteland, a wasteland which is post-Nietzschean but pre-Freudian: post-Nietzschean, in the sense that the Christian conceptions of salvation have become problematic; but pre-Freudian in the sense that Rilke cannot accept the secular gospel of well-adjusted emotional relationships as a valid alternative.

The poetic quest — for Rilke as for Kafka and others of his generation — is thus destined to fail: to fall between the two stools of a self-transcendence that is unattainable and a self-fulfilment that is felt to be inadequate, even if it could be attained. In this secularized version of the Pilgrim's Progress the Third Elegy represents the Slough of Despond. It is the darkest of the Elegies, haunted by images of night; and yet it has a remarkable clarity of structure. It is less fraught than any other Elegy with unresolved ambiguities, with undefined states of anxiety or deprivation. The anxiety is certainly there, but for once it is clearly defined — in images that blend residues of romantic love poetry with a language of the body that is disturbingly psychoanalytic.

Unlike the majority of the Elegies, the Third has a clear five-part structure. Indeed, it can be interpreted as a five-act drama. The protagonists in this drama are the Young Man and the Young Woman ('Jüngling', line 3, and 'Mädchen', line 5). The action involves a struggle to come to terms with what (in the language of Freud or Jung) we may call the 'archaic heritage'. The pauses between the acts are marked by the four line-breaks inserted by Rilke himself, dividing the dramatic action into five sections of unequal length. It is even possible to indicate the movement of each act by highlighting a crucial image: Act I: Turmoil ('Aufruhr', line 7); Act II: Initiation ('sich beginnen', line 25); Act III: Descending into the Depths ('hinabsteigen', line 58); Act IV: Recognition ('Sehen', line 66); and Act V: Containment ('verhalten', line 85).

My commentary will trace this five-phase movement from conflict towards resolution, showing that it depends (as in psychoanalysis) on a creative reworking of memories of childhood. Act I, 'Turmoil', is structured by a series of confrontations:

EINES ist, die Geliebte zu singen. Ein anderes, wehe,
jenen verborgenen schuldigen Fluß-Gott des Bluts.
Den sie von weitem erkennt, ihren Jüngling, was weiß er
selbst von dem Herren der Lust, der aus dem Einsamen oft,
ehe das Mädchen noch linderte, oft auch als wäre sie nicht,
ach, von welchem Unkenntlichen triefend, das Gotthaupt
aufhob, aufrufend die Nacht zu unendlichem Aufruhr.
O des Blutes Neptun, o sein furchtbarer Dreizack.
O der dunkele Wind seiner Brust aus gewundener Muschel.
Horch, wie die Nacht sich muldet und höhlt. Ihr Sterne,
stammt nicht von euch des Liebenden Lust zu dem Antlitz
seiner Geliebten? Hat er die innige Einsicht
in ihr reines Gesicht nicht aus dem reinen Gestirn?

ONE thing it is to sing the beloved. Another, alas,
that hidden guilty river-god of the blood.
That one she knows from afar, her young man, what does he know
himself of the lord of pleasure, who often from within his lonely being,
before the girl could soothe him, often as if she did not exist, dripping
from what unknowable depths, raised the god-head,
arousing the night to infinite turmoil?
Oh, Neptune of the blood, oh, his terrible trident.
Oh, the dark wind of his breast out of the convolute shell,
Hark, how the night takes on hollows and curves. You stars,
do you not impart the lover's delight in the face
of the beloved? Does not his rapt contemplation
of her pure face derive from the pure stars?

Although the protagonists are introduced as 'Jüngling' and 'Mädchen', this is clearly not simply a story of boy meets girl. The most significant confrontation occurs at the level of language, introduced by the opening contrast between love and lust. The traditional task of the lyric poet, 'to sing the beloved' (line 1) is contrasted with a theme that resists representation: the 'river-god of the blood'. That resistance is signalled in the second sentence by the absence of a verb. The concept of 'singing' ceases to be appropriate, not simply because the 'god of blood' is 'guilty', but above all because he is 'hidden' (line 2). The poet's task, like that of the psychoanalyst, is to find a language for impulses which elude verbalization because they originate in the realm of the unconscious and unknowable: 'das Unkenntliche' (line 6).

The disturbing paradox is that sexuality becomes aroused within the young man in solitude ('aus dem Einsamen'). The male sexual drive is so self-sufficient, so little dependent on a specific female partner that it often seems 'as though she did not exist'. It is not, however, the Freudian concept of libido that is invoked to describe the forces which plunge the young man into turmoil and reduce the girl to insignificance. It is the more dramatic figure of a 'Neptune of the blood', rising from the depths of classical mythology with 'his terrible trident'; that 'lord of pleasure' who is capable of 'arousing the night to infinite turmoil'. These phallic images nevertheless owe their impact to the way they blur the boundaries between poetic and psychoanalytic discourse, 'Neptune' and 'the unknowable', creating further turmoil in the mind of the reader.

The power of these images disrupts the poetic decorum established by the final section of the Second Elegy. In place of sculpted gestures of Greek serenity, it is now Neptune, a Roman deity, who rears his unruly head, dripping with unspecified seminal fluids. The theme of sexual turmoil is thus intensified by the tension between semantic codes. The romantic mode of 'singing the beloved' (line 1) recurs in lines 12-13 in images of spiritual purity: 'Does not his rapt contemplation / of her pure face derive from the pure stars?'. But these ethereal images represent a form of wishful thinking which pales by comparison with the primitive power of the lord of pleasure and the irrepressible energies which derive from a barely conscious biological heritage.

To resolve this turmoil, we are taken in Act II through a process of 'Initiation'. This section explores the tensions between the male self and the female other — the intimate 'du' of line 14:

Du nicht hast ihm, wehe, nicht seine Mutter
hat ihm die Bogen der Braun so zur Erwartung gespannt.
Nicht an dir, ihn fühlendes Mädchen, an dir nicht
bog seine Lippe sich zum fruchtbarern Ausdruck.
Meinst du wirklich, ihn hätte dein leichter Auftritt
also erschüttert, du, die wandelt wie Frühwind?
Zwar du erschrakst ihm das Herz; doch ältere Schrecken
stürzten in ihn bei dem berührenden Anstoß.
Ruf ihn... du rufst ihn nicht ganz aus dunkelem Umgang.
Freilich, er **will**, er entspringt; erleichtert gewöhnt er
sich in dein heimliches Herz und nimmt und beginnt sich.
Aber begann er sich je?
Mutter, **du** machtest ihn klein, du warst, die ihn anfing;
dir war er neu, du beugtest über die neuen
Augen die freundliche Welt und wehrtest der fremden.
Wo, ach, hin sind die Jahre, da du ihm einfach
mit der schlanken Gestalt wallendes Chaos vertratst?
Vieles verbargst du ihm so; das nächtlich-verdächtige Zimmer
machtest du harmlos, aus deinem Herzen voll Zuflucht
mischtest du menschlichern Raum seinem Nacht-Raum hinzu.
Nicht in die Finsternis, nein, in dein näheres Dasein
hast du das Nachtlicht gestellt, und es schien wie aus Freundschaft.
Nirgends ein Knistern, das du nicht lächelnd erklärtest,
so als wüßtest du längst, **wann** sich die Diele benimmt...
Und er horchte und linderte sich. So vieles vermochte
zärtlich dein Aufstehn; hinter den Schrank trat
hoch im Mantel sein Schicksal, und in die Falten des Vorhangs
paßte, die leicht sich verschob, seine unruhige Zukunft.

Not you, alas, nor was it his mother
who stretched the bow of his brows to such expectation.
It was not you, girl, that felt him, not you
who caused his lip to curve into more fruitful expression.
Do you really suppose it was your gentle approach
that stirred him so deeply, you who move as light as the morning breeze?
True, it was you who struck fear in his heart; but more ancient terrors
assailed him as he stirred to your touch.
Call him... you will never quite call him away from those sombre companions.
Of course, it's his **wish**, he escapes; relieved, he accustoms himself to
your intimate heart and takes and begins himself.
But did he ever begin himself?
Mother, **you** made him small, it was you who started him;
for you he was new, you inclined to his new
eyes the friendly world and shielded him from the world that was strange.

Where, oh where have the years gone when you simply
with your slender figure stood before surging chaos?
Many things thus you concealed from him; the menacing room at night
you made feel safe, and your heart full of refuge
added a realm more human to his realm of night.
No, it was not into the darkness but into your innermost being
that you placed the night-light, so that it seemed to glow with friendship.
There was no creak you could not explain with a smile,
as if you had always known **when** *the floorboards would move... And he*
listened and felt soothed. That much
your consoling presence could do; from behind the wardrobe stepped forth
his tall cloaked destiny, and into the folds of the curtain
fitted, gently swaying, his restless future.

This complex passage explores the origins of identity and the experiences of infancy. The female other, the intimate 'du' of line 14, is no sooner introduced than it is undercut by an abrasive negative: 'Du nicht' — 'Not you'! Neither the mother nor the girl has strung the bow of erotic expectation which shapes the young man's brow. It is not the 'gentle approach' of the girl but some 'more ancient terrors' (lines 18-20) that assail him. Through responding to the call of the love he hopes to escape those terrors and find a new point of departure in the girl's 'intimate' heart ('heimliches Herz' in line 24 plays, in a way that would have appealed to Freud, on the double meaning of the word 'heimlich', implying both 'familiar' and 'mysterious').[6]

However, in line 25 the whole notion of the young man as an autonomous subject, capable of 'beginning himself', is called into question: 'aber begann er sich je?' This abrupt question is followed by a silence: an empty space on the page which breaks the metrical rhythm. We are jolted back into a radically different time scale. In exploring the processes of individuation, the poem now invokes the primacy of the relation between mother and child. It is the mother who in a literal sense 'started' or 'made' him when he was small; and it is she whose 'slender figure' mediates for him the forces of 'surging chaos' (lines 26-30).

Once again Rilke's poetic vision borders on psychoanalysis in assigning to the pre-Oedipal experience of mothering such formative power. The mother is the original 'du', the intimate other who prefigures the 'du' of the beloved. At the same time Rilke's imagery of the relationship between mother and child has a pre-Freudian delicacy. The analyst (as Rilke wrote to Lou Andreas-Salomé in September 1914 during a course of medical treatment) encourages the patient 'just to bring up childhood in chunks' ('die

Kindheit so in Brocken von sich zu geben'). But his own creativity depends on a more inward resolution of unruly feelings and on their transposion into imaginative forms. Once again he concludes that 'analysis is fateful for all productivity' ('Analyse für alles Produktive verhängnisvoll ist').[7]

However, if writing poetry is consistently seen as an antithesis to undergoing analysis, this does not preclude the possibility of assimilating sophisticated psychological insights into the process of poetic self-therapy, not least in the recall of childhood. There is indeed, in the Third Elegy, a tension between lyrical images of protective motherhood and psychoanalytic intimations of the mother-child relationship as charged with erotic significance. At first the position seems reassuring. The floorboards may creak in the darkened room, but the mother explains it away with a smile. But the pivotal ambiguity occurs in line 30: the poignant lament for the mother who 'with you slender figure stood before surging chaos' ('mit der schlanken Gestalt wallendes Chaos vertratst'). In this line the image of maternal slenderness ('schlank') is counterbalanced by a word which suggests an overwhelming plenitude ('wallend'). And Rilke's soothing dactyls echo the language of the classical Goethe (one is reminded of the reassuringly stable metrics of Weimar Classicism). At another level the hypnotic sequence of 'a' sounds, 'mit der schlanken Gestalt wallendes Chaos vertratst', is reminiscent of that lullaby: 'Schlaf Kindlein schlaf, dein Vater war ein Graf', which works like a charm on children.

On a closer reading, however, the line 'mit der schlanken Gestalt wallendes Chaos vertratst', like the experience of mothering which it embodies, proves to be treacherously ambiguous. The 'slender figure' of the mother does not simply protect the child from chaos, for 'vertratst' too has a double meaning. It suggests the ambiguous way in which the mother's body both distances and makes manifest some dimly perceived danger. At this secondary level the mother's figure also represents, perhaps even *embodies* 'surging chaos', with the emphasis on her slenderness carrying a hint of seductiveness. Thus the night-light which her presence places in the dark realm of sexual foreboding may appear gentle and soothing; but it cannot protect the growing boy from his phallic destiny, that tall figure which emerges in the final lines of Act II from behind the wardrobe or among the folds of the curtain.

Through these richly suggestive motifs: the night-light, the creaking floorboards, the mother's slender figure, the inescapable destiny emerging from behind the wardrobe, Rilke poignantly succeeds in fusing adult reflection with the impressionability of childhood, conscious image with intuitive apprehension. At the same time, there is an imaginative residue — something lurking in the folds of the curtain — which resists rational exegesis. This is Rilke's poetry at its finest: a fusion of thought and feeling in images which resonate in the memory. Such images are not easy to elucidate and certainly cannot be explained away.

The Archaic Heritage

At other points, however, Rilke's diction decays into a hybrid between poetry and psychoanalysis, with a loss of both conceptual clarity and of imaginative vigour. This seems particularly true of certain passages in Act III of the Third Elegy, which invites the rather melodramatic title of 'Descending into the Depths' ('hinabsteigen', line 58). Here, the residues of 'self-therapy' become almost too obtrusive, while the images at times fall short of poetic 'autonomy':

Und er selbst, wie er lag, der Erleichterte, unter
schläfernden Lidern deiner leichten Gestaltung
Süße lösend in den gekosteten Vorschlaf—:
***schien** ein Gehüteter... Aber **innen**: wer wehrte,*
hinderte innen in ihm die Fluten der Herkunft?
*Ach, da **war** keine Vorsicht im Schlafenden; schlafend,*
aber träumend, aber in Fiebern: wie er sich ein-ließ.
Er, der Neue, Scheuende, wie er verstrickt war,
mit des innern Geschehns weiterschlagenden Ranken
schon zu Mustern verschlungen, zu würgendem Wachstum, zu tierhaft
jagenden Formen. Wie er sich hingab —. Liebte.
Liebte sein Inneres, seines Inneren Wildnis,
diesen Urwald in ihm, auf dessen stummem Gestürztsein
lichtgrün sein Herz stand. Liebte. Verließ es, ging die
eigenen Wurzeln hinaus in gewaltigen Ursprung,
wo seine kleine Geburt schon überlebt war. Liebend
stieg er hinab in das ältere Blut, in die Schluchten,
wo das Furchtbare lag, noch satt von den Vätern. Und jedes
Schreckliche kannte ihn, blinzelte, war wie verständigt.
Ja, das Entsetzliche lächelte... Selten
hast du so zärtlich gelächelt, Mutter. Wie sollte
*er es nicht lieben, da es ihm lächelte. **Vor** dir*
hat ers geliebt, denn, da du ihn trugst schon,
war es im Wasser gelöst, das den Keimenden leicht macht.

And he himself, as he lay, unburdened, under
drowsy eyelids shaped by your gentle touch,

absorbing sweetness into the first taste of sleep,
***seemed** well protected... But **within**: who could resist,*
prevent the floods of origin within him? Alas, within the sleeping boy
*there **was** no restraint; sleeping,*
but dreaming, but febrile: how deep was his downfall.
He, so new, shying away, how he became entangled,
with ever-encroaching tendrils of inward processes
twisted to patterns, to throttling growths, into forms
straining with animal energies. What self-abandon —. Loved. Loved his
inner self, his inner jungle,
the primeval forest inside him, upon whose silent overthrownness
his heart stood bathed in green light. Loved. Left it, went through his
own roots into primitive origin,
where his little birth was already outlived. Loving,
he descended into the more ancient blood, into ravines
where terror lurked, still gorged with his fathers. And every
dread knew who he was, winked, knowingly.
Yes, what was baleful smiled... Rarely
have you smiled so tenderly, mother. How should
*he not love it, when it smiled at him. Long **before** you*
he loved it, for even as you were carrying him
it was dissolved in the waters that sustain the germ of the child.

In this third section it becomes clear that the initiation of the child through maternal love provides an illusory security: the drowsy boy '*seemed* well protected'. But '*within*' — the use of repetition and emphatic type seems rather forced — 'within' he is defenceless against the 'floods of origin', Rilke's metaphor for the archaic heritage. Sleeping, dreaming, he becomes entangled in a lush botanical imagery which the poet does not really seem to have under control. It is certainly not the language of dreams — the language that Trakl and Kafka use with such evocative power. Rilke's picture of the 'jungle' of the young man's inner self (lines 50-54) is reminiscent of those Jugendstil book illustrations which show 'ever-encroaching tendrils' and 'throttling growths' creating a 'primeval forest' that is too picturesque to be entirely convincing. And there is something rather stagey about those terrifying ravines into which he descends ('Schluchten, / wo das Furchtbare lag', lines 57-8). The celebrated translation by J. B. Leishman and Stephen Spender, to which several generations of English readers owe their introduction to the Elegies, at this point reads: 'ravines / where Frightfulness lurked'. This sounds like a stage-set for a third-rate production of Wagner. Indeed, the capital letter used for 'Frightfulness' betrays the perplexity of the translators when confronted by such Germanic monsters.[8]

Just occasionally Rilke in this section strikes a richer vein — in images like 'stummes Gestürztsein' ('silent overthrownness', line 54). This hints at Heidegger's language of existential insecurity — that 'Geworfensein' which suggests that at birth we are 'precipitated' into a universe we cannot comprehend. But by contrast with the abstract language of Heidegger, Rilke's image of 'overthrownness' gains a palpable presence through the link with the 'primeval forest' — the hint of ancient tree trunks overthrown to reveal a space 'bathed in green light', where new shoots may grow. This imagery of roots and vegetation has the effect of subverting the romantic idiom of love. In lines 52-55 the word 'loved' is itself redefined within this process of a return to primitive biological origins. Set in isolation against the cumulative power of the imagery of 'Wachstum' and 'Ursprung', it becomes only too clear that 'liebte' is a weak verb. The word is repeated no less than three times in four lines, but with an ever-decreasing power of conviction: 'Loved. Loved his / inner self [...] Loved.' This gives a new slant to the celebrated Rilkean conception of love without a personal object, by grounding it in a conception of the archaic heritage that is strongly reminiscent of the theories of Jung. This biologically determined concept of a libidinous drive that predates all individuation, let alone any commitment to a particular person, is reduced grammatically to a single solitary word: 'Liebte', without subject or object.

Within this sombre realm, to 'sing the beloved' ceases to be plausible. Indeed there is no beloved in sight, no reference whatsoever to the girl in the whole of Act III. The action unfolds entirely *within* the man: 'innen' (line 45); 'in ihm' (line 54). The young man, and by this stage he is a very Jungian young man, is trapped by the tendrils of primeval sensuality, as he descends into 'the more ancient blood' of his ancestral heritage. The sexual drive is here pictured in a language of archaic terror. And the fears aroused by this descent into the 'ravines' may even be associated with revulsion about female genitalia.[9]

This disproportion between poetic stage-set and emotional scenario at times verges on the melodramatic. Imagery of 'blood' forms a leitmotif in this Elegy, from the 'river-god of the blood' (line 2) to the 'veins' of the young man in line 80. The word 'blood' signals a confluence between sexual arousal and genetic inheritance. It may seem pedantic to point out that this is pre-scientific (it was not, after all, until the 1930s that the different blood groups were identified and it became clear that blood was not the transmittor of heredity). Such turgid celebrations of 'blood-consciousness' were extremely prominent in the literature of this period (one thinks of D.H.Lawrence as well as Ernst Jünger and Gottfried Benn). And it was commonplace to attribute specific behaviour patterns to unalterable character traits which a person allegedly had 'in his blood'. However, in noting these affinities we may well wonder what a poet of Rilke's sensibility is doing in such company. The notion of 'the more ancient blood' seems oppressively deterministic. And the Jungian invocation of primal 'fathers' (in the plural) evades a more crucial issue: the question whether the poet, so haunted by maternal memories, is not evading the challenge of coming to terms with an individual father. The cluster of feelings associated with the word 'Vater', a word which does not occur in the singular in the Third Elegy, is not explored until the Fourth, and then only in a desexualized context. Despite the melodramatic invocations of primal ancestors, there is no attempt in the Third Elegy to engage with the full complexity of the Oedipal configuration.

The language of this third section thus seems simultaneously strained and evasive. But it is enlivened at the moment of recognition by disconcerting touches of black humour: 'And every / dread knew who he was, winked, knowlingly. / Yes, what was baleful smiled... Rarely / have you smiled so tenderly, mother. How should / he not love it, when it smiled at him.' (lines 59-63). That smile, so much more powerful than the consoling smile of the mother, has a seductiveness which transfixes, luring the young man towards his genetic destiny. The final images of this section reaffirm the primacy of the womb: 'the waters that sustain the germ of the child' (line 65). Yet it is hard to escape the conclusion that the imagery of the Third Elegy is overwhelmingly phallocentric.

In other Elegies the poet poignantly explores human destiny as a whole, including the female of the species. In the Third Elegy the girl's emotional viewpoint, her subjective experience of sexuality, is consistently marginalized. The woman's response, when confronted by the awesome spectacle of male sexual awakening, is pictured in a way that is positively Victorian. Whether as mother or as girlfriend, she is assigned a Florence Nightingale role, with even a hint (in line 35) of the lady with the lamp. The mother's role is to comfort, the girl's to soothe, and her approach is seen as 'gentle'. She is in line 21 just about allowed to 'touch'; but Rilke's fundamental theme is that the dynamics of male sexuality unfold (line 5) 'as though she did not exist'. This perspective is reinforced by a use of pronouns which is heavily weighted against any conception of active female involvement. The young man is consistently referred to in the third person, as 'er', the undoubted protagonist in the drama of individuation. But the girl is almost invariably addressed in the second person singular, as 'du', a passive spectator whose powers of action — and indeed of comprehension — are strictly limited.

This lack of symmetry results in a rather unbalanced picture of gender roles. The deconstruction of the romantic image of love is certainly honest and timely. It acknowledges, in terms which were rather daring at this date, that the power of the phallus predates the young man's first encounter with the girl. But the invocation of male potency has as its concomitant a prettification of female emotions. The girl is never given a chance to feel anything herself; her role is that of the 'girl' that 'felt him', subordinating her subjectivity to the emotional needs of the male.

Taming the Phallus

The patronizing tone persists in Act IV, 'Recognition'. Here the focus does shift back to the girl, but she is apostrophized in a form ('O Mädchen', line 68) that cannot be literally translated without sounding archaic. Moreover, she is still being addressed didactically, especially in lines 66-68, as if she were being given a sex talk by a rather pompous teacher:

Siehe, wir lieben nicht, wie die Blumen, aus einem
einzigen Jahr; uns steigt, wo wir lieben,
unvordenklicher Saft in die Arme. O Mädchen,
***dies:** daß wir liebten in uns, nicht Eines, ein Künftiges, sondern*
das zahllos Brauende; nicht ein einzelnes Kind,
sondern die Väter, die wie Trümmer Gebirgs
uns im Grunde beruhn; sondern das trockene Flußbett
einstiger Mütter —; sondern die ganze
lautlose Landschaft unter dem wolkigen oder
*reinen Verhängnis —: **dies** kam dir, Mädchen, zuvor.*

Look, we do not love, like flowers in one
single year; where we love, there rises
immemorial sap in our arms. Girl,
***this** is what matters: that we loved in ourselves, not simply one*
object, something to come, but
unceasing ferment; not just a single child,
but the fathers lying within our depths
like fragments of a mountain range; the dried-up river-bed

of former mothers; the whole
soundless landscape beneath our cloudy or
clear destiny —: ***this****, girl, was there before you.*

The tone of lines 66-68 is almost that of a botany lesson, in which an audience of schoolgirls is told about the birds and the bees, or rather warned not to confuse the language of flowers with 'the immemorial sap' which rises in our arms 'where we love'.

The crucial question is who is speaking in these lines and who is meant by the words 'we' and 'us'. Does the sex talk relate only to the man's genetic heritage? If we are to understand that it is only in the arms of *males* that the sap rises, this would surely limit the poem, by excluding a *shared* involvement the processes of procreation. Since (as we have seen) pronouns are particularly revealing in this poem, it is worth considering whether there is a progression from Act I to Act IV. An attentive reading soon establishes that different pronouns predominate in each section. In Act I it is the masculine 'er', the young man seen rather externally. In Act II it is the feminine 'du', the female other as apostrophized by the poet. Act III unfolds 'within him' ('in ihm', line 54); and it takes us, in pivotal lines 55-65, into the realm of the impersonal neuter pronoun 'es' — that 'it' (whatever it is) that the young man so dreads and loves. In German, of course, the 'es' is Freud's word for what in English is normally translated as the 'id'.

Finally, at the beginning of Act IV (line 66), the sequence culminates in the word 'we' — the 'wir' of shared experience. Since this is the first time the word 'wir' occurs, it hints at the possibility of an advance towards mature individuation, which presupposes a reprocity between self and other. In lines 66-68 it is still the poet speaking, offering a general statement about the human condition, expressed in the universalizing present tense. But the shift to the more personal past tense in line 69 ('wir liebten'), indicates a change of voice. The remainder of Act IV may be read as a dramatic monologue in which the young man conveys to the girl his rather bleak view of sexuality. Here the perspective changes and the word 'we' surely signifies 'you and I', the two young lovers. Thus for a moment the meaning opens out to include the girl within the dramatic scenario. And the young man's insights into the archaic heritage embrace the whole procreative process, mothers no less than fathers. The problem is that the voice of the young man is almost as patronizing as that of the poet. The possibility of childbirth, that specifically female dimension of sexual experience, is played down by his insistence that love is *not* directed towards 'a single child'. The aim may be to emphasize the impersonality of the act of procreation, but the effect is to devalue the experiences of pregnancy and motherhood by tracing them back to an abstract 'destiny'. And in line 75 the girl is once again addressed as if she were situated outside the sexual ferment, a late arrival on the scene of love who needs to have it all explained.

Thus the drama ends, in Act V, on a note of anti-climax. The poet begins prosing once more, concluding his address to the girl with an exhortation to restraint, rather than a promise of of fulfilment. It is clear that the young man's quest has not led to a recognition of what psychoanalysis would call 'mature genitality', since his sexual destiny, as recapitulated by the poet, remains in the realm of the archaic heritage. The vision of primal fathers ('Väter', line 59), extended in lines 71-73 to include 'former mothers', now acquires associations that are overwhelmingly negative:

Und du selber, was weißt du —, du locktest
Vorzeit empor in dem Liebenden. Welche Gefühle
wühlten herauf aus entwandelten Wesen. Welche
Frauen haßten dich da. Was für finstere Männer
regtest du auf im Geäder des Jünglings? Tote
Kinder wollten zu dir... O leise, leise,
tu ein liebes vor ihm, ein verläßliches Tagwerk, — führ ihn
nah an den Garten heran, gieb ihm der Nächte
Übergewicht.....
Verhalt ihn.....

And you yourself, what do you know — , you stirred up
times long ago in your lover. What feelings
welled up out of beings now vanished. What
women hated you in him. What sinister men
you aroused in the young man's veins. Dead
children reached out to you... Oh, gently, gently,
carry out a loving daily task before him, a reliable task, — lead him close
to the garden, outweigh the nights
for him.....
Restrain him.....

In this concluding section the girl is reminded not of the creative maternal heritage, but of women who 'hated' her, of 'sinister men' and of the 'dead children' whom she has unwittingly stirred up in the young man's veins. Out of this arid pre-historic landscape there is, it seems, to be no rebirth.

This final section also signals a regression in the ascending sequence of pronouns, from 'er' through 'du' and 'es' to 'wir'. For the pronoun with greatest significance for the process of individuation is the one that does not occur in the Third Elegy, the first person singular 'I' ('ich'). The frustration of the young man's quest is emphatically signalled by the failure to attain an 'ich', an autonomous ego. He finally has to be content with a passive role, as recipient of the girl's restraining influence. This absence of the pronoun 'ich' is all the more striking because the first person singular is prominent in all the other Elegies, with the solitary exception of the Eighth, a more impersonal philosophical poem.

The First Elegy begins with the question: 'Who, if I cried, would hear me'. And the Tenth Elegy also privileges the first-person singular pronoun in its opening line: 'May the time come when [...] I '. Since the opening lines of the Tenth were also part of Rilke's original draft, written in January 1912, it is clear that from the start the goal of the Elegies was the attainment of individuation, of the ability to say 'I' in an affirmative voice that could command the assent of the angels. The process is inhibited not only by existential insecurities, but also by the fallible nature of self-articulation itself, which the Elegies so richly explore in all its variants (crying, singing, saying, praising, lamenting). The inability to say 'I' in the Third Elegy marks a significant setback in the pilgrim's progress: a regression from that sufficiency of self, glimpsed in the mirror of the other, which Michael Minden has elucidated in his commentary on the Second Elegy.

In short, the protagonists of the Third Elegy fail to attain either individual fulfilment or a genuine reconciliation between the sexes. The young man of line 80 seems emotionally as immature as in the opening sequence which introduced him, although intellectually he now *knows* more that he originally did about the 'lord of pleasure'. As for the girl, she seems to be left with a choice between abandoning herself to primitive processes of 'fermenation' or opting for a consoling 'restraint'. 'Mädchen' still in line 70, the girl is not permitted to mature into a woman ('Frau'). How she is ever to achieve adult identity, let alone fulfil her role as mother, remains something of a mystery.

Nevertheless, it is she who is assigned the task of coping with the young man's unresolved emotional turmoil. Caught between fascinated love of his 'inner jungle' and horrified revulsion, he has clearly failed to come to terms with his sexuality. It seems that the girl must accept responsibility for him and bear the burden of his failure. In accordance with patriarchal sexual theory, it is her task to 'tame the phallus'. Rilke's poem envisages a similar solution, although he finds more delicate images for this process: 'lead him close to the garden, outweigh the nights for him..... Restrain him.....' Although the meaning of 'der Nächte Übergewicht' remains ambiguous, the image of the 'garden' seems to signal the taming of the 'jungle' within more civilized forms. But it is unclear how flowers, whose love lasts only 'one single year', are to blossom from the 'primeval forest'. In this poem the bodily self (to recall that formulation from Rilke's letter to Lou Andreas-Salomé) still seems a 'caricature' of the spiritual self, split into a polarized opposition between male overthrownness and female restraint. But the girl seems far too frail and disembodied to provide an effective counterweight. The image of 'restraint' with which this Elegy concludes thus comes as an anti-climax. It was not until he completed the Fifth Elegy, the very last to be written, in 1922 that Rilke succeeded in construing the interaction between lovers as a precarious equilibrium.

---

[1] Rainer Maria Rilke—Lou Andreas Salomé, *Briefwechsel*, ed. Ernst Pfeiffer, p. 240.

[2] Rainer Maria Rilke, *Briefwechsel mit Benvenuta* (Esslingen, 1954), p.127.

[3] Jacob Steiner, *Rilkes Duineser Elegien*, p.54. For a more sympathetic account of the links with psychoanalysis, see David Kleinbard, *The Beginning of Terror: A Psychological Study of Rilke's Life and Work* (New York, 1993).

[4] Ingeborg Schnack, *Rainer Maria Rilke: Chronik seines Lebens und seines Werkes* (Frankfurt am Main, 1975), pp. 439-40.

[5] Rilke, *Briefwechsel mit Benvenuta*, p. 127.

[6] See Freud's analysis of the multiple meanings of 'heimlich' in his essay on 'The Uncanny' ('Das Unheimliche', 1919), in *Studienausgabe* (Frankfurt/Main, 1969-79), IV, pp. 241-74.

[7] Rainer Maria Rilke—Lou Andreas-Salomé, *Briefwechsel*, p. 353 and 363-4.

[8] *Duino Elegies*, p. 45.

[9] See Steiner, *Rilkes Duineser Elegien*, p. 64.

ELEGY FOUR

A Dantist's view

Patrick Boyde

My soul, sit thou a patient looker-on;
Judge not the play before the play is done:
Her plot has many changes; every day
Speaks a new scene; the last act crowns the play.[1]

Happy those early days, when I
Shined in my angel-infancy!
Before I understood this place
Appointed for my second race,
...
When on some gilded cloud, or flower,
My gazing soul would dwell an hour,
And in those weaker glories spy
Some shadows of eternity.[2]

'To the cobbler there is nothing like leather', so I hope I may be forgiven if I approach my elegy via a famous passage in the *Vita nuova* which describes the genesis of a poem that was to mark a turning-point in Dante's development. The poet was walking 'beside a very clear stream' when a 'desire to write came upon him'. The desire was so powerful that he immediately took thought about his audience and decided to address himself to noble-minded women who understood the nature of love. Then, he tells us: 'my tongue spoke as if it were moved by itself and said: "Donne ch'avete intelletto d'amore". These words I stored in my mind with great joy, thinking that I would take them as my beginning'.

It is important to notice that Dante's theme was already determined. He had just resolved to stop writing self-centred poems of lamentation expressing the torments of unrequited love. Love for Beatrice was now to be its own reward. His new 'matter' was to be simply 'praise of this most noble lady' and his mission was to devise a style to achieve this high purpose, 'lo stilo de la sua loda', which he would later call a 'sweet new style'. He also goes on to make it clear that he waited 'several days' before composing the canzone which begins with the inspired line; and his detailed analysis of the structure of the poem calls attention to the meticulous planning of the whole.[3]

Anyone who knows anything about the *Duino Elegies* will see the parallels immediately. In Rilke's terminology, there was to be no more 'Werbung' and therefore no more 'Klage'; the poet had accepted an 'Auftrag', which was simply 'Rühmung'. But the most important reason for dwelling on this passage is that it offers one of the classic statements about the nature of poetic inspiration. Poetry, Dante reminds us, cannot be written to order. There can and should be preparation and meditation; one can and must take a decision about tone and the intended audience; but nothing will happen until a particular mood 'comes upon' the writer and 'the tongue speaks of its own accord'. That is what happened at Duino in January 1912 when a voice in the wind from the sea seemed to speak the opening line of the First Elegy; and that is what must have happened in Munich in November 1915 when an inner voice addressed a mysterious question to a no less mysterious audience in the line of verse that we know as the beginning of the Fourth Elegy:

O Bäume Lebens, o wann winterlich?

Rilke had had to wait a long while for inspiration to return after the delayed completion of the Third Elegy in 1913. In that time he had read widely, travelled widely, translated poetry from French and Italian, and fallen in and out of love with women who seemed to promise an ideal relationship (notably the pianist Magda von Hattenberg and the much younger painter Loulou Albert-Hasard). But he had not published a major collection of poems since the second volume of *Neue Gedichte* in 1908 and his principal source of income had become the royalties from the 1912 pocket edition of the prose poem he had begun as long ago as 1899, *Die Weise von Leben und Tod des Cornets Christoph Rilke*. Europe went to war while he waited; and the universal glorification of patriotism, danger, heroism and the sacrificial letting of blood gripped even Rilke for a time, as we know from three fragments written in August 1914, in which one recognises the tone and rhythms of the first three elegies. But these were an aberration and by the middle of 1915 the thirty-nine-year old poet was only too aware that he was likely to be called up into the Austrian army to fight against the two countries that had done most to shape his culture and imagination, Russia and France. His first medical, scheduled for May 1915, was postponed; but the second was set for 24 November (in the event he was passed as fit for service in the army reserve and did three painful weeks of basic infantry training before being posted to a 'chairborne' job in the War Ministry). It was a 'winter of discontent'. But the prospect of military service seems to have concentrated his mind and the first weeks of November saw a renewed surge of creative energy, culminating on the 22nd and 23rd with the composition of what became the Fourth Elegy.[4]

How or when did Rilke realise that his new poem was going to be part of the planned cycle? The Second and Third Elegies had begun by taking up one of the key-words of their predecessor ('Jeder *Engel* ist schrecklich'; 'Eines ist, die *Geliebte* zu singen ...'); and their opening words already display that mixture of dactylic and trochaic pulses through which they proclaim their distant relationship to the quantitative metre of the classical elegiac couplet. But our poem opens with 'trees' and 'winter'; and the following lines confirm that it is written in blank verse of the kind that Rilke had used with wonderful suppleness in some of the finest poems in *Neue Gedichte*: in other words, the rhythm is purely binary and the number of syllables strictly limited (ten to the line if the last word is oxytone, eleven if it is paroxytone, exactly as in the Italian hendecasyllable and the English iambic pentameter).

But perhaps the question is ill-conceived or ill-phrased. Rilke clearly did have a general plan of campaign and the first fifteen lines of the Tenth Elegy, composed in 1912, could be compared to a parachute drop on the final objective in advance of the main column. Moreover, nothing is more characteristic of Rilke than the conceptual leap to one side or the unexpected doubling back on his tracks in order to throw any plodding reader off his scent. It is also broadly true that his whole poetic output consists of loosely made micro-cycles and macro-cycles; by which I mean that in each of his earlier printed works the poems tend to fall into little groups, and that the same themes or subjects reappear from one collection to the next — themes such as childhood, the Great City, angels, love and lovers, and subjects such as buildings, works of art, animals and flowers (especially roses), or characters and episodes from the Old and New Testaments.

Enough, however, of these generalisations. For better or worse, my inclinations as a reader are like those of Theodor Fontane, who wrote that 'the merely generic, the heading, the indication of content can never rivet the attention: all the interest lurks in the detail'.[5]

O Bäume Lebens, o wann winterlich?
Wir sind nicht einig. Sind nicht wie die Zug-
vögel verständigt. Überholt und spät,
so drängen wir uns plötzlich Winden auf
und fallen ein auf teilnahmslosen Teich.
Blühn und verdorrn ist uns zugleich bewußt.
Und irgendwo gehn Löwen noch und wissen,
solang sie herrlich sind, von keiner Ohnmacht.

O trees of life, when is wintertime?
We're not at one. We don't have instinct
like migratory birds. Overtaken and late,
we suddenly cast ourselves upon the winds
and land on some unwelcoming pool.
Flowering and withering are known in the same moment.
And somewhere lions are still roaming and know
no weakness, while they are in their prime.

The opening words could hardly be more common: 'trees', 'life', 'wintry', 'O', 'when'. The figures of speech — apostrophe and rhetorical question — make one fear the worst. But there is an authentic 'strangeness' or 'otherness' in the language which has made the first line very familiar in Germany, where I have heard it quoted — as an automatic response to the name of Rilke — by people who cannot otherwise get beyond 'Herr: es ist Zeit. Der Sommer war sehr groß', the opening quatrain of *Der Panther* or the recurring 'white elephant' in *Das Karusell.* Perhaps this feeling of strangeness arises because one seems to hear a biblical quotation ('the tree of life'), because one would expect to combine 'Baum' and 'Leben' in German as 'Lebensbäume', or because 'winterlich' means 'wintry', so that a closer translation of the line might be 'O life-trees, O when wintrily'. But whatever the causes, the line seems 'inspired'.

If you ask 'what does it mean?', the answer must be that it is almost always a bad idea to demand complete intelligibility immediately from any poet worthy of the name, least of all from Rilke. We should think of his poems as being like barrels of 'real ale', alive and still in ferment unlike the lagers and keg bitters of today. They are in perfect condition when they leave the brewery, but get shaken up in the very process of being unloaded into our consciousness, so that they became 'cloudy' — what Rilke would call 'trübe' or 'beschlagen'. All we have to do is to let the 'cloudiness' settle down in the cellars of our minds while we read on, and we will find that they soon become 'clear' again — what the English landlord so poetically calls 'bright'.

So let us leave the meaning of the tree image and the full force of the question in suspension for a moment and move on to the following lines, where 'we' — apparently, mankind as a whole — are compared, to our apparent disadvantage, first with migratory birds, then with flowers, and finally with some very heraldic lions. They all live in a state of harmony with the rhythms of the cosmos. Birds 'know' instinctively when to leave for the south with a favourable wind; plants blossom and wither at the appropriate time of year (ordinary deciduous trees shed their leaves by late November in readiness for 'wintry' weather); lions simply do not know the meaning of weakness when they are in their lordly prime.

The syntax is almost ostentatiously simple, the tone deceptively relaxed. But there is already a hint of technical audacity in the tmesis of 'Zug-vögel'; the contrast between 'sich aufdrängen' and 'einfallen' is expertly managed; and the fifth line with its final sequence of long vowels is hauntingly beautiful: 'und fallen ein auf teilnahmslosen Teich' (one could say a great deal about the 'indifference' of ponds in Rilke). The essential thought, however, comes in line 2: 'Wir sind nicht einig'. And after the counter-examples — from what we dare to call the *sub*-human world — the meaning of this 'lack of oneness' is illustrated in examples and images from the sphere of human experience, where we are forced to recognise 'enmity' and 'opposition'.

Uns aber, wo wir Eines meinen, ganz,
ist schon des andern Aufwand fühlbar. Feindschaft
ist uns das Nächste. Treten Liebende
nicht immerfort an Ränder, eins im andern,
die sich versprachen Weite, Jagd und Heimat.
Da wird für eines Augenblickes Zeichnung
ein Grund von Gegenteil bereitet, mühsam,
daß wir sie sähen; denn man ist sehr deutlich
mit uns. Wir kennen den Kontur
des Fühlens nicht: nur, was ihn formt von außen.

But as for us, even when we are committed to one thing, totally,
we feel the whole force of the other. Conflict
is never far away. Lovers

keep on running into barriers in the other,
where they had hoped for open country, hunting and a home.
Even for a sketch to be done in an instant
the surface must be prepared with a contrasting ground, laboriously,
so that we may see it; because things are spelled out
quite clearly for us. We don't know the contour
of our feelings, only what forms it from outside.

Before I paraphrase the ideas here, let me again call attention to Rilke's language and especially to the progressive tightening and slackening of the syntactic pulse as we pass in an arc from 'wir' in line 9 to the next 'wir' in line 16. At first the movement is halting and ruminative, with 'Eines' echoing the 'einig' of line 2, and 'ganz' placed just where one puts it in speech, when thinking aloud. There follows a dense, newly-invented proverb, artfully straddling the line-break ('Feindschaft / ist uns das Nächste'). Lines 11-13 offer a slightly more complex structure (there is actually a relative clause; and what begins like a question ends without a question mark, as a statement of fact). Then comes the most ambitious sentence yet, with the main verb in the passive ('wird ... bereitet') and an adverbial clause of purpose with its verb in the imperfect subjunctive ('sähen'). But in the last lines of this passage Rilke reverts to the most basic syntax, using the plainest of constructions for his first tentative conclusion.

So what is he saying? That the human brain interprets the world, 'deutet die Welt' (cf. I, 13), only thanks to a series of binary oppositions. 'Left' means 'not right', and 'right' means 'not left'; 'night' draws its meaning from 'day' and vice versa. Or, if we may introduce an Italian technical term, 'chiaroscuro', taken from the art of drawing ('Zeichnung', 14), 'chiaro' is perceived as 'chiaro', 'clear', thanks to a contrast with 'scuro'. In our poem 'winter' is the opposite of 'summer' and 'blossoming' of 'dying back'. Even the briefest of intellectual insights makes sense only against a contrasting background of concepts ('ein Grund von Gegenteil', 15), and these were not assembled in a moment, but 'mühsam'. Lovers delude themselves at first into thinking that they will find a world in which they will be united and undivided, but in their metaphorical roaming and hunting on the open moors ('Weite, Jagd'), they keep coming up against boundary-fences ('Ränder', 12).[6] Worst of all — to go back to the image of drawing — we do not even know what we feel, what is going on inside ourselves, except by reference to the external cause of those feelings. The line

('Kontur') which defines the shape of our feelings seems to belong not to them but to the background against which we perceive them.

In the first eight lines of the elegy, a brief proposition was illustrated with a profusion of imagery. In the ten we have just examined, a dense argument was actually conducted through successive images. Nevertheless, the opening of the poem still belongs fairly clearly to the genre of philosophical or meditative poetry. The central section of the poem, by contrast, will abandon general statement for the description of a vision and for autobiography. So, this may be a good moment to pause and take stock, and to see if we can relate what Rilke has just been saying to the earlier poems in the cycle.

As we have been reminded in the first three essays in this volume, Rilke uses language to express what he declares to be inexpressible in language. In describing a condition common to him and to all mankind, he too is compelled to paint a 'ground of contraries', so that we may be able to see 'clearly'. He has in fact been comparing and contrasting our common lot with three *non*-human classes of being: angels (who have a 'stärkeres Dasein'), animals (including 'Zugvögel', obviously, who are resourceful,'findig'), and to a lesser extent, plants[7]. We ordinary mortals have also been contrasted with three categories of *super*-human or *rare* human beings: lovers (the unrequited but undemanding lovers like Gaspara Stampa, I, 45), saints (who remained on their knees, even when the voice of God lifted them bodily from the ground) and heroes (whose death in battle is 'another' or 'last' birthday). On the whole, these 'super-humans' have been located in the classical or medieval past, or, in the case of angels, in a past framework of belief, with the result that there is also a contrast between a lost innocence, or lost 'Einigkeit', and the present age of consciousness and guilt, in which we have been disinherited from a unity of perception and feeling which should have been ours.

We, the living, have also been contrasted with the dead — or, rather, with the '*living* dead', for Rilke seems to posit a vague belief in personal immortality, even though this too may belong to the past for him and many of his readers. And these 'living dead' have been subdivided into those who lived out their full span and those who were 'snatched away' or 'destined to cross over early'. But in the case of the dead we have been warned not to distinguish too sharply: the angels themselves find it hard to know which 'Bereich' they are moving through (I, 80-85). Later in this Fourth Elegy, also, we shall be reminded of what we learnt in the First —

that the 'Früheentrückten' (I, 86) are not the victims of an injustice, because they, like the heroes, were rightly unaware of any clear 'boundary', any 'opposition', between life and death. And, as we will soon be told (lines 65-75), all of us have experienced a state — childhood — in which we too enjoyed this primitive, unitary awareness, living in an enduring and happy present tense without a past or a future.[8] The lovers will return in Elegies V and VII, the heroes in VI, the animals in VIII, the dead in X, whereas our poem will centre on the child and on the pathos — or false pathos — of death in childhood. (Rilke himself, you will subsequently be able to infer, is simultaneously 'hero', in the sphere of his art, 'lover', of the renouncing kind, and eternal 'child'; but he is also, mercifully, one of us, one of 'the dispossessed' — hence the tone of 'elegy', of 'Klage', of 'lamentation without protest'.)

The best way to approach the body of our poem (lines 19-75) is to imagine that you are listening to a close friend telling you about a dream he had the previous night, a dream which has stirred him deeply and which he feels sure must be significant. You would expect there to be some abrupt transitions, because you are used to the problems of recounting your own dreams; but you are willing to put yourself into the state of mind of the dreamer-narrator, to whom every successive image seemed perfectly coherent at the time he was dreaming.

Your friend tells you that he found himself in a theatre. The curtain went up on a familiar scene; a dancer appeared to whom he took a violent objection, and this led him into a long harangue in praise of the *puppet* theatre. Then he was somehow actually in front of a puppet stage, doggedly refusing to leave, even though the lights went out, the heating was turned off, and the rest of the audience had gone. Next, he found himself defending his behaviour to his father, although he was well aware that his father was dead. Then he was having the same argument with various women friends, justifying himself all the time for his pig-headed resolve to stay on until something happened on stage. His excuses and self-justifications were cut short, however — and his patience was rewarded — because an angel suddenly came down, picked up the wires on the puppets and began to perform a play. And in the very moment when the angel jerked the puppets into life, he knew he had found not only the perfect theatre, but the key to the meaning of everything. The angel told him that the dying enjoy this same clarity of vision — this ability to pierce the veil and see the pattern — which is not all that surprising, because they have simply recovered the pure, undivided, 'open' state of mind they had known as children. Then the dreamer awoke (as in the best medieval poems) with a phrase on his lips in which you may recognise a fusion of two passages in the Bible: Christ's command (Mark x.14), 'Suffer the little children to come unto me ..., for of such is the kingdom of God'; and a line in the Book of Proverbs (viii. 23), where the figure of Wisdom says that she had been 'ordained from all eternity'.

Considered as a dream, there is very little in what your friend has told you that would remotely surprise a modern psychoanalyst; and there is nothing at all that would have surprised a medieval connoisseur of the human dream such as Chaucer or Dante — especially not in that series of implied contrasts between human beings, angels and inanimate objects, (above and below us on the Scale of Nature), or in the sense of a continuity between the living and the dead, which is so marked in Dante's representation of Purgatory, or — to stay with Dante — in the notion that one could have a decisive 'visionary experience' at the age of nine.

Let us now retrace our steps and go more slowly through all the stages of this dream-like middle section.

Wer saß nicht bang vor seines Herzens Vorhang?
Der schlug sich auf: die Szenerie war Abschied.
Leicht zu verstehen. Der bekannte Garten,
und schwankte leise: dann erst kam der Tänzer.
Nicht ***der****. Genug! Und wenn er auch so leicht tut,*
er ist verkleidet und er wird ein Bürger
und geht durch seine Küche in die Wohnung.

Who has never sat in dread before the curtain of the heart?
Up it went. A backdrop of departure.
Easy to understand. The familiar garden,
stirring slightly. Only then did the dancer make his entrance.
Not him! Enough! For all his pirouettes,
he's dressed for a part, and he'll turn into an ordinary mortal
and enter his house through the kitchen.

As has been pointed out, the pronouns are always important[9]. Here they shift away from the first person plural of meditation, used in the opening lines, towards the third person singular, used in narration (lines 20-25), through a third person interrogative 'who' in line 19 which still seeks to involve all of us. And I feel sure that every reader will indeed recognise from personal experience the mystery and the immediate rightness of that image of a 'curtain in the heart' — a curtain kept drawn to protect us from all the scary things in the subconscious which we learnt about in the Third Elegy (in Rilke's poetry, curtains always conceal horrors that fascinate).

The syntax becomes even more telegrammatic than it had been in the opening, but Rilke is now using language in a way that is no longer close to that of ordinary discourse, since we are told in line 20 that the 'scenery', the 'backdrop', was a 'leavetaking'. What does that mean? The full significance of this extraordinary phrase will become 'clear', or 'bright', only in the last line of the Eighth Elegy, so for the moment we must simply accept the dreamer's assurance that it was 'easy to understand'. Not that it is all that difficult to guess at the literal meaning. The backdrop showed 'the familiar garden' (the sort of thing, one imagines, that would do for a hundred plays in repertory in a provincial or touring theatre company); and the fact that it 'swayed' or 'stirred' revealed that it was painted canvas, not real. (A similar point is now to be made about an actor's costume and make-up).

After some delay a dancer appears on the empty stage; and the poet's reaction is one of immediate derision — catcalls, boos, 'O God! Not him!'. And the reason for this disdain is given immediately. Let the dancer pretend as much as he likes to be free from the restraints of gravity, this is not possible. He is 'in disguise', which is to say that instead of the costume and the man being one, 'einig', the audience is aware simultaneously of the actor and the character he is acting. Indeed, in a lovely moment of clairvoyance, Rilke can already see him turn back into an ordinary citizen, and enter the kind of suburban home where the back door leads directly into the kitchen.

Ich will nicht diese halbgefüllten Masken,
lieber die Puppe. Die ist voll. Ich will
den Balg aushalten und den Draht und ihr
Gesicht aus Aussehn. Hier. Ich bin davor.
Wenn auch die Lampen ausgehn, wenn mir auch
gesagt wird: Nichts mehr —, wenn auch von der Bühne
das Leere herkommt mit dem grauen Luftzug,
wenn auch von meinen stillen Vorfahrn keiner
mehr mit mir dasitzt, keine Frau, sogar
der Knabe nicht mehr mit dem braunen Schielaug:
Ich bleibe dennoch. Es giebt immer Zuschaun.

I won't endure these half-filled masks,
I'd rather a puppet. At least it's full. I'll put up
with the stuffed skin, and the wires, and the
blankly-staring face. Here. In front.

Even if the lights go out; even if I'm told:
'That's all'; even if emptiness
drifts from the stage in that grey draught;
even if not one of my silent ancestors
still sits with me, no woman, not even
the boy with the squint in his brown eye:
I'll stay on. One can always watch.

In the next section, and indeed right down to line 54, the dominant pronouns are those of the first-person singular. Rilke seems to launch into a tirade against the bourgeois theatre in a passage that reminds an Italianist very much of Pirandello's *Six Characters in Search of an Author* (1923), and which reminds all Germanists of a famous essay by Kleist, not to mention one by Rilke himself.[10] But this is not the place to explore these ideas in detail and the literal meaning of the text is in any case clear enough. Rather than look at an actor pretending he is not an actor, the poet would prefer to watch a 'Puppe' any day. ('Puppe' in German can mean 'doll', or any kind of 'puppet'; but in the context here it must refer to a marionette, a puppet on a string or a wire). He would rather watch a figure which is unmistakably a skin with stuffing inside ('Balg' is a word you might use of the skin of a stuffed animal in a natural history museum); he would rather watch a figure suspended on a clearly visible 'wire'; a figure whose painted 'expression' never changes, but which is not perceived as a mask over an actor's face.

So convincingly spontaneous is this outburst that it is easy to overlook its connection with the themes adumbrated in the opening lines of the poem. The links and the development might be paraphrased somewhat as follows.[11] The very fact of sitting and observing the feelings in our hearts, as if we were spectators in a theatre (19), is yet another sign or consequence of our divided existence. However, to recognise the conventionality, banality or falseness of our feelings (20-25) is to take the first step towards the rejection of this unnatural state (26-29). It is preferable to live clear-sightedly but impassively (30-32) in the awareness that a happier past is beyond recall (33-35). But if we will only endure, if we will only go on observing and feeling honestly (36), then one day we may be 're-united with ourselves' thanks to the return of the lost powers of the imagination, the creative imagination, symbolised by the coming of the angel in lines 56-57.

You may have thought we had met the shortest sentence in the verbless 'Nicht *der*. Genug!' in line 21, but now we come down to just three syllables, 'Die ist voll', and then to one word, 'Hier'.

The metre remains perfectly regular, but the rhythms of lines 26-29 seem as 'offbeat' as some of those in Beethoven's scherzos. And yet from these we launch, *attacca subito*, into a glorious *andante un poco mosso* — one of Rilke's typical long periods, where the apparent complexity vanishes when you realise that it consists of four, artfully varied, but co-ordinated 'if'-clauses, each introduced by 'wenn auch', leading up to the single main verb placed after a colon ('Ich bleibe', 36), which reiterates, so to speak, the earlier: 'Hier. Ich bin davor' of line 29. The music of these lines is superb, but its beauty does not lend itself to analysis in words. So we must limit ourselves to noting the little touches which lift the language out of the everyday, for example, an emptiness 'comes' from the stage, with a draught that is coloured 'grey'! We should also notice the appearance of the dead (paradoxically, through the denial of their presence) — the poet's ancestors, certain women in his life, and a very particular boy with a cast in his eye. And here it does perhaps help to know that the boy was his cousin, Egon, who died in childhood. He had been the subject of some moving pages in *Die Aufzeichnungen des Malte Laurids Brigge* and was to be the dedicatee of one of the loveliest poems in the later *Sonette an Orpheus* (II, viii).[12]

To know this is to be ready for the appearance of the theme of 'Der Kindertod' at the end of our elegy. It is also to be prepared for the fact that the voice which is using the pronoun 'ich' in this passage is closer to the 'real' or 'historical' Rilke than any 'ich' we have encountered up to this point in the cycle. In the Third Elegy (lines 26, 38), we met the figure of a mother — in principle, anyone's mother. Now we are going to learn about Rilke's father. I remind you that his parents had lost an infant daughter before René (as he was christened) was born in December 1875; and it is important to know that his mother dressed him and brought him up as a girl until he went to school. His parent's marriage was not a success, and after an over-protected childhood, dominated by his mother, he was packed off to a military academy from the age of 11 to the age of 15 (you may well be remembering a famous line by Philip Larkin about the disastrous effects that parents have on their offspring).

Primed with this information, we are ready to move on to the passage of defiant self-defence, the first part of which is addressed to his dead father.

Hab ich nicht recht? Du, der um mich so bitter
das Leben schmeckte, meines kostend, Vater,

den ersten trüben Aufguß meines Müssens,
da ich heranwuchs, immer wieder kostend
und, mit dem Nachgeschmack so fremder Zukunft
beschäftigt, prüftest mein beschlagnes Aufschaun, —
der du, mein Vater, seit du tot bist, oft
in meiner Hoffnung, innen in mir, Angst hast,
und Gleichmut, wie ihn Tote haben, Reiche
von Gleichmut, aufgiebst für mein bißchen Schicksal,
hab ich nicht recht?

Aren't I right? You who on my account always found life
so bitter, as you took a sip of mine, father,
tasting again and again, as I grew up,
the first cloudy infusion of my will — you who,
troubled by the aftertaste of so strange a future,
would look searchingly into the opacity of my gaze,
father, you who, now you are dead,
are often afraid, deep within me, in my hopes,
and give up a serenity such as the dead enjoy,
kingdoms of serenity, for my modicum of fate,
aren't I right?

We have now reached the start of the *Adagio* — a long, 'Bruckner-like' melody which unfolds (with just a single bar of 'Generalpause') right down to line 57. Syntactically, the adagio is far more complex than anything we have encountered in this elegy; and you may find it easier to follow when you realise that the bones of the first part of the sentence are the repeated vocatives to his father (lines 38 and 43), which are qualified by a pair of relative clauses: ' Du... Vater, ... der... prüftest...', and 'Vater, ... der du Angst hast... und Gleichmut aufgiebst...'.[13] However, the single most striking feature of the language here is the sustained metaphor from the sense of taste, (even more daring than the earlier example in the Second Elegy) which is applied to every aspect of the father's experience of his son. René's strong will to be different, his 'must', his 'Müssen' — early and persistent — is compared to the first pouring of newly-made herbal infusion, 'Aufguß' — or a pot of coffee perhaps — which is 'cloudy', full of sediment, 'trübe'; and the metaphor combines with the description of the boy's 'beschlagenes Aufschaun' to suggest that his nature was enigmatic, impenetrable and strange ('beschlagen' means 'misty' in the sense of 'steamed up', but it can also mean 'knowing'). 'Tasting' or 'sipping' ('kostend'), the 'strange future', to which this 'Müssen' will lead, already leaves an '*after*taste',

'Nachgeschmack', a bitter aftertaste, which will embitter his father's experience of life (37).

That, then, is the image of the father surviving in the poet's memory — a mouth pursed in distaste and incomprehension. But we have learnt that there is no clear divide between the living and the dead; and now we discover that the image of his dead father is still 'alive', often appearing to the grown man — Rainer now, not René — deep down inside him, in his hopes. The difference is that his expression has changed to one of anxiety, concern and fear. Instead of enjoying the 'equanimity', 'Gleichmut', to which the dead are entitled, he seems to become involved and to torment himself about his son's 'fate', that is, about his very destiny as a poet which the father had failed to understand. But of course the two images — the 'then' and the 'now', the pursed mouth in the memory, and the puckered brow in his dreams — also imply two portraits of the poet himself, as child and man, because he is the cause of the expressions on his father's face. And since it always seems to be true that 'qui s'excuse, s'accuse', we may hear in this insistent 'Hab ich nicht recht?' an expression of Rilke's feelings of guilt at having denied love to his father and at having stifled his father's potential love for him.

Let us read on to the end of the sentence:

und ihr, hab ich nicht recht,
die ihr mich liebtet für den kleinen Anfang
Liebe zu euch, von dem ich immer abkam,
weil mir der Raum in eurem Angesicht,
da ich ihn liebte, überging in Weltraum,
in dem ihr nicht mehr wart .....: wenn mir zumut ist,
zu warten vor der Puppenbühne, nein,
so völlig hinzuschaun, daß, um mein Schauen
am Ende aufzuwiegen, dort als Spieler
ein Engel hinmuß, der die Bälge hochreißt.
Engel und Puppe: dann ist endlich Schauspiel.

And you,
who loved me because of my first show of love to you,
a love from which I always turned away, because the space
in your features, even as I loved it, dissolved into cosmic space,
in which you were no longer present ....: aren't I right when I feel
impelled to wait in front of the puppet-stage, no,
to stare with such intensity that, in the end,
to counterweigh my gaze
an angel must be sent as actor

to jerk the stuffed skins into activity?
Angel and puppet: then at last we have a play.

Self-exculpation, together with the inseparable self-accusation, continues in this second half of the sentence which opens with another vocative — the familiar plural, 'ihr' — addressed this time perhaps to the various women who had opened their hearts to him in response to his own first, faint-hearted indication that he was attracted to them, and who were naturally resentful at his having pulled back from the relationship when it threatened to become a commitment. His line of defence here (lines 50-52) may sound like one of the most ingenious and least convincing excuses that any male has ever dreamed up for bringing an affair, or a marriage, to an end; and I really ought to explore the notions of 'Raum' and 'Weltraum', which we first met in Elegy One, to lend it an air of greater plausibility. But instead I will simply invite you to connect the whole of this passage with Edward Timms's analysis of the final part of the Third Elegy and to remember the apparent failure of the poet (not so surprising, in the light of his parents and upbringing) to achieve 'individuality' and with it the ability to relate to other individuals. And if I were to shift the emphasis slightly, it would only be to make three points. First, it is not in any way a weakness in an artist to represent our frailty with this kind of finesse and suggestiveness and this kind of artistic control (otherwise, I would have to deny greatness or relevance to Petrarch — whom any self-respecting psychoanalyst would have to consider as another case of 'arrested development', with all his 'vane speranze' and 'van[o] dolore').[14] Second, most of us, deep inside ourselves, 'innen in uns', are in much the same situation as Rilke was. And third, passages like this are therapeutic for us as well for the author, partly because they reveal that we are not alone in our feelings of inadequacy, but also, more important, because they can help us to find at least a moment of equilibrium, 'Gleichgewicht', or an instant of serenity, 'Gleichmut', thanks to a verbal music which, to quote from the First Elegy, 'enchants and consoles and helps'.

It would not be surprising if you have by now totally forgotten what the behaviour is that Rilke is so concerned to justify. The answer comes in line 52 when the long wave of the melody, having built up to its climax in the 'Generalpause' (represented by the dots), plunges forward like a breaking wave towards its resolution.

Let us take the literal meaning first. The poet is asking 'is he not right' to go on waiting so obstinately in the cold, grey, deserted puppet theatre — to go on staring with total concentration until the very intensity of his gaze will conjure into existence the performance he is waiting to see. If only he endures, an angel will be despatched to act as puppeteer, to twitch the sagging marionettes into life and to give the perfect performance of the perfect play: 'dann ist endlich Schauspiel'.[15]

Symbolically, it is not in the least difficult to interpret this final image as a figuration, or pre-figuration, of Rilke's life and art in the years from 1912 to 1922. He felt, as we learnt in the First Elegy, that he had been given a 'mission', an 'Auftrag'. He was prepared to sacrifice family, marriage, friends and lovers for the sake of that mission. He was willing to wait, 'on his knees' so to speak, for another six years if necessary. And the moment of inspiration (the 'voice of God' envisaged in I, 58-59) would come not in response to a call for help (the 'Schrei' or 'Lockruf' of I, 1 and 8) but in response to the intensity of his vigilance, the power of his gaze. Rilke was seeking 'in-sight', (he had already written the line in which he looked forward to the 'Ausgang der grimmigen *Einsicht*', X, 1). He wanted to become like the archetypal poet of earlier ages — blind Homer, the Hebrew prophets, the sybils, Dante — that is, he wanted to become a 'seer'. And it is a pity that we cannot match in English the crucial word-play between the verb 'schauen' (and all its many compound forms such as 'aufschauen', 'zuschauen', 'hinausschauen'), and the ordinary word for a 'play' in German — 'Schauspiel'.

In the next section Rilke carries his imagined role through to its logical conclusion (for your convenience, line 57 is repeated).

Engel und Puppe: dann ist endlich Schauspiel.
Dann kommt zusammen, was wir immerfort
entzwein, indem wir da sind. Dann entsteht
aus unsern Jahreszeiten erst der Umkreis
des ganzen Wandelns. Über uns hinüber
spielt dann der Engel. Sieh, die Sterbenden,
sollten sie nicht vermuten, wie voll Vorwand
das alles ist, was wir hier leisten. Alles
ist nicht es selbst.

Angel and puppet: then at last we have a play.
Then there comes together what we always
split simply by being here. Only then do
our seasons reveal the cycle

in all these transformations. Then the angel
plays high above us. Think, shouldn't
the dying be able to intuit how everything
we accomplish is full of pretence. Nothing
is itself.

The vision which the 'seer' has been granted is universally true. It is valid for all of us — 'wir' and 'uns' are repeated insistently — and it must be shared with us. The poet's role is that of a mediator between the world of being and the world of appearances. The seemingly impossible 'coming together' of sub-human and super-human actors in the puppet-play marks an end to the opposition between 'Zeichnung' and 'Grund' and a transcendence of 'Feindschaft'. And this transcendence involves the discovery of the complete 'cycle' underlying all 'our seasons' (underlying, that is, all the sharp distinctions which we as humans make in interpreting reality). This is the 'Umkreis' which is known by instinct to the migratory birds and the trees of the opening lines. Rilke here describes (if I may be allowed to combine images from the First Elegy with a famous terzina from the last canto of Dante's *Paradiso*), a moment of supreme insight when everything that seemed to be 'fluttering about so randomly in space' comes back into a state of 'relationship', of 'Bezug', a moment when all the 'leaves of the book, which are scattered through the universe' are seen to be 'bound together, by love, in one volume'.

Freilich ist es seltsam, die Erde nicht mehr zu bewohnen, ...
...Seltsam
alles, was sich bezog, so lose im Raume
flattern zu sehen. (I, 69, 76-78)

Nel suo profondo vidi che s'interna,
legato con amore in un volume,
ciò che per l'universo si squaderna.
(Paradiso 33, 85-87)

At a moment like this, an angel might well be said to 'play in the sky over our heads' (61-62) like the 'celestial host' who appeared to the shepherds 'watching their flocks'.

But although Rilke uses the present tense as if he were describing something recurrent, the event described in lines 58-62 really lies in the future — in that extraordinary February of 1922, when inspiration would return and he would write the Sonnets to Orpheus and finish the Elegies. The effect of the poet's attempt to involve us in his vision is to bring him back to the 'gedeutete Welt', where 'everything is not itself' (64), and where the dying — those who are soon to cross over into the other 'Bereich' — are granted a not particularly consoling vision as they come to suspect that everything they have done — and everything we go on doing — was 'full of pretence' (or 'pretext'). But we are not about to return to the resigned, 'elegiac' mood of the opening. There is to be a change in perspective — signalled by a change to the past tense — a perspective which depends on the quintessentially human faculty of memory.[16]

O Stunden in der Kindheit,
da hinter den Figuren mehr als nur
Vergangnes war und vor uns nicht die Zukunft.
Wir wuchsen freilich und wir drängten manchmal,
bald groß zu werden, denen halb zulieb,
die andres nicht mehr hatten, als das Großsein.
Und waren doch, in unserem Alleingehn,
mit Dauerndem vergnügt und standen da
im Zwischenraume zwischen Welt und Spielzeug,
an einer Stelle, die seit Anbeginn
gegründet war für einen reinen Vorgang.

Oh those hours in childhood,
when behind the figures there was more than simply
what was past, and no future stretched before us.
It's true we were growing and sometimes strove
to be grown-up quickly, half to please those
who had nothing else in life than adulthood.
And yet in our solitude we found
contentment in what endures; and we lived there,
in the borderland between world and toy,
in a spot that had been ordained
from the very first for an innocent event.

The past to which Rilke directs us back is that of childhood (65), a childhood as mythologised by the Romantics, but also, very specifically, his own childhood in Prague. What he is saying is that you do not have to wait single-mindedly for a personal vision, or to wait for a poet or prophet to reveal the truth: it is enough to recall your own childhood. Even when you were young, you may have had a tendency to drive or 'force' yourself prematurely towards 'grown-up-ness'.[17] But if you were lucky — as I was — you were not then preoccupied by past and future (67); and when you played alone by yourself — in the fields of wartime

Essex or wherever — you were in a no-man's land of the imagination (73), a pure space where you could find contentment with what does really endure (unlike the lovers of the Second Elegy, lines 58-59, who deluded themselves that they were experiencing 'das reine Dauern').

As I have hinted, this is very much an early nineteenth-century vision of childhood, 'trailing clouds of glory'. It cries out for extensive quotation from Wordsworth or Leopardi to set it in its proper context. Here, however, I will merely comment that I find this one of the loveliest passages in the elegies — especially perhaps lines 71-73, which for me describe not only my literal childhood, but the experience of reading modern languages in the 1950s at Cambridge (that was the 'Zwischenraum'), studying for papers on both Dante and Goethe (that was 'das Dauernde'); whereas line 70 evokes aspects of university life in the 1990s when, in Wordsworth's phrase, 'the world is too much with us', and we are badgered by people, 'die andres nichts mehr [haben], als das Großsein'.

The 'we' of these lines is perhaps not quite the same as in the previous section, since the poet seems to be thinking primarily of himself and a few childhood playmates, his 'Gespielen', who played in the 'scattered gardens' of Prague, completely cut off from the 'passing adults' and the 'houses' and 'carriages' in a world where only the 'curves of the balls' in the air were 'real':

> *Wenige ihr, der einstigen Kindheit Gespielen*
> *in den zerstreuten Gärten der Stadt:*
>
> *Und wie zergings unter allen den gehenden Leuten*
> *und im Bangen des langen Jahrs.*
>
> *Wagen umrollten uns fremd, vorübergezogen,*
> *Häuser umstanden uns stark, aber unwahr, — und keines*
> *kannte uns je.* ***Was*** *war wirklich im All?*
>
> *Nichts. Nur die Bälle. Ihre herrlichen Bogen.*
> *Auch nicht die Kinder... Aber manchmal trat eines,*
> *ach ein vergehendes, unter den fallenden Ball.*
>
> *(Sonette an Orpheus, II, 8, 1-2, 7-14)*

These lines are from a sonnet dedicated to the memory of one of those friends, his cousin, Egon, the boy 'mit dem braunen Schielaug' of line 35, who never made it to adulthood. It is one of the cycle he later wrote as a 'funeral monument' for Wera Ouckama

Knoop, who died as an adolescent in 1919; and it forms a perfect bridge to the last section of our elegy.

Wer zeigt ein Kind, so wie es steht? Wer stellt
es ins Gestirn und giebt das Maß des Abstands
ihm in die Hand? Wer macht den Kindertod
aus grauem Brot, das hart wird, — oder läßt
ihn drin im runden Mund, so wie den Gröps
von einem schönen Apfel?...... Mörder sind
leicht einzusehen. Aber dies: den Tod,
den ganzen Tod, noch vor dem Leben so
sanft zu enthalten und nicht bös zu sein,
ist unbeschreiblich.

Who can portray a child as he is? Who can place him
in his constellation, or put into his hands the measuring-rod
of distance? Who can mould a child's death
out of grey bread which grows hard? Or leave it
in the hollow of his mouth like the core
of a lovely apple?...... It's easy to see
into a murderer's mind. But this: to contain death —
death in its entirety — even before life has begun,
to contain it so gently, and not to feel resentment,
this lies beyond the power of words.

There is nothing particularly difficult to understand in the first two and a half lines which assert (in the form of rhetorical questions) that it is impossible either to portray a child in its concrete reality, 'wie es steht', or to give it the definitive praise or reward that is its due (the ancients believed that heroes were 'set' in constellations in the sky). But the third question (lines 78-81) switches direction to reach the theme of 'death in childhood'; and the language becomes eerily concrete, passing, if I have it straight, from the practice of primitive 'sympathetic' magic (the making of an image to be hurt — an image made not in wax, but in moist rye-bread that will be left to dry hard) to the story of Snow White, where Sneewittchen (in the version by the brothers Grimm) was left for dead by her wicked stepmother thanks to the poisoned 'Apfelgrütz' which stuck in her mouth.[18]

At first sight, perhaps, the sequence of ideas is not very surprising. If childhood is such a precious gift, what evil force could cause a child to die, or what providence could allow it to happen? But that is far too banal; and Rilke corrects himself immediately. The hostile forces, the 'murderers', are in fact easy to understand, as easy as the 'backdrop of departure' in the theatre of the heart. What is really 'indescribable' — for example, in a child slowly dying of leukaemia — is the extraordinary lack of fear or resentment shown by the child, the gentle, uncomplaining acceptance, the refusal to see life and death as opposites, the ability 'not to distinguish too sharply'.

It would be fruitful to follow this train of thought forward to the Sixth Elegy, where we are told that those who die young 'are wonderfully close to the hero' (or, to be more accurate, the other way round: 'Wunderlich nah ist der Held doch den jugendlich Toten', VI, 21). From there the path would lie open to the eighth elegy, also in blank verse, with its celebration of the animals who are 'free from death', and its final condemnation of human beings, of all of us who 'live our lives as if we were always taking our leave' ('so leben wir und nehmen immer Abschied', VIII, 75). This in turn would throw further light on line 20 of our poem — 'die Szenerie war Abschied' — especially if it were taken together with a famous sonnet in the second part of the Orpheus cycle (II, 13), 'Sei allem Abschied voran', which links the theme of leave-taking, or its avoidance, with that of winter (as in line 1 of our elegy), and is perhaps the fullest statement of the heroic 'Auftrag' which Rilke assigned to the poet in general and to himself in particular. But to make those connections here would be to spoil the deliberately quiet and downbeat ending of the poem. Rilke does after all say that the child's acceptance of death, the whole of death, is 'unbeschreiblich'.

---

1 Francis Quarles (1592-1644), Epigram, *The New Oxford Book of English Verse*, chosen and edited by Helen Gardner (Oxford, 1972), p. 252.

2 Henry Vaughan (1621-95), 'The Retreat', lines 1-4, 11-14, *The New Oxford Book of English Verse*, cit., p. 342. The whole poem, together with its companions such as 'The World', 'Man' and 'The Waterfall', (ibid. pp. 345-9), can throw light on the pre-Romantic, Christian antecedents of Rilke's feelings and ideas.

3 *Vita nuova* XVIII, 3-9—XIX,1-3 in the light of *Purgatorio* 24, 49-62. The phrase 'lo stilo de la sua loda' is used in *Vita nuova* XXVI, 4.

4 D. Prater, *A Ringing Glass. The Life of Rainer Maria Rilke* (Oxford, 1986), pp. 237-75; W. Leppmann, *Rilke, A Life*, translated from the German by R. M. Stockman in collaboration with the author (Cambridge, Lutterworth Press, n. d.) (original: *Rilke. Sein Leben, seine Welt, sein Werk*, Berne and Munich, 1981), pp. 283-312.

5 'Das bloße Allgemeine, die Rubrik, die Inhaltsangabe fesseln so gut wie nie; alles Interesse steckt im Detail'.

---

[6] Jacob Steiner, *Rilkes Duineser Elegien*, pp. 78-79, notes that any 'Rand' limits the notion of 'Weite', and that, in Rilke's view, lovers come to the end or 'boundary' of their promised 'Jagd', 'hunting', if they ever catch and possess their prey as ordinary hunters do; similarly, they cease to live in their true 'Heimat', 'home', if they try to settle down like ordinary mortals.

[7] For the lowly plants, see: I, 71; II, 39, 53, 75; III, 49-50, 55, 65-67, 83.

[8] It may helpful to summarise these paragraphs by setting out the nine terms of comparison in three sets of three (like 'der Engel Ordnungen' in the middle ages): a) the non-human: angels, animals, plants; b) the superhuman: saints, lovers, heroes; c) the living dead, both old and young, and children.

[9] See Peter and Sheila Stern, as well as Edward Timms, above, pp. 7 and 48, and E. L. Stahl, *Rainer Maria Rilke's **Duineser Elegien*** (Oxford, 1965), introduction, p. x.

[10] Kleist, 'Über das Marionettentheater'; Rilke, 'Puppen', SW, VI, 1063-74.

[11] Peter Krumme is particularly helpful in interpreting this part of the elegy in his *'Eines Augenblickes Zeichnung'. Zur Temporalität des Bewußtseins in Rilkes Duineser Elegien* (Würzburg, 1988), pp. 84-93. I was able to consult his excellent study only in the very last stages of revising this essay.

[12] In the prose work he is clearly the inspiration for 'Erik': see *Die Aufzeichnungen des Malte Laurids Brigge*, SW, VI, 732, 792, 818-23; see also below, p. 71.

[13] David Midgley reminds me that 'schmeckte' is here used transitively with 'Vater' as its subject. He suggests that the verb might be translated as 'flavoured' — with the implication that it was the father who introduced the bitter taste to life 'around' the boy.

[14] Petrarch, *Canzoniere*, I, 6.

[15] On this passage, see also E. L. Stahl, op. cit. in note 9, pp. xiv-xv, xxii-xxv.

[16] Dante makes it clear that angels have no memory because they never have any need to remember (cf. *Paradiso* 29, 79), and in his work the word 'mente' can mean either 'mind' or 'memory', a sign that there is no human understanding without some awareness of the past.

[17] In line 70 'drängten' recalls 'sich aufdrängen' of line 4; and the placing of 'bald' makes it mean something like 'as soon as possible' rather than simply 'soon'.

[18] For E. L. Stahl, Rilke simply 'likens [death] to stale grey bread and to the indigestible core of a sweet apple', op. cit. in note 9, p.xix. But both bread and apples are things on which a young child can choke itself to death (cf. *Sonette an Orpheus*, I, 13); and Peter Krumme points out (op.cit, p. 105) that, for Rilke, a fruit knows nothing of 'Gegenteil'; it consists of both sweet pulp and inedible core, life and death, and the child contains them both.

ELEGY FIVE

Naomi Segal

Rilke's Fifth Elegy was written on 14 February 1922. As the last of the Elegies to be composed, it is in one sense his final word, though he found it its appropriate place as the middle word instead, replacing the Elegy he had put in fifth place, which has thereafter been published separately, as 'Gegen-Strophen'.[1] I chose this Elegy for two main reasons. The first is that, more tailored to my own research interests, its scale is human. Here for the first time, the Angel appears as the indirect object of praise, just as it will in the Seventh and Ninth Elegies: that is, as the audience, not the object of the poet's address. This is not a metaphysical utterance but a meditation rooted in Rilke's own restlessness, and specifically harks back to two experiences of temporary residence: his stay in Munich in 1915 in the apartment of Hertha Koenig (to whom the poem is dedicated), who at that time owned Picasso's *Les Saltimbanques*;[2] and, looking back a further thirteen years, his painful early days in Paris in 1902, when he arrived, with little French and less worldliness, hoping to make contact with his wife's teacher Rodin, whose inept secretary he later briefly became.

Let me declare my bias. My Rilke — as it were — is the Paris Rilke.[3] It was out of the Paris experience that he wrote his extraordinary fiction, *Die Aufzeichnungen des Malte Laurids Brigge (The Notebooks of Malte Laurids Brigge)* (1910), a text that anticipates and in certain ways exceeds the final rhetorical position of the Elegies, the aim to transform the visible. In *Malte*, the reader follows the progress of the eponymous narrator through a terrorising material world into and beyond a linguistic state, creating first narratives of memory, later free-standing fictions out of the debris of personal recollections. At the same period (and the same time that Picasso was working on the *Saltimbanques*) Rilke wrote some of his finest short poetry, the *Neue Gedichte* (*New Poems*) (1907, 1908), small, light pieces on the model of C. F. Meyer's 'Dinggedichte', in which an available material object is recreated from an unfamiliar angle: Saint

Sebastian seen as if he were lying down, blue hydrangeas having the faded colour of a child's pinafore, a flight of steps compared to a king's train, climbing up a tower as if it were an ascent from the centre of the earth; or, in the uncanny 'Der Ball' — to which I shall return in a moment — the fulness of a globe described simply by the arc of its rise and the expectation of a pair of cupped hands... Typically in these poems, space and movement work to represent each other, the shape of a solidity is turned into a hollow form, or presence suggested by the mark of a material absence. There is nothing grand or prophetic in these pieces: they have the sly perfection of Gautier's *Emaux et camées*, without ever losing Rilke's endemic seriousness. The *Neue Gedichte* supply the objectification Rilke had in mind when he wrote desperately to Lou Andreas-Salomé of his need to 'Dinge machen aus Angst' (to make things out of fear).[4] They also anticipate the gem-like exactness of the *Sonette an Orpheus* (*Sonnets to Orpheus*) (1923), which in a burst of creativity provided the impetus for the 'miraculous' completion of the Elegies in Muzot. In both the *Neue Gedichte* and the *Sonette*, Rilke fulfils the command made in the euphoric closure of the Elegies: 'die Dinge sagen' (to say objects). Similarly, in this Elegy, his attention is directed not to the metaphysical heights or the abstraction of the general sweep, but towards the bodies of visible figures — half people, half movable objects, the *saltimbanques*.[5] The second reason connects, through the comparisons with these other texts, to the first. Speaking of the materiality and simplicity of human suffering in the persons of the acrobats, Rilke also speaks of the most difficult thing to describe or even imagine: the idea of exactitude. As he wrote in *Malte*: 'er war ein Dichter, und haßte das Ungefähre' ('he was a poet, and hated the approximate').[6]

The Fifth Elegy is about possibility and ability, 'being able to do' a thing. Doing it perfectly, exactly, can still somehow be oddly graceless. The acrobats execute their leaps without error — most of them — but also without joy or authenticity. They are caught, like the ball, in a circular movement not of their own making and thus tending to be empty. Against this false adequation, this failure of aesthetic precision, two moments will stand out. First, the boy's pain, the smile that fails to connect but still shows forth, going beyond its object and outside the circle, straight to the poet and thence to the Angel. And then the ultimate moment when, in the final image of the poem, imagined lovers find a perfect, graceful, fully connecting and satisfying act. The whole shape of the Elegy rests on the question marked out by the arc-shape of flight and return: in the perfect circle, when can we see fulness and when only hollowness? What is it that might make solidity out of the arc traced by a repetitive movement, what can create the ball out of the shape of the throwing-catching gesture? In other words, this poem, I suggest, re-enacts the shape of the earlier *Neues Gedicht* — Rilke's own favourite among his compositions[7] — humanising and thus problematising the 'Figur' of a rounded rise-and-fall.

Picasso's *Les Saltimbanques* (Fig. 1) hung in Rilke's room in Hertha Koenig's apartment. Picasso probably began work on it in late 1904 and completed it in the autumn of 1905.[8] I will begin my discussion of the Fifth Elegy in a moment by talking about this picture and its background. But first I should point out that Rilke not only rearranged, re-clothed and repositioned Picasso's acrobats, mixing them, as I shall suggest, with other figures of the artist's production in this period — he also blended them together with troupes of travelling *saltimbanques* whom he had seen in Paris. On 14 July, so his wife Clara reports, the two of them stopped to watch a troupe perform on their mat at the corner of the Luxembourg and the Boulevard St Michel.[9] He describes the mat, the chair and a pile of coats thrown over it, and then gives detailed descriptions of two of the players: the old Père Rollin, once the weightlifter and leader of the troupe, now sitting drumming pathetically, and his grandson, still learning his craft, and silently holding back tears just on the point of falling. The old man's son-in-law and daughter are also mentioned.[10] I shall return to these figures as they appear in the poem.

The real acrobats he had seen in the early years in Paris and then again in 1907 are surely the reason for Rilke's attachment to the Picasso painting. But in this fascination for the individual members of the troupe, and the human being behind the performer, Rilke joins a tradition which Picasso himself had developed from earlier artists of the theme.

Just perceptible underneath the present *Family of Saltimbanques*, analysis has discovered a watercolour version of the same subject-matter.[11] In it we see figures of all ages, both sexes, some in couples, some separate. The theme of the lonely Pierrot or Harlequin did not begin with Picasso, of course, but can be seen in such works as Watteau's *Italian comedians* of 1720 (Fig. 2) and Manet's *The Old Musician* of 1862. In both these paintings, a sad-looking figure dressed all in white dominates a group and stands out from it. The man at the centre of the Watteau, Gilles, a star of the Italian commedia dell'arte in Paris, is portrayed here just a few years after the troupe had been dismissed from the court for frivolity by Mme de Maintenon, Louis XIV's puritanical mistress. Sunk suddenly from the status of royal entertainers back to their origins as jugglers and acrobats, the elegant Pierrots and dancers begin to be represented as the lost, isolated artist — a theme that was developed by both painters and writers throughout the nineteenth century and later.[12] In two undated pictures, Daumier's *Wandering Saltimbanques* and Tiepolo's *The Spring Shower* (Figs. 3 and 4),[13] we see family groups closer to Picasso's. In the Daumier, they have started to set up the performance, and are drumming to attract an indifferent crowd; in the Tiepolo, rain has stopped the performance. Both groups show the same isolation, vulnerability and poignant functionality.

The word *saltimbanques* comes from the Italian *saltimbanco*, jumping on a bench; in French the travelling players were more commonly known as *bateleurs*, jugglers. They were street performers, skilled or half-skilled, associated in the popular mind with, on the one hand, the *forains* or travelling merchants, who used performers to entice customers to a sales pitch; and on the other with gypsies, a vague attachment that carries all the 'orientalist' connotations of the sinister and exotic habitually associated with the Romany. Such small groups of performers could be seen in rural or urban settings. Neither Rilke nor Picasso was original in signalling the poignancy of their crude skills and hand-to-mouth existences, the irony of the combination in one body of unhealthiness and muscularity. But the stress on the family structure seems to have caught Picasso's particular interest.[14]

In 1901, Picasso produced a number of paintings such as *Harlequin and his Companion* (Fig. 5) and the better-known *Au Lapin agile*; both of them are bar-room scenes in lush colours, representing sad couples, the man in harlequin-costume, the woman staring glumly away from him; these paintings are considered by critics to have a fairly direct autobiographical content. Around 1904-5, there followed a number of interior family scenes, such as *Harlequin's Family* and *The Acrobat Family* (Figs. 6 and 7). These have a certain perfunctoriness and weirdness — such as the unexplained presence of the monkey — but, almost for that very reason, they are cosy: the familiar nudity as the wife does her hair while the husband holds the baby, or the shared dandling of the child while the monkey looks on. Altogether they are icons of a wistful domesticity created against the instability of the wandering life. Even the dreamy *Death of Harlequin* shows a united family relation, portrayed at a moment of peaceful bereavement.[15] Soon after this, Picasso began to paint family pairs who become increasingly divided, lost and separated.

In *Girl on a Ball* and *Two Acrobats with a Dog*, (Figs. 8 and 9), which were painted in the same period as the large *Saltimbanques*, we recognise the same figures. The man watches the boy, the two lads hold hands, their heads are pointed towards each other; but in both cases the impact of the picture depends on their separation, contrasting figures, faces and gestures within a structure of combination. Gradually, in 1905, as we see in *Young Acrobat and Child* and *Mother and Child* (Figs. 10 and 11), the families are starting to appear split, divided, staring off in opposite directions, 'selten zärtlich/ seldom tender', as Rilke puts it. Looking again at the final version of the *Saltimbanques,* we see the same figures, unsmiling, staring away from each other (the three right-hand figures all with the same turn of the head and expression), lost in an ungiving landscape.

The Fifth Elegy has of course, like all of them, been much commented upon by critics, and I shall cite these in the course of my reading where they have been particularly useful. As far as its place and function in the whole cycle is concerned, some critics show how it marks an exact mid-point, or turning-point;[16] others see it as primarily the last-written Elegy or as the nadir of the poet's mood,[17] still others show how it connects directly to the themes of the Fourth Elegy — or even the Third — despite being written seven years later.[18] In my own reading, I want to stress four aspects of the poem in particular: first, those two I pointed to earlier: the question of 'das Können', exactitude and its spatial corollary, the completed arc; then, the question of the *site* of this possibility, designated by such nouns as 'Stelle' 'Ort', 'Platz' and 'Teppich' and the interrogative pronoun 'wo'. Finally, marked in both imagery and thematics, the motif of sexuality and love, which leads from the flawed bodies of street-entertainers to the closing scene where the bodies of the perfect lovers are on display to the eyes of the imagination.

Wer aber ***sind*** *sie, sag mir, die Fahrenden, diese ein wenig*
Flüchtigern noch als wir selbst, die dringend von früh an
wringt ein **wem,** ***wem*** *zu Liebe*
niemals zufriedener Wille? Sondern er wringt sie,
biegt sie, schlingt sie und schwingt sie,

wirft sie und fängt sie zurück; wie aus geölter,
glatterer Luft kommen sie nieder
auf dem verzehrten, von ihrem ewigen
Aufsprung dünneren Teppich, diesem verlorenen
Teppich im Weltall.
Aufgelegt wie ein Pflaster, als hätte der Vorstadt-
Himmel der Erde dort wehe getan.

But who ***are*** *they, tell me, these travellers, a little*
more fleeting even than we, driven from early years, wrung by a
*(****whose****, for* ***whose*** *sake?)*
ever unsatisfied will? Yet it wrings them,
bends them, slings them and swings them
throws them and catches them again; as out of oiled
more slippery air they come down
on the threadbare carpet, thinned by their everlasting
leaping-up, this forlorn carpet
lost in the universe.
Laid on like a plaster, as if the suburban
sky had injured the earth there.

To whom is the opening line addressed? Rilke's pronouns are, here as elsewhere, left vague and work rather to suggest a psychological position than a consistent *dramatis personae*. The 'sag mir', rather than invoking a particular interlocutor, echoes the opening line of Homer's *Odyssey*.[19] And who are they? The stress is on their fleetingness, movement not of the acrobatic acts but of their whole life; and surely the 'wir' with whom they are compared is not artists in general or Rilke in particular, as some critics insist, but humanity who, for good or ill, has transitoriness as its basic premise. Like the puppets of the preceding Elegy — but with less autonomy, it seems — these bodies are manipulated by some faceless will, which is itself acting 'jemandem zuliebe', for someone else's sake.[20] In a few lines, this power will be implicitly identified with a careless and thuggish tyrant, August der Starke, later on with an infant 'Leid', still later with the creepy milliner 'Madame Lamort'. In three stages, then, the will is embodied in the figures of man, child and woman, every time stressing the Brobdignag-like scene of a world in which the human scale is nothing. The powerful row of verbs (all assonant with the implicit and later much repeated verb 'springen')[21] build up the rapid and helpless motion of the figures; the adjective 'geölt' suggests their machine-like function. Like the ball of 'Der Ball', they glide down — but unlike it, they land with an impact violent enough to wear away the mat which is their makeshift stage.

In a brief but highly original article, Ronald G. Brown points out that what wears out the mat here is not, as the image leads us to expect, the landing but the '*Auf*sprung' of the acrobats; he follows through the frequent occurence of the preposition 'auf-' all through this Elegy and the blending of the ideas of 'up' and 'on' which it implies;[22] in this single prefix, we could infer, the tortuous circularity of these acts is already inscribed. The mat on which this landing-and-leaping takes place is the focusing of a somewhere and a nowhere — like the central motif of a children's film, in which a stamp is simultaneously a magic carpet — it is located both in the cosmos and at the same time in a 'Vorstadt' in which, as a stuck-on plaster, it marks the spot of a graze (suggestive of the bleak sky-scrapers of the Paris suburbs?) and the potential of a healing.

Und kaum dort,
aufrecht, da und gezeigt: des Dastehns
großer Anfangsbuchstab..., schon auch, die stärksten
Männer, rollt sie wieder, zum Scherz, der immer
kommende Griff, wie August der Starke bei Tisch
einen zinnenen Teller.

And no sooner there,
upright, here and presented: the big capital
D of Display ..., at once even the strongest
men are rolled again, in sport, by the ever-
returning grasp, as Augustus the Strong once at table
doubled a pewter plate.

Like all good gymnasts, they no sooner land than they straighten up in a erect, shown-off position — and as they do, they become, like an illuminated letter in a manuscript (we are still at the start of the poem and the performance), a great capital D.[23] What happens here, I think, in one of Rilke's familiar conceits, is an almost imperceptible slip from the individual performer to the group, and beyond it to the abstraction of an idea. The capital D, as many critics note, picks up on the shape made by the whole left-hand group in Picasso's painting. But the connexion of shape and meaning in the 'D/Dastehn' is crucial, as translators have despairingly found: Mitchell has 'Destiny', Cohn 'Duration'; Leishman and Spender sacrifice form for content with T for 'Thereness'. It is, I think, misguided to elide 'Dastehn' with the more portentous 'Dasein', as many critics do.

The very idea of 'standing-there' is itself the sort of concrete possibility that fascinated Rilke like an abstraction. The erect posture is, also, the first of a series of images of phallic completion that appear only to be collapsed in the course of this poem. As for Augustus the Strong (elector of Saxony and later king of Poland in the early eighteenth century) his dinner-party trick represents the terrifying playfulness of every ogre of folktale.

Ach und um diese
Mitte, die Rose des Zuschauns:
blüht und entblättert. Um diesen
Stampfer, den Stempel, den von dem eignen
blühenden Staub getroffnen, zur Scheinfrucht
wieder der Unlust befruchteten, ihrer
niemals bewußten, — glänzend mit dünnster
Oberfläche leicht scheinlächelnden Unlust.

Alas and around this
centre the rose of an audience:
blooms and unpetals. Around this
pestle, this pistil, caught by its own
blossoming pollen, fertilized
again to a sham-fruit of boredom, yet
never conscious, — gleaming with thinnest
surface-light sham-smiling boredom.

This complex image of the rose and its scattering of sterile pollen falls into three parts. In the first, the centre, the site of performance, creates around it the flower of that gathering/thinning/regrouping circle, the audience. In the second, the focus returns to the erect figure of the most powerful acrobat (one of the 'stärksten Männer' of the last extract) or 'stamper' who marks the core of the central space: the German nouns 'Stampfer' and 'Stempel', etymologically linked like the English 'pestle' and 'pistil', bring together the simultaneous rhythms of a pounding and a fruitless casting-forth. In the third part, we note the repeated negatives of the prefixes 'Un-' and 'Schein-', both of which serve in one of the simplest and cleverest devices of the German language, to preserve the positive while 'bracketing' it with a negative that both amplifies and alters.[24]

The opening image of the rose reminds this and most other readers of Rilke's many rose-poems, in particular of his stunning epitaph:

Rose, oh reiner Widerspruch, Lust,
niemandes Schlaf zu sein unter soviel
Lidern.

Rose, oh pure contradiction, desire
to be no one's sleep under so many
lids.[25]

where, similarly, the power of the rose's beauty lies in its apparently modest enigma: what is there *inside* the overleafed skirts of petals? The answer in the epitaph is death, seen as a peaceful absence — no-one's sleep. In the Elegy, the petals, imitating the brief lifespan of the bloom, are the arriving and departing onlookers; their centre, it is implied, is nothing in the disguise of everything. With the brevity of their interest, nothing can pass between the audience and the performer. Thus — and the question of the relation of elements in a circumscribed atomic space will recur and increase in importance — the central figure of the stamper, as he metamorphses into the pistil/pestle pounding at the heart of the flower,[26] can cast only pollen that either returns to himself — Politzer sees this as a critique of a certain masturbatory creativity Rilke disapproved of[27] — or else creates nothing but false fruit, the product of fake or negative 'Lust' (the noun means both 'desire' and 'pleasure'). One last thing is false here — only superficial or 'scheinend', apparent — this is the smiles of either the performers or the audience or both, again the outward show of an inner desultoriness, a pleasure without depth.[28]

From this medium shot, Rilke comes into close focus, describing in turn four of the acrobats. Before considering the first, let us take a look at two more Picasso paintings of the same period, *The Organ Grinder (Old Jester and Harlequin)*, and *Seated Saltimbanque with Boy* (Figs. 12 and 13). In them we see two figures who seem to have combined in Rilke's mind (along with Père Rollin, of whom more in a moment) to produce the old drummer. Actually the fat man — who appears in *Les Saltimbanques* and a number of other paintings and drawings — is the only one of Picasso's figures whom we know by name. Known as 'El tio Pepe don José', he is featured with all sorts of family members, bursting out of a red costume and wearing a jester's hat. (In a biographical reading of the painting, he is identified with Apollinaire, while the cross-looking Harlequin is Picasso himself.)[29]

1. Pablo Picasso, *Family of Saltimbanques,* 1905. Chester Dale Collection. Photograph © Board of Trustees, National Gallery of Art, Washington. © DACS 1996

·ntoine Watteau, *Italian ·nedians,* 1720. ·nuel H. Kress Collection. ·tograph © Board of Trustees, ·ional Gallery of Art, ·shington.

3. Honoré Daumier, *Wandering Saltimbanques,* c. 1847/50
Chester Dale Collection. Photograph © Board of Trustees, National Gallery of Art, Washington.

4. Domenico Tiepolo, *The Spring Shower,* undated.
J.H. Wade Fund. Cleveland Museum of Art.

5. Pablo Picasso, *The Saltimbanques: Harlequin and his Companion,* 1901. Pushkin Museum, Moscow/The Bridgeman Art Library, London.
© DACS 1996

ablo Picasso, *The Harlequin's Family,* 4–5.
ACS 1996

7. Pablo Picasso, *The Acrobat Family,* 1905.
Goteborgs Konstmuseum, Sweden/The Bridgeman Art Library, London. © DACS 1996

8. Pablo Picasso, *Girl on a Ball,* 1905.
Pushkin Museum, Moscow/The Bridgeman Art Library, London. © DACS 1996

9. Pablo Picasso, *Two Acrobats with a Dog,* 1905. Gift of Mr and Mrs William A.M. Burden. Photograph © 1996 The Museum of Modern Art, New York. © DACS 1996

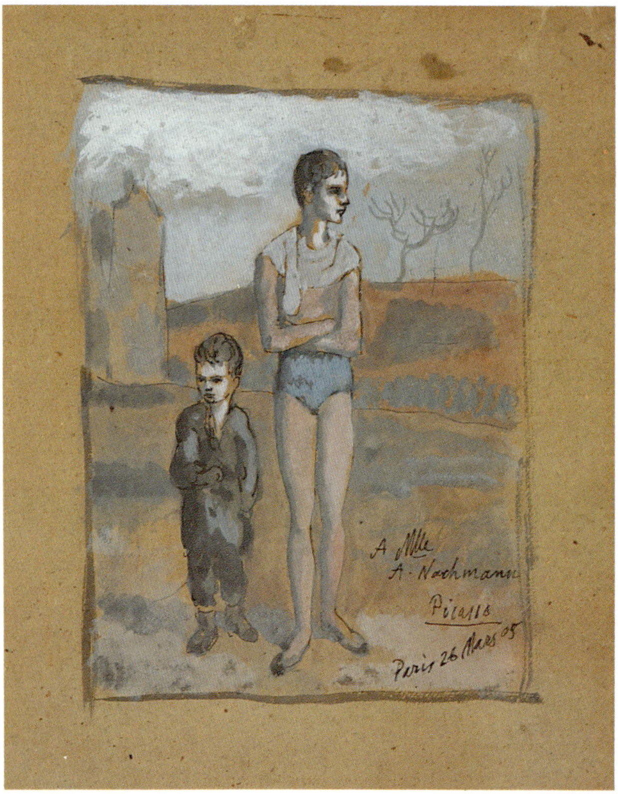

10. Pablo Picasso, *Young Acrobat and Child,* 1905.
Solomon R. Guggenheim Museum. Gift Justin K. Thannhauser, 1987. Photograp by David Heald © The Solomon R. Guggenheim Foundation, New York. © DACS 1996

11. Pablo Picasso, *Mother and Child,* 1905.
Staatsgalerie, Stuttgart. © DACS 1996

Pablo Picasso, *The Organ Grinder,* 1905.
sthaus Zürich. © DACS 1996

13. Pablo Picasso, *Seated Saltimbanque with Boy,* 1905.
The Baltimore Museum of Art. The Cone Collection, formed by Dr Claribel Cone and Miss Etta Cone of Baltimore, Maryland. BMA 1950.270. © DACS 199

14. Pablo Picasso, *Young Girl with a Dog,* 1905.
Location unknown. © DACS 1996

Da: der welke, faltige Stemmer,
der alte, der nur noch trommelt,
eingegangen in seiner gewaltigen Haut, als hätte sie früher
***zwei** Männer enthalten, und einer*
läge nun schon auf dem Kirchhof, und er überlebte den andern,
taub und manchmal ein wenig
wirr, in der verwitweten Haut.

There, the withered, wrinkled weight-lifter,
an old man, who only drums now,
shrivelled back inside his mighty skin, as if it once
*had contained **two** men, and one*
already lay in the churchyard, and he was outliving the other,
deaf and sometimes a little
bewildered, in his widowed skin.

Here, in translation,[30] are some of the lines on the old trouper seen in the Luxembourg:

Père Rollin, who was once so famous at all the fairs, is no longer 'working'. He has stopped lifting those monstrous weights and — once the most eloquent of all of them — is now quite silent. He has been given the drumming to do. He stands there, touchingly patient, with his athletic face looking too big now, its features hanging loose and disarrayed, as though in each one the heavy weight that kept it tense had been hung out. Neatly dressed, with a sky-blue knitted tie around his colossal neck, he has withdrawn at the height of his fame into this suit and this modest position, on which, so to speak, the bright light of glory no longer shines. But if there is anyone in this audience of young people who has seen him before, he knows that in those sleeves there are still those famous muscles whose slightest movement could set the weights to leaping. He has a clear memory of some such master-stroke, and whispers to his neighbour, and points, and then the old man feels their gaze upon him, pensive, vague and respectful. It's still there, that strength, you young people, he thinks; it's not at the tip of my fingers, that's all; it's gone down into the roots, that's where it is, somewhere there, all in a knot. It's much too much for the drumming. He sets to with the sticks. But he drums much too often, and then his son-in-law whistles at him warningly from the other side; he was just in the middle of a speech. And the old man stops, shocked, and apologises with his heavy shoulders and shifts himself ceremoniously onto the other leg. But the next moment there is another whistle. Hell. Père! Père Rollin! He had started drumming again. He is hardly aware of it. He could go on drumming for ever; as long as they don't think he is getting tired... The old man drums away like fourteen drummers. Père Rollin! hey, Père Rollin!, calls out someone from the audience who has just arrived and recognised him. But he just nods without taking any notice; drumming is an honour and he takes it seriously.

In the Elegy, there is more humour and more pathos, the latter consequent on the grotesquenenss of the imagery. Like that of a delivered woman, this man's skin is too big for him because, it seems, it once contained two people — but what he has given birth to is the death of another himself.[31] Terms like 'welk', 'faltig' and the physical and psychological equivalents 'taub' and 'wirr' all stress the loss of virile strength, now present only in a set of reminiscences in which he — lacking hearing and insight[32] — has no part. Where we *see* the loss of manhood, he has long gone away from the surface on which his comical skin betrays him.

Aber der junge, der Mann, als wär er der Sohn eines Nackens
und einer Nonne: prall und strammig erfüllt
mit Muskeln und Einfalt.

But the young one, the man, as if he were the son of a neck
and a nun: taut and strapping and full
of muscles and innocence.

In contrast and next in age is 'the man', a Schwarzenegger type who fills his skin to bursting — but has the same simplicity as the hero of *The Twins* if not of *Terminator 2*. The central image in this line has caused endless discomfort to critics for its grotesque disproportion, even though it fits in quite logically to a familiar caricature of the masculine — the muscular neck — and the feminine — nun-like innocence. The Catholic Guardini and the well brought-up Politzer alike object to the impugning of the nun's virtue, though Leishman and Spender suggest Rilke may be thinking of the Portuguese nun, who features elsewhere as one of his 'großen Liebenden'.[33] But, as Komar points out, such commentators tend to ignore the more peculiar parent, the neck.[34] Now I have an original contribution to offer here, though there is no question of ascertaining direct influence. In Hebrew the phrase 'son of a neck' (*ben anak*) means a giant. Translations of the Biblical phrase, which occurs repeatedly in the first six books and elsewhere,[35] often simply give 'the Anakites' (German: 'die Enakiter') and from this there has developed the false etymology of an ancestor called Anak. However, how or whether Rilke could have come across this strange phrase, which means exactly what he uses it for here, I can only wonder.

I want to pause here to consider how the theme of centredness and fulness develops in this poem towards what I called earlier 'the relation of elements in a circumscribed atomic space'. In the early sections of the poem, Rilke has looked at masculine images: the pistil or pestle, Augustus the Strong, the former strength of the weightlifter and phallic muscularity of the young man. In the second part of the poem, it is children who take over, and with them and their special kind of forlornness, we discover another kind of centre which consists not of fulness but relatedness. Thus within the apparently solid object, inside the skin, at the heart of the metaphor, there is not solidity but rather something like a nucleus, in which separations orbit around each other, just as the acrobats leap and fall in their choregraphed arcs. To anticipate the shape of the poem's argument again: in the final image of the lovers we will find the least phallic of centres: from the image of the feeble acrobats arises the idea of risk, success that is success precisely because there is no guarantee and no certainty, and the chance coincidence of bodies related in the moment.

Oh ihr,
die ein Leid, das noch klein war,
einst als Spielzeug bekam, in einer seiner
langen Genesungen....

Oh you,
that a sorrow, small still and young
once received as a toy, in one of its
long convalescences....

Here the power that controls the acrobats has become a Brobdignagian child; Rilke may be thinking of a folktale here, or of his own childhood convalescences, full of delirium like those of Malte, or followed by a long-promised visit to the circus.[36] The critics differ as to who they think are addressed by this suddenly direct appellation of 'ihr': whether all the acrobats, the two men described earlier,[37] or, as makes best sense to me, the two children whose description now follows. It is as if the poet bends down (with his not unaccustomed sentimentality towards the very young) and addresses them on their scale: suffering too is a little child. But inverting that very softening of the puppeteer figure that controls them to infant scale, we see another side to the analogy: the pain of the lives of children lived under the yoke of a merciless work-ethic that puts them perpetually on display.

In the next seventeen lines, we have the central image of the poem (perhaps, as Schwerte suggests, of the whole cycle): the youngest of the acrobats, not yet able to perform well or without pain, and the strength with which he holds in *but also lets out* his frustrated need for his mother. A comparison of the mother/son pairs in Fig. 11 and *Les Saltimbanques*, is instructive: in the former, the couple sit side by side, despairing and apart; in the latter, they stand, offering the identical face and head-position, both right hands holding a cloth, his left hand hanging, hers caressing her own hair in a strangely awkward bend, he looking at her exactly the same way as she is staring into the distance.

A striking pair of photographs is reproduced in Ingeborg Schnack (ed.), *Rainer Maria Rilke: Leben und Werk im Bild*.[38] In the first picture we see Rilke aged five wearing a white knee-length dress and with his hair curling down to his shoulders; in the second, taken two years later, he is in shorts and plain shirt, with short hair and a huge bow-tie, awkwardly holding a riding-crop. Only the cross-ankled stance and the sad, empty expression are the same. Now dressing little boys in girls' clothing was not unusual at the time, especially as infants, but this is extreme. Shortly after the second photo was taken, his parents separated and he was sent to a particularly oppressive military boarding school, which he never later spoke of without distress. In *Malte* there are some haunting and chilling passages where the mother dresses her son up in girls' clothes, smiles with him over the happy disappearance of the naughty Malte, and together they unreel long spools of lace. Rilke's loathing of dolls (in contrast to puppets, though they share the same noun in German) is thought by some biographers to have originated in this gender ambiguity of early childhood and his mother's habit of passing him around among her friends for admiration like a big doll.[39] We should bear these images in mind when reading the next two tableaux of the poem.

Du, der mit dem Aufschlag,
wie nur Früchte ihn kennen, unreif,
täglich hundertmal abfällt vom Baum der gemeinsam
erbauten Bewegung (der, rascher als Wasser, in wenig
Minuten Lenz, Sommer und Herbst hat) —
abfällt und anprallt ans Grab:
manchmal, in halber Pause, will dir ein liebes
Antlitz entstehn hinüber zu deiner selten
zärtlichen Mutter; doch an deinen Körper verliert sich,
der es flächig verbraucht, das schüchtern
kaum versuchte Gesicht... Und wieder
klatscht der Mann in die Hand zu dem Ansprung, und eh dir
jemals ein Schmerz deutlicher wird in der Nähe des immer
trabenden Herzens, kommt das Brennen der Fußsohln
ihm, seinem Ursprung, zuvor mit ein paar dir
rasch in die Augen gejagten leiblichen Tränen.
Und dennoch, blindlings,
das Lächeln.....

You who, with the thud
that only fruit know, unripe,
daily drop hundredfold from the tree of the movement
they build up together (the tree that, faster than water, in few
minutes has spring, summer and autumn) —
drops and rebounds on the grave:
sometimes, in half-pauses, a sweet
face tries to appear to send across to your seldom
tender mother; yet on your body it's lost,
spent on the surface, that shy
scarcely attempted look... And then once more
the man claps his hands for the leap, and before even
a pang can be clearer to you in the nearness of the ever
galloping heart, the burning soles of your feet,
running even before its source, chasing suddenly
into your eyes a few bodily tears.
And yet, all blindly,
the smile.....

Here is how this boy is described in the Rollin narrative: he sits down every now and then on the chair piled high with coats because

he needs that, he is just a beginner, so they say, and his feet hurt at the sharp spring with which he lands, from the high leaps, back onto the earth. He has a large face, big enough to hold a quantity of tears, but sometimes they hang on the edge of his wide-open eyes. And then he has to hold his head ever so care-

fully, like an over-full cup. It does not make him sad, not at all; he would not notice it if he were; it is simply the pain which is weeping, and this must be allowed him. With time it becomes easier to bear and in the end it disappears altogether. His father has not known what this pain was for a long time, and as for the grandfather — no, he forgot it sixty years ago, or else he would never have got so famous.

The boy's vulnerability is as the fruit at the top of the tree — the pyramid of the generations that holds the newest, lightest one aloft — which is not false ('Scheinfrucht') but instead 'unreif': immature/unripe. The tree is a favourite image of Rilke's especially in the fruit-laden poems of the *Sonette an Orpheus*. Again, and especially in its brevity, this is a sexual image,[40] again it has no product but the pain of the weakest element. Falling to earth, the boy is both touching his grave and also, like Antaeus, seeking strength from his mother.

Again here, a circle is described, from high to low and up again; but in the instant of landing, on the surface of his body, a countenance appears — the word 'Antlitz' is used normally in the Elegies only of the Angels — and is at once gone again. Timid, scarcely attempted, the miracle is not the rarity of his achievement but that of his remaining ability to go on trying for simple relatedness against such compulsive odds. For, as he leaps up against the pain, there appears on his face not just a few 'leiblichen Tränen' but once again, 'das Lächeln'.

'Das Lächeln ist nichts', Rilke once wrote, 'als das Consentement des Geistes, in uns zu sein' ('a smile is nothing but the consent of the soul to be in us').[41] As for the earlier term 'leiblich', he wrote also: 'auch der Leib ist leibhaft erst im Geiste' ('even the body becomes corporeal only in the spirit').[42] The body, then, is a surface on which expressive movements of the spirit are sometimes shown. This spatial metaphor can be linked to his use of the motif of love. Both are movement in an outward direction ('O Lächeln, wohin?' 'O smile, where to?') — which can either be stopped by reciprocation — the received smile, requited love — or else stream forth so powerfully that they surpass their motive. In *Malte*, it is said of the protagonist's young aunt Abelone, 'sie sehnte sich, ihrer Liebe alles Transitive zu nehmen', 'she longed to take all that was transitive out of her love'.[43] By this idea of surpassing requitedness, we find the very transitive element becoming objectless. Projection, directionality, is all.

This child's martyred smile is pure direction. His mother is there but she does not return his gaze — perhaps because, like the mother in Picasso's painting, she is absorbed in her vanity, perhaps because, like Père Rollin's daughter, she is now running the troupe and is too busy to look.[44] Rilke, whether for autobiographical or other reasons, gives the mother the short shrift of a single phrase. Her son, however, is the only one of the figures given a psychology, however rudimentary, the only one capable of feeling through his body the inexorable will of which they are playthings and at the same time of opening the way beyond that circuit, and he does it by a wish for connection that cannot yet find closure. By the end of the poem, Rilke will get beyond even this powerful but cruel idea, offering the aesthetic of pure gratification in the place of the image of martyrdom which so often tempts him.

Engel! o nimms, pflücks, das kleinblütige Heilkraut.
Schaff eine Vase, verwahrs! Stells unter jene, uns ***noch*** *nicht*
offenen Freuden; in lieblicher Urne
*rühms mit blumiger, schwungiger Aufschrift: »****Subrisio Saltat.****«.*

Angel! O gather it, pluck it, that small healing-herb.
Make a vase, keep its bloom! Set it among those joys not ***yet***
open to us; in a charming urn
*honour it with florally soaring inscription: '****Subrisio Saltat.****'.*

Here the Angel is positively invoked — indeed, instructed — for the first time in the Elegies. Note the imperative 'schaff' ('create'), rather than 'verschaff' ('provide');[45] but note also that the vessel is both a vase and an urn: preservation implies death. The imagery of fruitfulness turned positive here, the tiny moment of feeling has become a herb with healing properties, and, with the final flourish of the conceit, the poet gives it a name with the typical abbreviation of an apothecary's label. On the Middle Latin phrase here, a lot of drafts were lavished: the final version, *subrisio saltat.*, short for 'subrisio saltatoris', 'smile of the acrobat' carries implied in its shortened ending the potential extra meaning: 'the smile leaps'.[46]

Before going on to the next description, it is enlightening to make another comparison with Picasso's work, in particular with two earlier versions of the little girl. *Study*, now held in the Pushkin Museum, Moscow, and *Young Girl with a Dog* (Fig. 14) show the same child as in the *Saltimbanques*. In the first, the mother's place is taken by a dog (the very dog, one presumes, that appeared in Fig. 9). In the second sketch, the girl's hand rests gently on the dog's head. Despite the familiar forlornness, despite her faceless posture, we have here a minimal contact between human and animal.

If we turn again to the *Saltimbanques*, we remark how the dog has been removed and, without the slightest change in the girl's gesture, the flower-basket — similar to the mother's hat — is put in its place. Artifice replaces the animate, vanity replaces contact, the parallels between the two females serve to divide them.[47] In Rilke, the poignant icon is (familiarly) that of mother/son; the little girl is evoked as vulnerable precisely and only in her incipient feminine vanity.

Du dann, Liebliche,
du, von den reizendsten Freuden
stumm Übersprungne. Vielleicht sind
deine Fransen glücklich für dich —,
oder über den jungen
prallen Brüsten die grüne metallene Seide
fühlt sich unendlich verwöhnt und entbehrt nichts.
Du,
immerfort anders auf alle des Gleichgewichts schwankende Waagen
hingelegte Marktfrucht des Gleichmuts,
öffentlich unter den Schultern.

Then you, pretty one,
you, whom the most charming joys
dumbly leap over. Perhaps your
fringes are happy for you —,
or over your young
tight breasts the green metallic silk
feels itself endlessly spoilt and wants for nothing.
You,
never twice the same on all the faltering scale-pans of balance,
laid out market-fruit of serenity,
publicly shown among shoulders.

In his treatment of the little girl, the poet moves away from the moment of potential which he found in her brother back to a figure who, like the young man, is presented without consciousness.[48] But unlike Picasso, Rilke sees her from the front and in motion, raised aloft like her brother but in a passive posture, held out like fruit for sale. All the pleasure in her developing body is transferred, fancifully and somewhat coolly, to her clothing rather than herself. She is both decorated and decorative. The 'Gleichmut' here is surely less any kind of serenity or indifference attributable to the child than the skill of those shoulders that raise and carry her exactly balanced. Her own suffering is only implicit in the poet's tender address; like Picasso's girl with the basket, she is more fetish than human.

Wo, o ***wo*** *ist der Ort — ich trag ihn im Herzen —,*
wo sie noch lange nicht ***konnten,*** *noch von einander*
abfieln, wie sich bespringende, nicht recht
paarige Tiere; —
wo die Gewichte noch schwer sind;
wo noch von ihren vergeblich
wirbelnden Stäben die Teller
torkeln.....

Where, O ***where*** *is the place — I carry it in my heart —,*
where they ***could*** *not yet do it, by far, falling away still*
from each other like animals trying to mount, not properly
ready for mating; —
where the weights are still heavy;
where the vainly twirling
plates on their stems still
reel.....

The opening here proposes a place and offers a moment — the German 'wo' acts as both spatial and temporal connective; thus the moment before possibility is spatialized and can be carried like an image in the memory/heart.[49] The poet opens up the joyless exactitude of the acrobats' skills, as he has a moment ago with the child who had not yet got them perfected. Clumsiness is evoked in the image of the animals failing to mate, the juggling weights not yet quite able to defy gravity (as the ball divinely could) and the brilliant hanging position of the verb at the end, just about to drop… In the memory or image of a place/time of ineptitude, the poet urgently seeks (hence the italics) the paradox that all the positive elements are ones which fall outside the compulsively achieved performance. This is the meaning of the complicated conceit that follows:

Und plötzlich in diesem mühsamen Nirgends, plötzlich
die unsägliche Stelle, wo sich das reine Zuwenig
unbegreiflich verwandelt —, umspringt
in jenes leere Zuviel.
Wo die vielstellige Rechnung

zahlenlos aufgeht.

And then, in this wearisome nowhere, all of a sudden,
the wordless impossible place where the pure too-little
incomprehensibly turns — leaps round
into that empty too-much.
Where the many-figured sum
works out without remainder.

After the time of not-yet-being-able there must have been an instant of change — Rilke is always fascinated by the transformation of one state into another — when the purity of inadequacy was exchanged for the emptiness of an excess which is more precisely exactitude. He may, as some critics believe, be casting a scathing glance here at the facility of some poets, including himself in less sensitive times. But there is a difficult abstract idea at work here too. For all the temptation of exactitude ('er war ein Dichter und haßte das Ungefähre') it can be the very opposite of perfection, having something vain and almost ill-balanced about it. The sum is too long, the right answer gives nothing, no remainder and therefore no product. Exchanging the organic imagery (via the tree changed into a set of scales in the last tableau) for imagery of scientific abstraction, Rilke suggests a loss of making, repetition without reproduction.

Plätze, o Platz in Paris, unendlicher Schauplatz,
wo die Modistin, ***Madame Lamort,***
die ruhlosen Wege der Erde, endlose Bänder,
schlingt und windet und neue aus ihnen
Schleifen erfindet, Rüschen, Blumen, Kokarden, künstliche Früchte —,
alle
unwahr gefärbt, — für die billigen
Winterhüte des Schicksals.
. . . .

Squares, O square in Paris, infinite showplace,
where the milliner ***Madame Lamort***
fashions the restless paths of the earth, endless ribbons,
loops and winds them, invents from them new
bows, ruffles, flowers, cockades, artificial fruit —,
all
falsely coloured, — for the cheap
winter bonnets of fate.
. . . .

From there we return to Brobdignag, where the sinister figure of death personified as a milliner suggests a spiritless creativity; the cold squares of inner Paris replace the windier suburban spaces, and the 'Platz/Schauplatz' supersedes both 'Ort' and 'Stelle', leading back towards a completed circle at the final locus of the 'Teppich'. Mme Lamort ('Mrs Death', as Politzer bathetically calls her, while Komar more perspicaciously recalls Madame Lafarge)[50] is the subject of a series of verbs that echo the ones in the opening image, suggesting that she is a last version of the despotic will. At the same time, she is the culminating figure of fakery, with the artificial fruit she pins on her hats, and the art with which she curls the ribboned roads is tawdry, urban and cheap.[51] In this last glance at the Picasso original, we find the pretty mother's hat transformed into the leering vanity of death. Then the poem reaches its climax.

Engel!: Es wäre ein Platz, den wir nicht wissen, und dorten,
auf unsäglichem Teppich, zeigten die Liebenden, die's hier
bis zum Können nie bringen, ihre kühnen
hohen Figuren des Herzschwungs,
ihre Türme aus Lust, ihre
längst, wo Boden nie war, nur an einander
lehnenden Leitern, bebend, — und ***könntens,***
vor den Zuschauern rings, unzähligen lautlosen Toten:
  Würfen die dann ihre letzten, immer ersparten,
immer verborgenen, die wir nicht kennen, ewig
gültigen Münzen des Glücks vor das endlich
wahrhaft lächelnde Paar auf gestilltem
Teppich?

Angel!: If there were a square that we do not know of, and there
on a wordless impossible carpet, the lovers who here
never can quite do it, might show their bold
high-flying feats of the heart's swing,
their towers of desire, their two
ladders that long since, where ground never was, have leaned
only on each other, trembling, — and ***could*** *do it,*
before the gathered spectators, the numberless unspeaking dead:
  Would they then fling their last, ever saved up,
ever hidden, that we never know of, eternally
valid coinage of bliss before the finally
truthfully smiling couple on the quieted
carpet?

This Elegy ends, as it started, with an open question. Once again everything is centred on a performance on a mat, but at last it is one that reaches a full and satisfied conclusion, the 'lineaments of gratified desire'. The acrobats with their clumsy competence have given way to the couple in love,[52] who, unusually in Rilke, have surpassed even the ideal of unrequitedness and whose bodies allow them complete transitivity. It is now the freely motivated body that affords the 'high saltos' of the heart, with the same vulnerability — expressed in the marvellous image of the two ladders leaned trembling against each other on no ground.[53] Perfect satiation closes the text with the same focusing effect as in so many sections, on a single word that picks up from the preceding lines — but before it does, we must recognise the disturbing nature of this couple's sexual synchrony, which is after all played in front of an admiring and paying audience. Only the dead are vouchsafed this edenic performance; they pay with the long-saved coinage which is a version of the 'reine Zuwenig' a currency of true measure. What they and we see here can best be described by the word 'grace' — but what remains striking in this idea of love is that grace, the aesthetic, is represented as the perfect exactitude of the body, not the spirit, the surface of the self where it is visible to beloved and spectators alike, in the now completed smile.

---

1 *SW*, II, 136-8.

2 In a letter simply dated 'Freitag', Rilke asks Hertha Koenig 'ob Sie mich rasch und still für eine Weile beim großen Picasso in der Widenmayerstraße würden aufnehmen und verbergen wollen', offering to be the 'Wächter am Picasso', Rainer Maria Rilke, *Gesammelte Briefe in 6 Bänden, IV,* 46 and 48.

3 See my *The Banal Object: theme and thematics in Proust, Rilke, Hofmannsthal and Sartre* (London, 1981) and 'Rilke's Paris: "*cité pleine de rêves*"', in Edward Timms and David Kelley (eds.), *Unreal City* (Manchester, 1985), pp. 97-110.

4 Letter of 18 July 1903, *Briefwechsel mit Lou Andreas-Salomé*, p. 64. Dieter Bassermann identifies this time and this mood as that of the Fifth Elegy in *Der späte Rilke*, p. 477.

5 Paul de Man notes the same parallel of subject-matter among *Malte*, the *Neue Gedichte* and the Fifth Elegy in *Allegories of Meaning*, p. 22. On pp. 49*ff*, he discusses the complex and important relation between Rilke's messianic posture and 'a play of language that can only come about because the poet has renounced any claim to extra-textual authority' (p. 50).

6 *SW*, VI, 863.

7 See Elisabeth von Schmidt-Pauli, conversation with Rilke, quoted by Richard Jayne, *The Symbolism of Space and Motion in the Works of Rainer*

Maria Rilke (Frankfurt/Main, 1972), p. 74. For use of reference, it is worth reproducing this remarkable poem (written in Paris in July 1907):

Du Runder, der das Warme aus zwei Händen
im Fliegen, oben, fortgiebt, sorglos wie
sein Eigenes; was in den Gegenständen
nicht bleiben kann, zu unbeschwert für sie,

zu wenig Ding und doch noch Ding genug,
um nicht aus allem draußen Aufgereihten
unsichtbar plötzlich in uns einzugleiten:
das glitt in dich, du zwischen Fall und Flug

noch Unentschlossener: der, wenn er steigt,
als hätte er ihn mit hinaufgehoben,
den Wurf entführt und freiläßt —, und sich neigt
und einhält und den Spielenden von oben
auf einmal eine neue Stelle zeigt,
sie ordnend wie zu einer Tanzfigur,

um dann, erwartet und erwünscht von allen,
rasch, einfach, kunstlos, ganz Natur,
dem Becher hoher Hände zuzufallen.

[8] For this and other details on Picasso's *Saltimbanque* series, I am indebted to E. A. Carmean Jr., *Picasso, The Saltimbanques* (Washington, 1980), from which I have drawn most of the illustrations for this article.

[9] See Marion Faber, *Angels of Daring* (Stuttgart, 1979), p. 83.

[10] There are two sources for this account, the first a short narrative of 14 July 1907, the second a letter of the same date to Dora Heidrich, reproduced by B. J. Morse, 'The Fifth Duino Elegy', *The Welsh Review*, vol 3, no 2 (June 1944), pp. 122-9. Herebelow the narrative, from *SW*, VI, 1137-9:

Vor dem Luxembourg, nach dem Panthéon zu, hat wieder Père Rollin mit den Seinen sich ausgebreitet. Derselbe Teppich liegt da, dieselben abgelegten Mäntel, dicke Wintermäntel, sind über einen Stuhl gehäuft, auf dem gerade noch soviel Platz bleibt, daß der kleine Sohn, der Enkel des Alten, zwischendurch zu einem Viertel Hinsitzen kommt, ab und zu. Er braucht das noch, er ist ein Anfänger, heißt es, und die Füße tun ihm weh bei dem jähen Aufsprung mit dem er, aus den hohen Saltos heraus, auf die Erde kommt. Er hat ein großes Gesicht das eine Menge Tränen fassen kann, aber sie stehen doch manchmal bis an den Rand in den ausgeweiteten Augen. Dann muß er den Kopf ganz vorsichtig tragen, wie eine zu volle Tasse. Er ist nicht traurig dabei, garnicht, er würde gar nicht merken wenn er es wäre, es ist einfach der Schmerz der weint und das muß man ihm lassen. Mit der Zeit wird das leichter und schließlich ist es fort. Der Vater weiß längst nichtmehr wie das war, und der Großvater, nein, der hat es schon vor sechzig Jahren vergessen, sonst wäre er nicht so berühmt geworden. Aber, sieh da, Père Rollin, der so berühmt geworden ist auf allen Jahrmärkten, »arbeitet« nicht mehr. Er schwenkt nicht mehr die ungeheuren Gewichte und er (der Beredteste von Allen) sagt kein Wort. Er ist aufs Trommeln gesetzt. Rührend geduldig steht er da mit dem zu weit gewordenen Athleten-Gesicht, in dem die Züge locker durcheinanderhängen, als wäre aus jedem einzelnen das Gewicht ausgehängt worden, das ihn spannte. Bürgerlich angezogen, eine gestrickte himmelblaue Cravatte um den kolossalen Hals, hat er sich auf der Höhe seines ehrlichen Ruhms zurückgezogen in diesen Rock und in die bescheidene Stellung, auf die, sozusagen, kein Glanz mehr fällt. Aber wer, von diesen jungen Leuten, ihn mal gesehen hat, der weiß ja doch, daß in diesen Ärmeln die berühmten Muskeln stecken, deren leisestes Spiel die Gewichte zum Springen brachte. Der hat eine ganz bestimmte Erinnerung an ein solches Meisterstück und er sagt ein paar Worte zu seinem Nachbar und zeigt herüber und dann fühlt der Alte ihre Blicke auf sich, nachdenklich und unbestimmt und achtungsvoll. Sie ist schon noch da, diese Kraft, junge Leute, denkt er; sie ist nicht mehr so bei der Hand, das ist das Ganze; sie ist in die Wurzeln gegangen; da irgendwo ist sie noch, der ganze Klumpen. Und für das Trommeln überhaupt ist sie noch viel zu groß. Und er schlägelt los. Aber er trommelt viel zu oft. Dann pfeift ihm der Schwiegersohn von drüben und winkt ab; er war gerade mitten in einer Tirade. Und der Alte hört auf, erschrocken, und entschuldigt sich mit den schweren Schultern und tritt umständlich auf das andere Bein. Aber da muß schon wieder abgepfiffen werden. Diable. Père! Père Rollin! Er hat schon wieder getrommelt. Er weiß es kaum. Er könnte immerzu trommeln; sie sollen nur nicht meinen, daß er müde würde. Aber da, jetzt redet seine Tochter; schlagfertig und handfest und ohne Loch das Ganze und ein Witz über den andern. Sie hält überhaupt jetzt die Sache zusammen, es ist eine Freude zuzuschauen. Der Schwiegersohn arbeitet ja gut, da ist nichts zu sagen, und gerne, wie es sich gehört. Aber sie hat das Zeug im Blut, das merkt man. Damit muß man geboren werden. Sie ist fertig: Musique, schreit sie. Und der Alte trommelt los wie vierzehn Trommeln. Père Rollin, Heh, Père Rollin: ruft jemand aus den Zuschauern, der hinzutritt eben und ihn erkennt. Aber er nickt nur nebenbei; das Trommeln ist eine Ehrensache und er nimmt es ernst.

[11] *Circus Family*, shown in Carmean as Fig. 8, opposite p. 17.

[12] See Carmean, pp. 24-5 and Jean Starobinski, *Portrait de l'artiste en saltimbanque* (Geneva and Paris, 1970).

[13] Daumier 1808-1879, Tiepolo 1727-1804.

[14] The term 'family' may, however, often have been used metaphorically; see Carmean, p. 42.

[15] Rilke's comment on this painting, in a letter to Marianne von Goldschmidt-Rothschild, concentrates on the four diamonds of colour on the dying figure's

arm: 'Man möchte fast versucht sein, von diesem viertönigen Anschlag aus den späteren Picasso zu begreifen, als ob, nach Pierrots Tode, die zerschlagene Welt nur noch in solchen schönen Scherben zusammenkäme'; quoted in Herman Meyer, 'Die Verwandlung des Sichtbaren' in Rüdiger Görner, *Rainer Maria Rilke,* p. 158.

16 E.g. Erich Meuthen, *Bogengebete* (Frankfurt, Berne, New York, 1983), pp.182-93; and Hans Schwerte, 'Das Lächeln in den Duineser Elegien', *Germanisch-Romanische Monatsschrift* vol 35, (1954), pp. 289-98.

17 For the first of these, Heinz Politzer, 'Some aspects of "late art" in Rainer Maria Rilke's Fifth Duino Elegy', *Germanic Review*, vol 32, no. 4 (Dec. 1957), pp. 282-98; for the second, Theodore Ziolkowski, *The Classical German Elegy 1795-1950*, p. 247 and Kathleen Komar, *Transcending Angels*, p. 89. Komar is also unusual in giving a formalistic analysis of the Elegy's difference from the others and from the classical model, pp. 101-2.

18 E.g. E. M. Butler, *Rainer Maria Rilke*, p. 333; and B. Subramanian, *Engel und Mensch* (Berne, Frankfurt, New York, 1986), pp. 100-101.

19 In German: 'Sage mir, Muse, die Taten des vielgewanderten Mannes...', quoted by Meuthen, p. 183.

20 This is pointed out by Faber, p. 87.

21 See Käte Hamburger, *Rilke: eine Einführung*, p. 127 and Faber, p. 117.

22 Ronald G. Brown, 'Rilke's Fifth Elegy', *The Explicator*, vol 35, no 1 (Fall 1976), pp. 27-8.

23 Romano Guardini, *Rilke's Duino Elegies*, tr. K. G. Knight, p. 136, gives on the authority of 'someone who knew Rilke very well for a long time' a rather fanciful analogy with describing a woman who is no more than beautiful as being 'the initial letter of beauty'. This seems unnecessarily complicated.

24 For a brilliant explication of this linguistic resource, see Freud's 1919 article, 'Das Unheimliche', in *Studienausgabe* (Frankfurt/Main, 1969-79), vol IV, pp. 241-74.

25 *SW*, II, 185. The resonance of these dazzling lines is of course increased by the implied word-play on 'reiner/Rainer'and 'Lidern/Liedern'.

26 The cognate terms pestle/pistil and the ambiguous 'Stempel' suggest the same doubly phallic image in both German and English.

27 See Politzer, p. 291.

28 For a consistent and intelligent analysis of this image, see Schwerte.

29 See Carmean, pp. 50-52. Other putative originals are Fernande Olivier and a girl she briefly adopted (see note 44), André Salmon as the taller youth and Max Jacob as the boy, clutching the tip of a Jewish *tallit*!

30 This and other translations, unless otherwise attributed, are my own.

31 There is surely a hint here of one of Rilke's crazier fantasies, the figure of the male 'Tod-Gebärer' featured in the last section of the *Stundenbuch*, *SW* II, 273-76.

[32] The German 'doof' and English 'dopy' both etymologically take the idea of stupidity from the idea of deafness, just as hearing and understanding are equivalent in the French verb 'entendre'.

[33] See Guardini, p. 141 and note 1; Politzer, p. 289: 'his descent from a nun casts upon him a sheen of dubiousness and disrepute or, taking the nun's virginity into account, of a messianic, Christ-like, promise'; J. B. Leishman and Stephen Spender, *Duino Elegies*, p. 127, quoting J.-F. Angelloz, another of Rilke's translators.

[34] Komar p. 236, note 13.

[35] E.g., as *ben/b'nei anak* in Joshua 15:14, Numbers 13:33, Deuteronomy 9:2; and as *anakim* in Joshua 11:21 and 22, Joshua 14: 12 and 15 and Deuteronomy 2:10, 11 and 21. I am very grateful to my father, Professor Ben Segal, for this reference.

[36] *SW*, VI, 797*ff*. For the biographical inference see Hamburger, p. 128 and Heinrich Kreutz, *Rilkes Duineser Elegien* (Munich, 1950), p. 80.

[37] Komar rather inexplicably assumes the latter, p. 96.

[38] Ingeborg Schnack (ed.), *Rainer Maria Rilke: Leben und Werk im Bild* (Frankfurt, 1973), pp. 46 and 47.

[39] See the brilliant 1914 essay 'Puppen' (*SW*, VI, 1063-74) and the creepy story 'Frau Blahas Magd' (of 1899, *SW*, IV, 623-9); the latter connexion is made by E. M. Butler in her biographical study.

[40] See Subramanian, p. 107; this critic is almost alone in discerning the complex imagery of sexuality and fertility in this poem, see pp. 121-27.

[41] From the prose paraphrase of a poem unpublished in Rilke's lifetime, 'La Nascita del Sorriso' (The birth of the smile); quoted by Schwerte, p. 295, and Steiner, p. 114.

[42] This is the last line of a sonnet on Elizabeth Barrett-Browning; see Schwerte, loc. cit. Both poems were written in 1919.

[43] *SW*, VI, 937.

[44] Few critics have any time for the mother; among these are Katharina Kippenberg, *Rainer Maria Rilkes Duineser Elegien und Sonette an Orpheus* (Frankfurt, 1946), p. 50, and Subramanian, 108. Both assume that she too underwent a 'harte Jugend' and 'rigorösen Training' and therefore lost her innate softheartedness. This is endorsed in the Père Rollin text, where she appears as a daughter and manager rather than a mother: 'schlagfertig und handfest und ohne Loch das Ganze und ein Witz über den andern. Sie hält überhaupt jetzt die Sache zusammen, es ist eine Freude zuzuschauen. Der Schwiegersohn arbeitet ja gut, da ist nichts zu sagen, und gerne, wie es sich gehört. Aber sie hat das Zeug im Blut, das merkt man. Damit muß man geboren werden.'

[45] See Steiner, p. 115.

[46] This point is noted by Franz Josef Brecht, *Schicksal und Auftrag des Menschen* (Munich, 1949), p. 155, and Politzer p. 293, quoting Else Buddeberg, *Rainer Maria Rilke* (Stuttgart, 1955), p. 418.

[47] Carmean, pp. 52-54, tells the story of a little girl, Raymonde, whom Fernande Olivier and Picasso adopted from an orphanage but who was returned there after a few days, apparently on the decision of Olivier and against the wish of Picasso, André Salmon and Max Jacob.
[48] The epithet 'prall' is used of both of them in reference to aspects of their bodies, while with the boy it describes his bouncing fall.
[49] Some critics take the second phrase as an answer to the first — which makes little sense. But Steiner, p. 118, offers an interesting analogy with the idea of saying something 'liege mir auf der Zunge'; and Politzer points to the Rilkean concept of *Weltinnenraum*, p. 294.
[50] Politzer, p. 294; Komar, p. 104.
[51] A similarly powerful image, playing with changes of scale and the analogy earth/body, likens seams of ore to veins in the *Neues Gedicht* 'Orpheus. Eurydike. Hermes'.
[52] Subramanian, p. 122, suggests a more purposeful analogy between the two sets of performers: 'Es ist offenbar, daß hinter dem Bild der Saltimbanques das Bild der Liebenden im Liebesakt steht'.
[53] Faber, pp. 114-5 sets in parallel three quotations in which the writer is cited as 'bodenlos'. First, Kafka: 'Der Schriftsteller in mir wird natürlich sofort sterben, denn eine solche Figur hat keinen Boden, hat keinen Bestand, ist nicht einmal aus Staub'; and two letters written by Rilke in Dec 1921, just two months before he wrote this Elegy: [he exists] 'in der offensten und nun eigentlich bodenlosen Welt'... the artist must live for his art alone and relate to his audience with an 'akrobatische Geschicklichkeit'.

ELEGY SIX

David Midgley

It is often said of heroes that they were unknowable men. Whatever it is that drives them to perform illustrious feats — perhaps even to court death — also seems to set them apart from ordinary mortals. They are often secret beings, unconcerned with those social compromises that most of us are content to make in our lives.

That aspect of the hero is part of the mystery that Rilke explores in his Sixth Elegy, but only a part of it. The otherness of the hero provides, in a quite literal sense, the framing idea of the poem: the first line expresses the notion of something peculiarly significant, and the very last word of the poem characterises the hero as 'different'. Within that frame Rilke imagines the qualities of a human type capable of transcending the compromises of ordinary earthly existence. His theme is one that was briefly touched on in the First Elegy (l. 41f), where the hero is mentioned as one inspiring example amongst others for the poet's task. But as Rilke enlarges here on his sense of the hero's significance, he also confronts us with additional puzzles. The terms in which he evokes the hero are closer to those of ancient myth than to any commonplace perceptions of modern war heroes, and yet the allusions to antiquity are left intriguingly understated in the poem. He celebrates the hero as the realisation of a higher existential ideal, but in terms which may well arouse suspicion in late twentieth-century readers. And he introduces his subject with an image which appears at first sight to be curiously at odds with any conventional notion of heroism. That image is the fig-tree.

The fruit of the fig-tree is familiar to us as an emblem of sexuality. It is one which for English readers, moreover, Elizabethan drama has coloured with ribald associations. But Rilke has a rather different connotation in mind. As he explains in lines 2-7, he is picturing the arching curve of the branches of the fig-tree, and he is linking them with a botanical conundrum. The flowering of the fig-tree is a peculiarly discreet process. It takes place in concealment, it is — as Rilke puts it — almost skipped; and the fruit is disclosed ('entschlossen' is used here unusually in the sense of 'aufgeschlossen') seemingly ahead of its due season. The idea to which Rilke is attaching importance here is that the secret vitality of the fig-tree is driven, 'pure' and 'unproclaimed', into its fruiting, into fulfilment. He makes his point in diagrammatic terms, comparing the branch of the tree to the pipework of a fountain: the sap is led down and then upwards, erupting out of dormancy, without any intervening phase. The 'sweet achievement' that is evoked in line 7 is attained without the sexual union that would be associated with flowering. More specifically it is attained without the turbulence and anguish of adolescence as it is discussed in the Third Elegy. The anatomical picture that Rilke has constructed here is one in which vital forces are spontaneously converted into immediate fulfilment, into action without reflection, with scarcely any degree of self-consciousness. If we were to interpret the image in Freudian terms, then we would say that we were reading a description of the sublimation of libidinal energy into asexual activity:

FEIGENBAUM, seit wie lange schon ists mir bedeutend,
wie du die Blüte beinah ganz überschlägst
und hinein in die zeitig entschlossene Frucht,
ungerühmt, drängst dein reines Geheimnis.
Wie der Fontäne Rohr treibt dein gebognes Gezweig
abwärts den Saft und hinan: und er springt aus dem Schlaf,
fast nicht erwachend, ins Glück seiner süßesten Leistung.
Sieh: wie der Gott in den Schwan.

FIG-TREE, for how long now have I found it significant
that you almost entirely pass over your blossoming
and urge your pure mystery, unproclaimed,
into your early-disclosed fruit.
Like the curved pipe of a fountain, your arching boughs drive the sap
downward and up again; and almost without waking
it bursts out of sleep into its sweetest achievement.
See: like the god entering the swan.

The line-break that Rilke introduces at this point invites us to linger on the analogy of the god and the swan. The image is powerfully redolent of the world of ancient Greek myth, but it is left curiously undeveloped in the text of the poem. Zeus, of course, was notorious for his absence of sexual restraint, and for the inventiveness of the guises in which he sought the favours of mortal women. He transformed himself into a swan, we might recall, in order to deceive and possess one who was particularly noted for her faithfulness and chastity: Leda. The outcome for which that union is most commonly remembered was the birth of Helen of Troy. And the heroic acts with which Helen's name in turn is linked are commemorated in Homer's *Iliad*, with its famous celebration of the valour of Achilles, and also its account of the ignominous treatment to which Achilles subjects the body of Hector once he has defeated him in battle. Rilke's poem excludes all explicit reference to these matters, although the general qualities of the hero as the Sixth Elegy evokes them are entirely compatible with the way that Homer characterises both Achilles and Hector. Like them, Rilke's hero is physically strong, fleet of foot, and inclined to destructive acts; and just as Homer's heroes are preordained — by a higher fate (*moira*) to which even the gods are subject — to die young, so too is Rilke's hero linked to the notion of being destined for early death. But Rilke's more immediate concern is with another attribute of the hero which he may have recalled from Homer: the hero is also destined to outshine his peers, he is set apart from the common run of men.

The continuation of line 8 introduces a note of contrast, a contrast moreover with the shared reality in which the reader is presumed to live. 'We' do not experience that immediate fulfilment of the fig-tree. 'We' tarry and are seduced — very sweetly, by the gentle night air of line 13 — into the 'blossoming' that is associated with sexual dalliance, and when we finally reach maturity and do our 'fruiting' we arrive enfeebled, disappointed, disillusioned and betrayed (l. 10). There are few who are so fashioned that they can resist sensual distraction and achieve immediate fulfilment. They include heroes, and more generally those who are *fated* to die young, the 'frühe Hinüber*bestimmten*' (l. 15):

...... Wir aber verweilen,
ach, uns rühmt es zu blühn, und ins verspätete Innre
unserer endlichen Frucht gehn wir verraten hinein.
Wenigen steigt so stark der Andrang des Handelns,
daß sie schon anstehn und glühn in der Fülle des Herzens,
wenn die Verführung zum Blühn wie gelinderte Nachtluft
ihnen die Jugend des Munds, ihnen die Lider berührt:
Helden vielleicht und den frühe Hinüberbestimmten,
denen der gärtnernde Tod anders die Adern verbiegt.
Diese stürzen dahin: dem eigenen Lächeln
sind sie voran, wie das Rossegespann in den milden
muldigen Bildern von Karnak dem siegenden König.

......But for our part we linger,
alas, we are flattered into blossoming and we enter
the belated interior of our final fruit betrayed.
In only a few does the urge to action rise up so strongly
that they halt, glowing in their heart's abundance,
when, like the soft night air, the temptation to blossom
touches their youthful mouths, their eyelids:
heroes perhaps, and those destined to die young,
whose veins Death the gardener bends in a different way.
These plunge on ahead: in advance of their own smile
like the team of galloping horses before the triumphant
pharaoh in the mild hollowed reliefs of Karnak.

In the image of the pharaoh that appears in this second section of the poem we may detect a reminiscence of Rilke's Egyptian travels in the winter of 1911, and there may be a similar recollection behind the fig-tree image with which the poem began. But the reference to smiling in line 17 introduces a motif which invites interpretation from within the specific context of the *Duino Elegies*. In Elegies Two to Five, the smiling of lovers, mothers and performing artists has betokened an enclosing reciprocity which was evoked only to be rejected. Something which marks the hero, and the young dead generally, out as different is the fact that they are careering ahead of their own smiles; they are as if empowered to break out of that enclosure. This particular mark of distinction will be emphasised again in the last three lines of the Sixth Elegy, which belong, like the first thirty-one lines, to the early phase of composition (they were added in the autumn of 1913). There the hero is presented as someone who disdains the 'abodes of love' (l. 42), who storms through life, drawing impetus from the heartbeats of those who love him, and who can pass beyond the domain of smiles and all that it implies.

I shall discuss the particular resonances of that ending at the appropriate point. In the meantime we should note how, in line 16, Rilke has introduced an explicit indication of what it is that has made the hero, and the young dead, different from the rest of us. It is a personified Death — a gardener Death — that has moulded them, bending their branches (their tubes) to a purpose. The botanical conceit with which the poem began, then, is being developed into an argument which can make death confer a purpose on life. The solemnity of the moment is underscored by the rhythm of Rilke's versification. In lines 11-16 — exceptionally even within the *Duino Elegies* — he has begun to catch the effect of the elegiac couplet of antiquity, even if the first of each pair of lines tends to fall short of a true hexameter. The very metre, then, underscores the sense in which Rilke is evoking the model of the hero as he was depicted by classical authors; and in the phrase 'Fülle des Herzens' (l. 12) there is also a strong echo of an eighteenth-century poet who pioneered the imitation of ancient Greek metres in German verse: Klopstock.

What is peculiarly significant about the rhythmic effect of line 16, however, is that it is symmetrically constructed, placing a purposeful stress both on 'Tod', which immediately precedes the caesura, and on 'anders', which follows it:

> *Hèlden vielleìcht und den frühe Hinǜberbestìmmten,*
> *dènen der gä̀rtnernde Tòd || ànders die Àdern verbìegt.*

Rilke also reinforces the sense of a contrast between that kind of destiny and ours in his unconventional deployment of verbs. In line 10, 'we' are said to be obeying a *de*-personalised compulsion: 'uns *rühmt es* zu blühn'. The verb 'rühmen', like the verb 'preisen', represents an activity which is part of what poetry traditionally does: it sings in *praise* of something. That activity was part of the 'task' that Rilke set himself in the First Elegy (l. 40). It will be recalled again at the start of the Tenth Elegy; and it will be evoked as part of the celebration of great cultural achievements, and of mundane artefacts, that he strives for in the Seventh and Ninth Elegies respectively. Here, in the impersonal form 'es rühmt', the verb suggests a reified impulse that is existentially inferior to the impetus of the hero. By contrast with the discreetly 'unproclaimed' flowering of the fig-tree in line 4, 'we' succumb to the appeal of vanity and false pride (which is why I have translated Rilke's 'uns rühmt es' as 'we are flattered').

It is worth noting here, too, that when we come to the third section of the poem, we shall find a parallel instance in the unusual use of 'singen' as a transitive verb (ll. 24-5): the hero is *being sung*, what is 'singing' him is again a personified agency — a 'Schicksal' (fate) — and it is 'singing' him as an expression of *its* enthusiasm. Here again there are particular poetic effects to be noted in Rilke's versification, and once again they serve to emphasise the difference between the hero's destiny and ours. Firstly the unconventional placing of the relative clause before the noun to which it refers allows the word 'Schicksal' to be given prominence at the end of line 24 (which in this case is, arguably, a true hexameter). Secondly, the echo of the elegiac couplet in this instance confers stress in line 25 on 'his' (the hero's) world:

sìngt ihn hinèin in den Stùrm || sèiner aufràuschenden Wèlt.

There is much for us to admire in Rilke's poetic skill here, but how many of us can be content to follow his argument? It was one thing in the world of classical antiquity to interpret a life in terms of the death that ended it, and to say of one who died young that 'the gods so loved him that they took him early'. It may even have had meaning to do so in the heroic age of high Romanticism, when Byron wrote just such a line... But by the time Rilke was completing his Elegies, the great human catastrophe of mechanised warfare had made a nonsense of any notion of a 'hero's death' as the fulfilment of any personal destiny. We might find it puzzling that when Rilke returned to the composition of the *Duino Elegies* in 1922, he made no attempt to incorporate any reference to the impact of the First World War. But we would do well to remind ourselves that it took a long time for the poems which we now associate with the distinctive experiences of that war to be accepted into the canon of modern poetry. As late as 1936, when W.B. Yeats was invited to edit the Oxford Book of Modern Verse, he decided to exclude all poems about the First World War on the grounds that 'passive suffering is not a theme for poetry'.

When Rilke sought the seclusion of Muzot in 1921-22, he did so in order to recover the integrity of his original poetic vision after all the disruption that the war years and their aftermath had brought.[1] In the case of the Sixth Elegy, the idea he was trying to articulate through the theme of the hero, while not without its violent implications, had little to do with the experience of war as such. It is in the third section of the poem that we are given a clearer sense of connection between the Sixth Elegy and the purpose that Rilke outlined in the First Elegy. Let us consider his celebration of the hero in the light of that connection:

Wunderlich nah ist der Held doch den jugendlich Toten. Dauern
ficht ihn nicht an. Sein Aufgang ist Dasein; beständig
nimmt er sich fort und tritt ins veränderte Sternbild
seiner steten Gefahr. Dort fänden ihn wenige. Aber
das uns finster verschweigt, das plötzlich begeisterte Schicksal
singt ihn hinein in den Sturm seiner aufrauschenden Welt.
*Hör ich doch keinen wie **ihn**. Auf einmal durchgeht mich*
mit der strömenden Luft sein verdunkelter Ton.

Dann, wie verbärg ich mich gern vor der Sehnsucht: O wär ich,
wär ich ein Knabe und dürft es noch werden und säße
in die künftigen Arme gestützt und läse von Simson,
wie seine Mutter erst nichts und dann alles gebar.

Wondrously near is the hero to those who die young. Permanence
does not concern him. His rise is true being; constantly
he removes himself and passes into the altered constellation
of his perpetual danger. Few would find him there. But
Fate, which is darkly silent of us, grows suddenly excited
and sings him into the storm of his upsurging world.
I hear none like him. All at once I am pierced
by his darkened sound, borne on the rushing air.
Then how gladly I would hide from the longing: O would that
I were a boy once again, with my life before me, and could sit
leaning on future arms and reading of Samson,
how his mother bore first nothing, then all.

That 'wondrous' closeness between the hero and the young dead is a reminder that the evocation of the hero is part of the poetic task expounded in the First Elegy (l. 41f). There the hero was a source of inspiration for the overcoming of sorrow and loss. With a simple assonance, Rilke had linked the hero firmly with the notion of preservation: 'es erhält sich der Held' — he keeps well. And where does he 'keep'? The context of that line in the First Elegy permits us to infer that he is preserved in our recollection of him, in poetry ('Preisung'), in legend, in myth, in the stars: his demise ('Untergang'), we are told, is also a kind of birth, his entry into our commemoration of him. The 'picture' of the hero in the stars — his 'Sternbild' — is expressly evoked in the Sixth Elegy (l. 22) with a simple plasticity that is inevitably lost if we translate the word into English, as we must, with the abstract term 'constellation'. At the same time, the 'Untergang' of the First Elegy is rewritten as 'Aufgang' — again to the inevitable bewilderment of English translators. Rilke is able to use the standard German words for the rising and setting of stellar systems (as of the sun) in order to suggest the trajectory of the hero's career, his 'rise' in our estimation which is inseparable from the notion of his physical demise. The hero's 'Aufgang' (l. 21) is the moment of his rising up as a hero, it is the token of his fitness to mount the heavens, and it is simultaneously an expression of the apotheosis entailed in our act of commemorating him. It is also, in itself, 'Dasein' — a moment of true being. In the broad context of the conversion of negative experience into affirmation that Rilke is pursuing in the *Duino Elegies*, the hero represents the existential possibility of immediate transcendence of the lot of ordinary mortals.

The meaning inherent in that existential possibility is revealed in the way that the image of the hero as 'rising star' is elaborated. The hero can be treated as an antidote to the sense of loss that death brings us because he is unconcerned for permanence (l. 20f), and thus by implication also for our fond memories of him. It is not his nature to abide, he is constantly removing himself (l. 21f). The medium in which he exists is one of constant danger, where few can match him, and the constellation into which he enters is thus forever changing, indeed it is implicitly changed by his act of entering it (l. 22f). There is a clue here to the reason why, as we noted earlier, the names of specific heroes are kept out of the text of the Sixth Elegy — with one exception, as we are about to discover. The existential superiority of the hero resides in his dynamism, his capacity for perpetual transformation. That is why he is not to be recalled as any fixed image or particular identity. It is also why the reality of the hero's existence is ultimately to be perceived, not in visual terms, but as rushing sound (l. 26f).

There is, however, one particular hero who is named in the Sixth Elegy: Samson. Two points ought to be made straightaway about the grammatical context in which he makes his appearance. For one thing the desire to read about Samson is part of the yearning to return to childhood: the whole of the statement which follows the colon in line 28 expresses the content of the 'Sehnsucht', and the emotions evoked in that sentence are held at a distance by the persistent subjunctive forms in which they are expressed. (The effect of this cannot be exactly reproduced in English, but I have tried to reflect its implications in my translation.) Secondly, the experience of the hero as described in lines 20-27 is what would (subjunctive again) enable the speaker to escape from that yearning. To 'hear' the hero and to evoke his existential potency in poetry would, these lines appear to be saying, provide a safeguard against the kind of hero-worship that is presented here as a boyhood fantasy. But that said, the lines with which Rilke chose to continue the poem in 1922 are such as to emphasise the desperate nature of that fantasy:

War er nicht Held schon in dir, o Mutter, begann nicht
dort schon, in dir, seine herrische Auswahl?
Tausende brauten im Schooß und wollten **er** *sein,*
aber sieh: er ergriff und ließ aus —, wählte und konnte.

Und wenn er Säulen zerstieß, so wars, da er ausbrach
aus der Welt deines Leibs in die engere Welt, wo er weiter
wählte und konnte. O Mütter der Helden, o Ursprung
reißender Ströme! Ihr Schluchten, in die sich
hoch von dem Herzrand, klagend,
schon die Mädchen gestürzt, künftig die Opfer dem Sohn.

Denn hinstürmte der Held durch Aufenthalte der Liebe,
jeder hob ihn hinaus, jeder ihn meinende Herzschlag,
abgewendet schon, stand er am Ende der Lächeln, — anders.

Was he not a hero already inside you, mother? Did he not
begin his lordly selection there already in you?
Thousands seethed in the womb, wanting to be him,
but see: he took hold and let go, he chose, he could do it.
And if he sundered pillars, it was when he burst
from the world of your body into the narrower world, where again
he chose and could do it. Oh mothers of heroes, oh source
of raging torrents! You ravines into which
maidens have plunged, from the highest rim of the heart, lamenting,
henceforth in sacrifice to the son.

For the hero stormed forth through the abodes of love,
each one bore him up and away, each heartbeat that was meant for him,
till he stood, at the end of the smiles, turned away, — different.

The birth of the hero as it is evoked here is no longer the figurative one that enables him to live on in our memory of him, but the literal one that enables Rilke to speak of his heroism as an innate and preordained force. Samson — whose birth, incidentally, is one of those which the biblical account records as having been foretold by an angel (Judges 13) — is being presented as the incarnation of an absolute strength (l. 31) whom thousands of weaklings may envy (l. 34). His very birth is an eruptive act of the will, an exact parallel to the act of destruction for which he is commonly remembered, demolishing the house of the Philistines in which he was being paraded as a captive. The power that is exemplified in Samson is there from the outset and will not be denied. The hero is a 'raging torrent' that has its source in the womb; his inherent impetus is fed by the grief and lamentation that attends him on his way (l. 39f).

Here again, Rilke's image of the hero may be entirely compatible with what we find in the literature of antiquity, but it is here, too, that we may note the sense in which Rilke is writing in the spirit of his own time. Readers who suspect that there are echoes of Nietzsche in lines 32-41 are quite right, even if the echoes to be found here are vague and general. Rilke had shared in the keen fascination for Nietzsche's writings which was common among his generation in the 1890s. In 1896, at the age of twenty, he had written a short story called 'The Apostle', which draws on well-known motifs from *Thus Spake Zarathustra*, and more clearly still from *The Anti-Christ*, which had been published the previous year. At a banquet held for prominent members of central European high society, a mysterious stranger denounces their charitable projects as acts of Christian meekness and proclaims a doctrine of the strong individual whose 'divine power' and ruthless acts should be permitted to lead the human race on its path to a higher earthly destiny. Even that youthful mimicry of Nietzsche in prophetic mode is not entirely lacking in self-irony: the story ends with a banker mumbling, as he chews his lobster vol-au-vent, that the stranger must be 'only a fool or…' — and the cognoscenti of the time would have been able to complete the sentence with an allusion to Nietzsche's own words, '… only a poet'.[2]

Erich Heller, who has explored the relation between Rilke's poetry and Nietzsche's thought in a long and subtle essay[3], shows how delicately the *Duino Elegies* take up and re-work impulses which we might recognise as Nietzschean, and which Rilke had voiced more rapturously in various early writings. Heller investigates the historically illuminating affinities between Rilke and Nietzsche, their shared awareness of the spiritual hunger of the modern age, their sense of being 'commanded' to write — to write, moreover, in ways which aimed to overcome the dogmatic distinction between thought and feeling that was characteristic of their time — and their common purpose of transfiguring the world and its sufferings by finding the means to affirm them, to will them. He also reminds us that the 'will to power' as Nietzsche discusses it is an instrument of metaphysical inquiry rather than political assertion; and he speaks of Rilke, in so far as he may be placed among the disciples of Nietzsche, as 'the St. Francis of the will to power' (p. 131). But Heller omits all reference to the Sixth Elegy, and the omission is a telling one. For it is in the lines with which Rilke completed that Elegy in 1922 that we hear him speak, surely, in the language of a vulgarised 'will to power'. Whether we interpret Samson's 'selection' (l. 33) as an instance of his choosing, his exertion of authority over others ('herrisch'), or as an expression of his being chosen (by Fate), we are left with an image of him as the ruthlessly assertive male whom mothers are destined to bear and for whom maidens are destined to sacrifice themselves.

It is a brutish idol, then, that is conjured up in the closing section of the Sixth Elegy. Is there nothing to be said in mitigation of the impulse that the poem seems to be expressing?

There are a few things. Firstly there is the point we noted earlier, the fact that the image of Samson is introduced as a boyhood fantasy, as part of that yearning from which the speaker would gladly be screened by knowledge of the true significance of the hero's dynamic potential. In so far as the poem permits us to maintain an awareness of the strongly provisional force of those subjunctive verbs in lines 28-30 as we read on into lines 32-41, it might be said to acknowledge the regressive nature of the image of the storming hero that it is elaborating there. Secondly, a further grammatical observation might help us to keep a clear perspective on what we are reading. From line 32 onwards the poem is firmly couched in a narrative past tense: this *was* the mode of existence that characterised heroes of old, they *used to* storm through the abodes of love in this fashion (and this is how the boy Rilke might have read about them in his story books). Finally, to highlight that (albeit inobtrusive) distancing effect in the closing section of the poem is to remind ourselves that the hero has been evoked all along as a mode of being that contrasts distinctly with our own. His dynamism, his capacity for self-transformation, is an extreme existential possibility that is not available to 'us'; and in the final line the hero stands (stood) 'turned away', separated from us in his very difference.

In this perspective the Sixth Elegy might be said to join Elegies Two to Five as an expression of disappointment.[4] The hero, like the lovers and adorers he is said to transcend, embodies a mode of existence that the poet explores in order ultimately to discard it — because it represents an unattainable possibility, because it cannot truly bring the fulfilment that the Elegies are seeking to articulate. It was a necessary step in the elaboration of the task that had been set out in the First Elegy, but necessary, in the last analysis, as preparation for the gesture of renunciation and self-limitation which characterises the Seventh Elegy.

---

1 See *Materialien zu Rainer Maria Rilkes 'Duineser Elegien*, I, 14f., 213f.

---

2 The words 'Nur Narr! Nur Dichter!' occur in Part IV of *Also sprach Zarathustra*, in the section entitled 'Das Lied von der Schwermut'.

3 'Rilke and Nietzsche, with a discourse on thought, belief and poetry', in Erich Heller, *The Disinherited Mind* (London 1952), pp. 123-80.

4 Peter Krumme, whose excellent commentaries on the Elegies I was only able to read after I had completed my own account of the Sixth Elegy, similarly interprets the hero, along with the lovers of Elegy II and the acrobats of Elegy V, as an expression of the 'inadequacy of archetypal forms of existence': Peter Krumme, *'Eines Augenblickes Zeichnung'. Zur Temporalität des Bewußtseins in Rilkes Duineser Elegien* (Würzburg 1988), pp. 144-56.

ELEGY SEVEN

Peter Hutchinson

The Seventh Elegy was written in Muzot on 7th February 1922. Rilke revised the conclusion on the 26th of the same month, adding the final six lines. This is a totally different form of elegy — a breakthrough, in fact, in both its mood, which is more often exuberant than elegiac, and in its content, which is positive and constructive. In some respects it can be seen as an epiphany. It contains a profusion of themes, some of which echo and develop those which have preceded, but several of which are entirely new. It enunciates basic principles about life, fulfilment, and transcendence, and in its frequent digressive tangents, it aims to communicate Rilke's ideas on death, the modern age, and the cycle of history. More than in any other elegy, the negative is not accepted in a regretful manner: on the contrary, it is used as a form of self-encouragement and inspiration to positive ends. In this respect the poem may owe much to Hölderlin, under whose influence Rilke existed for long periods of his life, and who likewise saw his own generation as living in an age which followed a golden one. For Hölderlin the present darkness was temporary, however, and our vision of the past should therefore not be lost: the way to preserve it lay in poetry. In Elegy Seven Rilke may be seen as offering a form of response to his predecessor; certain lines here provide the golden beacon of the cycle.

This elegy stands out in other respects. It achieves, for the most part, a remarkably successful relationship between content, rhythm, and, equally importantly, sound. The latter two aspects enrich our experience of Rilke's untraditional use of imagery with its denseness, its provocative combinations of adjectives and nouns, its constant, unprecedented and extended metaphors, and its abrupt changes from concrete to figurative; the complexity of idea produced by such an approach is consolidated, in this elegy in particular, by constantly varying rhythms and intricate sound patterns. To achieve his effects Rilke is drawing on predecessors from well over a century before: most notably Hölderlin and Klopstock, with their subtle adaptation of classical metres, their effortlessly flexible use of the line, their constantly delayed subjects, objects, and verbs, and, particularly in the case of Klopstock, the highly suggestive, and sometimes aggressive, combination of consonant and vowel. As far as the language is concerned, we can in fact sense a delight in Rilke's usage in Elegy Seven, and this we would expect in what is actually the first of the cycle truly to endorse the uplifting aspects of human existence. For here, the poet continues the positive trend emerging in the sixth and can declaim triumphantly, almost at the mid-point, with alliteration and open vowels characteristic of this poem, 'Hiersein ist herrlich'. Human existence can be glorious, although darker aspects of our lives are not excluded from the poet's vision. Our aim must be to reconcile, to accept, and to praise what has been achieved by mankind, some of which merits the respect even of the Angel.

In what frame of mind do we approach a poem? In the case of one by an unknown author, our expectations are established by tradition, to which a poet can adhere, or which he can reject. In the case of Elegy Seven, our attitude, our mood, our expectations have been set above all by the preceding six pieces. Rilke will now adhere to certain patterns and concepts, but he will reject others, and it is for this reason that I feel the elegies as a whole, and in particular number seven, need to be seen as a cycle. If we approach this one only as an individual piece, we miss the referential dimension from which it draws much of its intellectual energy. Its images and ideas are dependent on, indeed, sometimes controlled by, what has preceded: and the better we know what has preceded, the more references we recognise: ideas, verbal echoes, linking images. A single word — angel, lover, fountain, night, the dead, or even a simple adjective of colour, grey — can trigger a sequence of interrelated concepts. More obviously, this elegy can only be bright because what has preceded has been dark.

We come to the first lines shaped by our previous reading, then, and we encounter, to use the words of Peter and Sheila Stern in their discussion of the First Elegy, a form of 'allusion and liberation'. The poet alludes to what has been a principal aim of the past, and immediately liberates himself from it. The 'Schrei' to which he here refers takes us back to the very first line of the whole cycle ('Wer, wenn ich schriee. . .'), but the immediate, and vigorous rejection of it proclaims this elegy will be different:

WERBUNG nicht mehr, nicht Werbung, entwachsene Stimme,
sei deines Schreies Natur;

WOOING no more, not wooing, oh voice which has outgrown it,
be the nature of your cry;

The poet's voice has now outgrown the need to woo, that is, to solicit another — we do not yet know whether lover or angel, and we do not know why the voice has outgrown this need — whether through constant failure in the past, or a new sense of maturity which makes wooing unnecessary. We should note, however, that the 'nicht' is not simpy repetition of 'nicht mehr': the emphasis here suggests that something else is to take its place. Again, we do not yet know what or why, and the explanation is in fact long delayed, for, in one of those extended digressions so typical of the elegies, the poet immediately begins to explain and to illustrate the exact nature of his former 'cry'.

zwar schrieest du rein wie der Vogel,
wenn ihn die Jahreszeit aufhebt, die steigende, beinah vergessend,
daß er ein kümmerndes Tier und nicht nur ein einzelnes Herz sei,
das sie ins Heitere wirft, in die innigen Himmel. Wie er, so
würbest du wohl, nicht minder —, daß, noch unsichtbar,
dich die Freundin erführ, die stille, in der eine Antwort
langsam erwacht und über dem Hören sich anwärmt, —
deinem erkühnten Gefühl die erglühte Gefühlin.

true, were you to cry as purely as the bird,
when that time of year uplifts him, that rising time, almost forgetting
that he's a creature of care and not just a solitary heart
which is thrown into azure, into innermost heavens. Like him
you too would probably woo, no less —, so that, still invisible,
your beloved friend would sense you, that quiet friend in whom a reply
slowly awakened, and, as it listened, grew warmer,—
the female form, flushed by your fortified feelings.

Quite apart from problems of meaning, the elegies regularly confront us with problems of grammar: is 'schrieest' a simple past, or the imperfect subjunctive? 'You cried', or 'if you were to cry'? (It is not until line 6 that the problem is resolved by a clear imperfect subjunctive.) Uncertainty is featured on several occasions in what is to follow, and it is part of the means by which Rilke confuses us as to which voice he is speaking in: the voice of the poet is merged with that of the bird, and such ambiguity is part of Rilke's occasionally *playful* approach. Now the word 'playful' may seem an unusual and possibly inappropriate adjective to apply to our poet, whose deep seriousness of purpose in never is doubt, and who thus far in the cycle has often seemed to border on despair; but a distinctly light-hearted element will indeed soon appear — in the description of the bird's trill.

The poet's wooing is depicted in dramatic terms, like the upward flight of a bird far into the sky. What strikes me most here, is the apparent helplessness of that bird, which, as several critics suggest, must be a lark, one of the earliest of spring's song-birds and the only one which sings, jubilantly, in flight. Rilke suggests this lark is not free, but *controlled by the season*, and the way in which it finds itself helpless as it is carried, indeed, *thrown* upwards, is reflected in the rhythm. Rilke here carries us too onwards far more than we would expect, causing us almost to lose our breath. We are driven over the end of the third line— as we would probably expect from a sentence which begins in the middle of a line — but we are propelled further on, first by parenthesis explaining the season, and then by an adverbial phrase which draws us into the following line. Rhythmically, we now expect a break (at the end of line 4); but we are forced, against our will, as it were, to complete the sentence, and our resultant breathlessness mirrors the sense of helplessness of the bird. Now this analogy suggests that the poet's wooing was involuntary. Like the bird in spring, like the readers of the poem, a higher force was in control. But this situation is to change. The poet now pledges to woo no more. *He* is taking control of his situation.

Another striking aspect of these lines, and again one overlooked by many critics, is that the sound is not actually that of a song, but of a *cry:* self-reference, of course, to the opening line of Elegy One, but here the poet goes out of his way to emphasize the nature of the act. The key vowel combination in these lines is that contained in the noun 'Schrei', that high-pitched 'ei', which occurs on no less than nine occasions in these three and a half lines. Rilke was well aware of the harshness of this combination, and uses it, with self-conscious excess, in one of the *Sonette an Orpheus.*[1] This slightly unsettling usage of vowels is, however, compensated for at the end of the section by the more soothing alliterative 'H' in three key nouns, 'Herz', 'Heitere', and 'Himmel'. Again, I would suggest this serves to reflect the poet's changing situation: the unpleasant high-pitch of the cry is balanced by the harmonious background against which it is heard. So this unexpected subordinate clause, which has forced our reading onwards, actually creates a more positive feeling — both in its sound, as well as in content, which suggest the beauty and depth of the heavens. Note that further ambiguity here in 'Himmel': in one of its senses, the traditional domain of the Angel.

Now, after this description of the bird, we return to the theme of wooing, or rather, of what the poet used to woo: not, perhaps to our surprise, the Angel, but a silent female friend, who would be slowly roused to an answer by the poet's cry. The personification of such abstracts as 'Antwort', 'Gefühl', and 'Gefühlin' is unfamiliar, and the vocabulary unorthodox: we find 'sich anwärmen' followed by a strange neologism, 'Gefühlin', a coinage which might well remind us of Klopstock's attempts to ensure that the language of poetry was clearly not that of prose![2] The suggestion here is of slow arousal, the connotations strongly sexual, and the sound, once again, a reflection of mood — here, that of controlled desire. These lines are quieter than the preceding. The poet is trying to intimate the intimacy, the sensuality of this communion. The length of the phrases is important: note the constant hesitation in 'daß — noch unsichtbar — dich die Freundin erführ — die stille —' there is a gradual straining forward here which is only now resolved in the flowing line and a half which follows, and then closed by the symmetrically balanced final parenthesis. The sound 'ü' is dominant: established first in the unusual 'erführ', it is echoed partly in the next line in 'über' and then flowers fourfold in the line 9. This particularly slow-moving succession of dactyls creates a sensation of reciprocated desire and longing held in check; it is quite different from the Third Elegy's urgent, passionate movement and phallocentric imagery. This line conveys balance and control. Not that impetuous and primarily sexual impulse on the part of one partner, but a sense of mutual satisfaction.

The slow, restrained movement of this sensuous line changes abruptly. The 'üh' is echoed in the 'Frühling'; a brief, confirmatory clause before the poet describes the stages through which the bird's song — and by analogy, his also — rises, leading to one of the many, long-delayed climaxes of the poem:

O und der Frühling begriffe —, da ist keine Stelle,
die nicht trüge den Ton der Verkündigung. Erst jenen kleinen
fragenden Auflaut, den, mit steigernder Stille,
weithin umschweigt ein reiner bejahender Tag.
Dann die Stufen hinan, Ruf-Stufen hinan, zum geträumten
Tempel der Zukunft—; dann den Triller, Fontäne,
die zu dem drängenden Strahl schon das Fallen zuvornimmt
im versprechlichen Spiel.... Und vor sich, den Sommer.

Nicht nur die Morgen alle des Sommers —, nicht nur
wie sie sich wandeln in Tag und strahlen vor Anfang.
Nicht nur die Tage, die zart sind um Blumen, und oben,
um die gestalteten Bäume, stark und gewaltig.
Nicht nur die Andacht dieser entfalteten Kräfte,
nicht nur die Wege, nicht nur die Wiesen im Abend,
nicht nur, nach spätem Gewitter, das atmende Klarsein,
nicht nur der nahende Schlaf und ein Ahnen, abends...
sondern die Nächte! Sondern die hohen, des Sommers,
Nächte, sondern die Sterne, die Sterne der Erde.
O einst tot sein und sie wissen unendlich,
alle die Sterne: denn wie, wie, wie sie vergessen!

Oh, and spring would understand —, there is no place
which would not carry the tone of annunciation. First that small
questioning note which, with rising stillness,
is surrounded by the silence of a pure, affirming day.
Then up the steps, those steps of notes towards that dreamt-of
temple of the future; then the trill, like a fountain
where the falling stream awaits the rising jet
in promising play.... And ahead of that day, the summer.
Not just the mornings of summer, each one —, not just
their changing to day, their gleam before sunrise.
Not just the days, so gentle to flowers below,
so mighty, so strong to the trees, fully formed, above.
Not just the worship and awe of those unfolded forces
not just the paths, not just the meadows at evening,
not just, after late evening storms, the pure breath of clearness,
not just approaching sleep and the longing of evening...
but also the nights! But also those limitless nights
of summer, but also the stars, those stars of our earth.
Oh to be finally dead and to know them forever,
all the stars; for how, how, how to forget them!

Spring, named as such for the first time, would reflect in every one of its aspects, the sense of proclamation, annunciation. 'Verkündigung' is a suggestive word: it points unambiguously towards 'Mariä Verkündigung', the visit by, of course, a *Christian* angel, to the Virgin Mary, announcing the birth of Jesus.[3] Its timing: the beginning of spring. The sense of joy in that news is now reflected in a jubilant outpouring of feelings. Yet, what, precisely, is the poet referring to here? The accusative case of 'jenen kleinen fragenden Auflaut' suggests apposition to 'den Ton der Verkündigung', but the broader idea is of the *sound* of bird and poet. (By this stage, though, the bird is diminishing in importance, and the poet increasing.) Not just sound is important, though: both sound *and* vision are crucial here, as, in synaesthetic manner, Rilke attempts to present that sound in visual terms: minimally in the sense of the day enclosing the very beginning of the song; boldly in the idea of rising steps to a climax; and then almost playfully, in the comparison of trill with fountain. The fountain has just featured in the preceding elegy, where it may well have sexually symbolic force; the adjective 'drängend' here could certainly be seen to have comparable connotations, as could, consequently, the succeeding 'Fallen'. At another level, we must admire the clear visualisation of the fountain by the poet, his grasp that we actually *anticipate* the fall of the jet as it rises. But the activity is playful, like the trill, probably the most obviously playful musical motif, which alternates so rapidly between two notes, rising and falling, constantly promising a resolution.

We have in this following long unit, stretching from line 18 to 29, a sense of *joie de vivre* hitherto unseen in the elegies; it is conveyed principally by the breathless enumeration, the parataxis, the increasing length of the sentences, the sense of delight in naming of elemental pleasures of existence. There is an exultation here in the simplest aspects of nature, and the language too is undemanding. Nor is there, for a change, any straining on our part to deduce sense, despite the lack of grammatical control: in the powerful surge in these twelve lines, we are not held back by any puzzling image, idea, or concept. Structurally, is this section in one sense Rilke's version of the poetic 'trill'? Like the rising and falling movement in the trill and the fountain, the movement here is equally 'versprechlich': it is not just the fact we have the repetition of 'nicht nur', on no less than eight times within eight lines, each one raising expectations, but each occurrence of that phrase also arouses in us an expectation of 'sondern auch'. The resolution, when it finally comes, is twofold: the nights and the stars, both traditional symbols of mystery, unknowability, but in the Elegies, of course, multivalent symbols, suggesting among other things, passion and permanence. The resolution to this section is marked out clearly in metrical terms too: we find a reduction in stresses in the penultimate line, and an extension in the final one. Another means, perhaps, of providing a resolution to the 'Triller'.

There may be another meaning attributable to 'night' here. Rilke is dealing with seasons and cycles. We have moved from spring to summer. We have also moved from the mornings, to the evenings, to the nights. And finally, we have moved from joy in life to joy in *death*. The section ends startlingly, with nothing less than a death wish. Paradoxically, only death will bring total knowledge of the ultimate. As in the Sixth Elegy, then, death is to be seen positively, as part of an organic development.

Once again, the next section begins with a contrastingly brief sentence, as the poet embarks on another explanatory, but far more jerky sequence:

Siehe, da rief ich die Liebende. Aber nicht ***sie*** *nur*
käme... Es kämen aus schwächlichen Gräbern
Mädchen und ständen... Denn, wie beschränk ich,
wie, den gerufenen Ruf? Die Versunkenen suchen
immer noch Erde. — Ihr Kinder, ein hiesig
einmal ergriffenes Ding gälte für viele.
Glaubt nicht, Schicksal sei mehr, als das Dichte der Kindheit;
wie überholtet ihr oft den Geliebten, atmend,
atmend nach seligem Lauf, auf nichts zu, ins Freie.

Look, I was calling the lover. But not only ***she*** *would*
come... Girls from frail graves would rise and would
stand there... For how, how could I restrict my call,
once made? Those who have sunk away still
seek our earth. — You children, one thing in this world, if truly grasped,
would stand for so many.
Do not believe that fate is more than the fullness of childhood;
how often you would run past your lover, breathless,
breathless in blissful pursuit of nothing but wide open spaces.

If the poet had attempted to call the person in love, his song would have been so effective that it would have reached far more than a single individual. The dead would have risen (and because he is a male, it is, of course, dead *girls* who would have responded), for they are still searching for something on earth. We now begin one of the central statements of this elegy, and move towards the poet's understanding of fulfilment. Rilke abruptly switches to why the dead girls should *not* return to earth, and he explains that fulfillment did actually occur, only it was not properly grasped by those involved. Somewhat patronisingly, he addresses the dead girls as 'Kinder', and claims that understanding a single thing on earth represents understanding many. The ambiguous 'Schicksal' and 'Dichte' have aroused considerable commentary, but to me their sense must be wholly determined by the need to explain why the dead need to return to earth: the dead seek fulfilment, their fate, destiny, full experience of life, but

Rilke is beginning his explanation, which will not be complete until l. 45, that the dead *did* experience fulfilment on earth. They are reminded that the hectic period of childhood is a packed, fulfilling experience. And now there is an example of a fulfilling moment, when the lover would, with a sudden burst of energy, pursuing nothing but the distance, run past the loved one. The breaking up of the sentence here conveys that very sense of panting which these lines denote.

This bliss in the simplest of things now brings forth the great proclamation of this elegy, and further illustration of periods of fulfilment:

*Hiersein ist herrlich. Ihr wußtet es, Mädchen, **ihr** auch,*
die ihr scheinbar entbehrtet, versankt —, ihr, in den ärgsten
Gassen der Städte, Schwärende, oder dem Abfall
Offene. Denn eine Stunde war jeder, vielleicht nicht
ganz eine Stunde, ein mit den Maßen der Zeit kaum
Meßliches zwischen zwei Weilen —, da sie ein Dasein
hatte. Alles. Die Adern voll Dasein.

To be here is glorious. You girls knew that, even those of you
who seemed wanting, who sank away —, those in the foulest
streets of the cities, festering, doomed to be cast out as rubbish.
For each of you had an hour, perhaps not quite
an hour, a point between periods,
barely perceptible —, when you truly existed.
When you had everything. Your veins full of life.

The boldness of Rilke's claim is almost as surprising as its unexpectedness. For the first time in the elegies we are given an unqualified approval of Life. 'This marks', suggests Kathleen Komar, 'the beginning of his recognition of his true poetic task — not transcendence and escape of this fleeting physical world, but transformation of the physical through consciousness'.[4] Yet Rilke's assertion is, I feel, considerably weakened by his choice of example. He turns not to the beauties of nature, which he has praised so lavishly in the second section of the poem, and which would seem an obvious means to make the point. He almost rebukingly reminds the girls who would rise from their graves that they too had their moment of such recognition. In an image strongly reminsicent of images in the *Aufzeichnungen des Malte Laurids Brigge*, even the most forsaken of all have had a moment of full existence. To make this point about the highest aspects of experience, Rilke selects imagery from the lowest: girls are seen as festering; ready to be thrown in with the rubbish. But, Rilke claims, they neverless reached a pinnacle at some point, even if its duration was remarkably brief.

For many readers, this claim may not carry conviction. Had Rilke been speaking for himself alone, had he praised existence as it had been experienced by *himself*, we could have maintained the poetic suspension of disbelief and continued the lofty train of thought. Yet with the 'Schwärende' and 'dem Abfall /Offene', the poet moves from the sublime to what borders on the naturalistic — even if the language is slightly precious, what is evoked is certainly not. The jump from the gloriousness of existence to the obvious miseries of existence is disconcerting. Further, by this stretching of his claim to include the whole of humanity, and by setting the briefest of experiences against whole lifetimes of misery, the poet may appear insensitive.

There are other difficulties to our wholehearted agreement with the poet's claim. By introducing a curious temporal span, by suggesting the moments of fulfilment may actually be briefer than an hour in the whole of a lifetime, Rilke is seemingly contradicting the spirit of permanence which he had initially suggested in 'Hiersein ist herrlich'. The continuing precious language here, with its delicate alliteration and assonance ('ein mit den Maßen der Zeit kaum/ Meßliches zwischen zwei Weilen'; and the rich 'da sie ein Dasein'), creates an even greater tension between the ugliness just described and the elevated language in which it is conveyed. Finally, there is another sense of contradiction here. If life on earth is so glorious, why has the poet so desperately wished for death in line 28? (Rilke's vision of life and death as a unity, of death as a transformation of life, will not become fully clear until Elegy Ten; the Elegies often give the impression that the poet is working out his conclusions as he actually writes, describing the gradual process of realisation.)

This experience of fulfilment is described only in terms of its intensity, but because it is so personal, Rilke sees a danger in our not recognising its value. We are tempted to treasure only the external or the material, what others can see or can covet:

Nur, wir vergessen so leicht, was der lachende Nachbar
uns nicht bestätigt oder beneidet. Sichtbar
wollen wirs heben, wo doch das sichtbarste Glück uns
erst zu erkennen sich giebt, wenn wir es innen verwandeln.

But we forget so easily what is not confirmed

or envied by our laughing neighbour. We must lift it
up, visibly, when yet the most visible joy reveals itself
only when we transform it, within.

Rilke here moves to a theme which will dominate much of the rest of the poem: he rejects the human obsession with outward appearance, with our satisfaction gained from the false or superficial laughter of others. The external world may be visible, but it is, paradoxically, insubstantial; the most valuable joys are internal. We have a clear echo of a biblical theme: the rich may actually be poor in spirit, while the poor can be fulfilled. True richness is to be achieved by transforming reality and thus transcending it. As the poet put it in the famous letter to his Polish translator Witold Hulćwicz, questioning his own use of the key verb here: 'Verwandelt? Ja, denn unsere Aufgabe ist es, diese vorläufige, hinfällige Erde uns so tief, so leidend und leidenschaftlich einzuprägen, daß ihr Wesen in uns "unsichtbar" wieder aufersteht. *Wir sind die Bienen des Unsichtbaren. Nous butinons éperdument le miel du visible, pour l'accumuler dans la grande ruche d'or de l'Invisible'* (*D*E, I, 320-1). ('Transformed? Indeed, for our task is to imprint upon our minds this temporary, frail earth so deeply, so painfully and passionately, that its essence may be resurrected "invisibly" within us. *We are the bees of the invisible. We desperately gather the honey of the visible, in order to hoard it in the great golden hive of the Invisible.*') The idea is developed further in the next section. The unspecified 'wir' must refer, at least in the first instance, to poets.

There follows another of those grand, authoritative proclamations of this elegy as Rilke praises the act of internalisation:

Nirgends, Geliebte, wird Welt sein, als innen. Unser
Leben geht hin mit Verwandlung. Und immer geringer
schwindet das Außen. Wo einmal ein dauerndes Haus war,
schlägt sich erdachtes Gebild vor, quer, zu Erdenklichem
völlig gehörig, als ständ es noch ganz im Gehirne.
Weite Speicher der Kraft schafft sich der Zeitgeist, gestaltlos
wie der spannende Drang, den er aus allem gewinnt.
Tempel kennt er nicht mehr.

Nowhere, beloved, can there be world but within us. Our life's
course proceeds in a process of change. Yet the outside
world is ever diminished. Where once was a house built to last,
a cerebral image now rises, obliquely, still part
of the mind, still quite in the brain.

Our age creates for itself vast garners of power,
soulless, like the force and the tension it draws from all things.
We can no longer recognise temples.

Although the poet has suggested the path to salvation, he seems more interested in dealing with the failings of the modern age. As in the previous section, a grand proclamation is undercut by the reflections which follow. Life, the poet claims, is to be experienced within us, ‘innen’; what he sees outside himself is depressing. We pass our lives in a process of ‘Verwandlung’, transformation, a concept which will not be explained fully until the end of this section. But the objects which we actually can ‘transform’ are decreasing in number. The paradox is well explained by Jacob Steiner, who suggests: ‘(*geringer* ist hier kein vermindemdes Adverb zum Verb, sondern meint: zu einem immer Geringeren schwindet das Außen.) In einer historischen Spätzeit muß schon das meiste der Welt anverwandelt sein, da sich nichts Neues der Verwandlung stellt oder das Neue ihr noch unzugänglich bleibt.’[5] The poet then explains precisely why the external world is diminishing, and the key word in the following lament is ‘erdachtes’. What is being constructed in the modern world is a product of the brain rather than, we must assume, the soul. The traditional landscape is changing. Houses, built with care and built to last, are being replaced by purely rationally designed structures, which give the impression of having emerged straight from the intellect.[6] The poet’s stress on the rational element is to be seen on three occasions within two lines: ‘erdachtes’; ‘Erdenklichem’; ‘Gehirne’. The spiritual dimension is absent. We are controlled instead by an anonymous force, ‘der Zeitgeist’, the spirit of our age, immensely powerful, and in some respects — to judge by its ability to create such great storehouses of power, and to draw quite so much out of everything — in some respects admirable. Yet at the same time our age is formless: everything is being robbed of its essential force, which is being turned into energy. It is presumably the utilitarian and exploitative element which Rilke seems to be so opposing here, in addition to the lack of reverence for tradition and the past. This latter aspect is now condensed in the simple, unambiguous, brief lament: we no longer know what a ‘temple’ is. Rilke has in mind here perhaps less an ancient, physical structure than a symbol of the divine and the beautiful, erected for the purpose of praising a higher being. We have lost, in his eyes, our capacity to recognise the need for such places of peace, prayer and contemplation. In a utilitarian era, they are luxuries. As he goes on:

Diese, des Herzens, Verschwendung
sparen wir heimlicher ein. Ja, wo noch eins übersteht,
ein einst gebetetes Ding, ein gedientes, geknietes —,
hält es sich, so wie es ist, schon ins Unsichtbare hin.
Viele gewahrens nicht mehr, doch ohne den Vorteil,
daß sie's nun ***innerlich*** *baun, mit Pfeilern und Statuen, größer!*

These, luxuries of the soul,
we save now more secretly than in the past. Nay, where one of
them still survives,
a thing that was worshipped, served, bowed down to —,
it reaches, just as it is, into the unseen world.
Many no longer perceive it, not taking advantage of
building it greater, with columns and statues, ***within****!*

Admiration for such things as temples is no longer common, hence the need for us to save them more secretly than before. We are in an age in which we are actually embarrassed by the pleasure to be drawn from such luxuries, precisely because they are those of the heart — the opposite of that 'brain' which so dominates us in the present world. Indeed, many are now so much controlled by cerebral processes, that to them such temples, even where they still exist, are virtually invisible. What could be done, of course, is to rebuild such a temple in our mind, creating it even grander than it originally was, with even more pillars and statues. So at the end of this section the poet returns to the point at which he began: the world is not without, but within.

A spatial break in the poem suggests a move to a different subject, but Rilke continues his reflection on the peculiar position of man in the present age. Our position is generalised, though, and seen in a grand historical context. We are by no means unique. We are simply caught in a period between cycles:

Jede dumpfe Umkehr der Welt hat solche Enterbte,
denen das Frühere nicht und noch nicht das Nächste gehört.
Denn auch das Nächste ist weit für die Menschen.

Each sluggish turn of our world has such disinherited minds,
to whom neither past nor yet future belongs.
For even what's coming is far for mankind.

The tone of the poem has changed again. We have gone through sections of praise, ecstasy, encouragement, lament, restrained admonition. There is now less emotion: we are reflective, philosophical. Here we have a statement of fact as much as an expression of regret; and in commensurate, abstract language; these three lines are, in addition, heavy and dull, almost verging on the prosaic through their accentuation of particular consonants and the frequency of monosyllables — a reflection, clearly, of the spirit of the times to which the poet refers. This period, Rilke suggests, is a historical turning point, an attitude shared by various other writers in the aftermath of the Great War. The moment is characterised as 'dumpf', suggesting a sense of dullness, indifference, sluggishness, and it is a period in which those who cannot relate to the past are totally deprived. These 'disinherited' are the ones who fail to see the temples of the past, cannot experience things inwardly, and who are dependent on the age yet to come for their salvation. But that is far off, and the poet turns in self-consolation to part of his poetic task: the existence of such disinherited should encourage those who can do so to preserve the past. The mood is reminiscent of Hölderlin's urgent question of *Brod und Wein*, where he too sees himself caught between two ages: 'wozu Dichter in dürftiger Zeit?' And Rilke's response is similar to that supplied by his forebear. The poet has a clear purpose in an age of darkness: it is to preserve knowledge of the past. He therefore moves on with confidence, encouraging himself, one feels, as much as others, with constantly enjambed lines reflecting a sense of vitality and providing a sharp contrast with the preceding:

__Uns__ soll
dies nicht verwirren; es stärke in uns die Bewahrung
der noch erkannten Gestalt. — Dies __stand__ einmal unter Menschen,
mitten im Schicksal stands, im vernichtenden, mitten
im Nichtwissen-Wohin stand es, wie seiend, und bog
Sterne zu sich aus gesicherten Himmeln.

This
must not confuse us; let it strengthen our memory
of forms which we still can perceive. This __stood__ once amongst us,
stood at the mercy of fate, the destroyer, stood in the midst of
not-knowing-where-next, as though it were living, and drew
the firm stars from their place in the heavens.

The fact that he lives in a period of change must be used as a form of encouragement — encouragement to '*uns*'. The pronoun, as we have seen, so crucial an element of the elegies, avoids the naming of those who are envisaged. But the encouragement can only be addressed to poets. The process is again reminiscent of Hölderlin's attempts to inspire himself by depicting the misery of his age. Just as Hyperion sings his amazingly negative 'Schicksalslied' when he is 'irre', and in order to '[sich] stärken', so too does Rilke urge that those like him avoid 'confusion' ('verwirren') and be 'strengthened' by the nature of their age — they must be inspired to preserve those aspects of the past which are still recognisable. Note how Rilke gives emphasis to the verb 'stand', not simply by italicisation, but by two-fold repetition. The idea is not that such things simply existed in the past; had Rilke wished to make that point, he would have emphasised 'einmal'. The emphasis on 'stand', the sense of power with which this simple verb is endowed, together with the rhythmic stress it carries, communicates a sense of grandeur: these physical structures possessed a quality which was lasting; they could endure the destructive power of destiny; they could survive the lack of purpose and direction in existence; they had a life of their own; and could even attract the stars from their apparently fixed positions. The stars, as we have already seen in line 29, are the greatest, most enduring manifestation of nature, and they here acquire prominence through carrying full rhythmic stress and being the first word in the line. We note, incidentally, that it is only rarely in the elegies that the first word of a line carries force, and the number of lines that actually begin with a noun is low: 15 out of 93 here, although this is actually — proportionately — the highest in the whole cycle. In verse as fluid as this, that is perhaps not surprising; but when the poet does choose to begin a line with a noun, it is usually a key one: 'Werbung', 'Tempel', 'Nächte', 'Mädchen', 'Hiersein', etc.

The poet is so convinced by the power of these past structures, he is so proud of them, that he can call on the Angel, that representative and judge of the absolute, for approval:

Engel,
***dir** noch zeig ich es, **da**! in deinem Anschaun*
steh es gerettet zuletzt, nun endlich aufrecht.
Säulen, Pylone, der Sphinx, das strebende Stemmen,
grau aus vergehender Stadt oder aus fremder, des Doms.

Angel,
let me show it to you, ***there!*** *in your gaze*
let it be finally saved, fully upright, at last.
Columns, pylons, the Sphinx, the striving upward thrust of the minster,
grey against background of fading, or foreign, town.

Even if these structures have no physical permanence on earth, the angel's gaze can nevertheless endow them with such, and the subjunctive 'steh' indicates the wish that they will indeed be finally valued. The wish that they can at last stand '*aufrecht*' in a way they deserve to be seen. Why is there such stress on this uprightness, and why is it that so many *vertical* structures, as supplied in the next line, are selected? Inevitably, certain critics have seen the phallic symbolism as important here, and it is indeed the case that the poet draws attention to nothing but the upward stretching in three of the four images which now follow. First of all pillars, or columns — presumably supporting something, but what they are supporting is obviously unimportant; second, pylons — not in the modern, but in the classical sense of the gateway to an Egyptian temple. Egypt features more obviously in the allusion to the Sphinx, that massive enigmatic stone figure, with body of lion and human head. In the Tenth Elegy the Sphinx is seen rather in its guardian role. Here attention is being drawn simply to its size. And finally, we have the 'striving' upward thrust of the 'Dom', most probably, given the adjective here, suggesting 'cathedral' and drawing attention to its tall spire. This stands out against its background, which is by contrast fading away or is strange to us. It is architecture, then, on which the poet concentrates here; structures significant for their sheer size, or which reveal striving towards the heavens, towards the stars, or towards the traditional domain of the Angel. The poet does not here show any interest in beauty; or intricacy; or music; or art; not even poetry. But in objects which tower above all around them, and mainly from a society which existed long ago. These objects have transcended time: that would seem to be their principal claim to the poet's attention. They arouse in him a sense of the miraculous:

War es nicht Wunder? O staune, Engel, denn ***wir*** *sinds,*
wir, o du Großer, erzähls, daß wir solches vermochten, mein Atem
reicht für die Rühmung nicht aus. So haben wir dennoch
nicht die Räume versäumt, diese gewährenden, diese
unseren *Räume. (Was müssen sie fürchterlich groß sein,*

da sie Jahrtausende nicht unseres Fühlns überfülln.)

Was that not marvellous? Oh gaze in wonder, Angel, for it was ***us****,*
oh Great Being, us, recount that we managed such things, my breath
cannot last for the praise which is due. So we have not, despite all,
neglected earth's spaces, those welcoming spaces, our very own
spaces. (How fearfully large they must be,
if not overflowing by thousands of years of our feelings.)

The poet's feelings are couched in shorter clauses, suggesting breathlessness and communicating almost a sense of disbelief. He has, after all, come a long way from the first two elegies. No longer is the Angel terrifying. He is called upon directly to express amazement at human achievement. The poet can therefore show his relief that mankind has not failed, and in a formulation again characteristic of the elegies, with their constantly unexpected metaphors, can proclaim that we have not wasted one of our gifts. Now we might expect the poet to suggest our *time* on earth had not been wasted, but he rather surprisingly suggests it is the *spaces* on earth which have not been neglected. Human achievement is actually seen in spatial terms. The bracketed after-thought is actually an important aspect of the poet's thinking, for it is here that he explains what has inspired these wonderful creations: our feelings. It is these which we have projected into creations which take up space, the space which we have been allotted on earth. Despite the sense of achievement, praise, and wonder, Rilke's final two words here may leave us uncomfortable ('Fühlns überfülln'). At points throughout the elegies there has been detailed, and rich echoing of sound — particularly in this one. Yet here the carefully constructed internal half-rhyme is created in what may appear a slightly artificial manner, while the elision of 'e' in both noun and verb — arresting to both eye and ear — reflects, perhaps, a sense of constriction and overflow.

The poet, however, can press on confidently, with further examples of human greatness, and now they are not simply architectural:

Aber ein Turm war groß, nicht wahr? O Engel, er war es, —
groß, auch noch neben dir? Chartres war groß —, und Musik
reichte noch weiter hinan und überstieg uns. Doch selbst nur
eine Liebende —, oh, allein am nächtlichen Fenster....
reichte sie dir nicht ans Knie —?

But a tower was great, was it not? Oh Angel, it was, —

great, even beside you? And Chartres was great —, and music
rose further still and even surpassed us. But simply
a girl in love —, oh, alone, at an evening window....
did she not reach as far as your knee?

Some commentators have found the reference to the tower suggestive of both physical and metaphysical: it may bring to mind, for example, 'die ins Unendliche hinaufschießenden Gipfelungen der Gotik',[7] or 'the timeless aspirations of man, his striving toward higher perspectives'[8]. I would have expected something more specific, some stage in a progression from the list of architectural features which have preceded; I find it functions as something of an anticlimax, reduced to a colloquial level by the prosaic 'nicht wahr?', and I feel a slight disappointment with the brief sequence which now follows, with its mixture of concrete and figurative, with what must be termed its hesitation and *half*-certainty over human achievements, and its rather rushed handling of Chartres, the whole of human achievement in music, a girl in love. It is particularly surprising that Chartres, a former source of poetic inspiration, receives no more than that simplest of adjectives which proliferates here, 'groß'[9]. I am also a little uneasy by Rilke's juxtaposing the girl in love and the angel in purely in physical terms. This seems to me to rob the Angel of the transcendental stature it has hitherto possessed. The image of the girl obviously suggests unfulfilled love ('allein'); it takes us back to the notion of love as an absolute suggested in the First Elegy with the reference to Gaspara Stampa.

Nevertheless, the poet's questioning is now replaced by firm statement, and we enter the final confident declaration. Perhaps to our surprise, the poet insists he has not been wooing, and thus takes us back to the opening line of the poem:

Glaub nicht, daß ich werbe,
Engel, und würb ich dich auch! Du kommst nicht. Denn mein
Anruf ist immer voll Hinweg; wider so starke
Strömung kannst du nicht schreiten. Wie ein gestreckter
Arm ist mein Rufen. Und seine zum Greifen
oben offene Hand bleibt vor dir
offen, wie Abwehr und Warnung,
Unfaßlicher, weitauf.

Do not believe I am wooing,
Angel, and even if I were! You do not come. For my
call is forever full of rejection; with such a strong current

you cannot make headway. Like an arm outstretched
is my call. And my hand, outheld,
ready for grasping, is open before
you, as if warding away and warning,
Ungraspable One, far above.

We would not be surprised that the Angel would not come, even if the poet were to woo. But we are certainly surprised by the reason given. Not for those we have encountered elsewhere in the elegies, in the presentation of the Angel: not because the Angel would not hear, or that he is too far removed, or too absolute to take notice. No, the Angel will not come because the poet *will not let him*, and so defiant is he, so great is his new-found power, that even the the Great One cannot succeed against it. Indeed, the poet's outstretched and upward-reaching hand is now warding off and warning the Angel. There is a final ambiguity here in the pun on 'Unfaßlicher': the Angel cannot be 'grasped', either literally or figuratively, and there is an equal ambiguity in the outstretched hand, which is warning away, but which is nevertheless 'open', as if it could still be grasped. The end may be seen to represent that unresolved conflict of ideas which drove Rilke to write the Elegies. The ambiguity expresses this conflict, but in a spirit of euphoria (perhaps hubris), at what he, the poet has achieved.

In the course of this elegy Rilke has moved from celebrating the beauties of the natural world to affirming the achievements of man in creating his own. It is aspects of the latter from which we can derive most satisfaction and self-justification, and which place us virtually on a par with the Angel. Indeed, in this elegy Rilke depicts man as capable of paralleling the achievements of that absolute being. As he put it in his letter to Huléwicz, who had asked for clarification on the nature of these Angels: 'Der Engel der *Elegien* ist dasjenige Geschöpf, in dem die Verwandlung des Sichtbaren in Unsichtbares, die wir leisten, schon vollzogen erscheint. Für den Engel der Elegien sind alle vergangenen Türme und Paläste existent, *weil* längst unsichtbar, und die noch bestehenden Türme und Brücken unseres Daseins *schon* unsichtbar, obwohl noch (für uns) körperhaft dauernd. Der Engel der Elegien ist dasjenige Wesen, das dafür einsteht, im Unsichtbaren einen höheren Rang der Realität zu erkennen.' (DE, I, 322) ('The Angel of the Elegies is that creature in which the transformation of the visible into what is invisible, an act which we have to undertake, already appears complete. For the Angel of the Elegies, all towers and palaces from the past exist, precisely because they have been invisible for so long, and those towers and bridges of our own age which still survive are *already* invisible, even though (for us) they physically endure. The Angel of the Elegies is that being which vouches for the recognition of a higher level of reality in that which is invisible.') Whether such a task can be realised by the reader remains questionable; but as he has triumphantly proclaimed, Rilke certainly saw it as the supreme goal, and, clearly, achievement of his own art — not least of the Seventh Elegy.

---

[1] II, 26. Discussed briefly by Jacob Steiner, *Rilkes Duineser Elegien,* p. 149.

[2] Steiner draws attention to Rilke's feminisation, elsewhere, of 'Jüngling[in]' and 'Liebling[in]' (p.151), to which might be added Hölderlin's 'Fremdlingin' in the opening stanza of 'Brod und Wein'. The effect, it seems to me, is comparable to that in Klopstock: a slight distancing of the reader from the poem.

[3] An earlier poem, 'Mariae Verkündigung', one of a cycle celebrating the life of Mary, was composed by Rilke at Duino early in January 1912, i.e. immediately before he began work on the elegies themselves. See SW, I, esp. pp. 669-70.

[4] Kathleen L. Komar, *Transcending Angels,* p. 129.

[5] Steiner, p. 163.

[6] Rilke gives fuller examples of what he deems the 'indifferent' modern approach in his letter to Hulėwicz. Here he declares his own age may be the last actually to experience such objects in an appropriate, *human* manner. See especially DE, I, 321.

[7] Suggested, alongside other possibilities, by Romano Guardini, *Rilkes Deutung des Daseins,* p. 286.

[8] Komar, p. 137.

[9] Rilke wrote a poem after a visit to Chartres. He was specifically inspired by, significantly, an angel bearing a sundial: 'L'ange du méridien. *Chartres*', contained in the *Neue Gedichte,* SW, I, 497.

ELEGY EIGHT

Terry Llewellyn

My situation, coming late in this sequence of readings, has certain advantages. One is that my colleagues have already done invaluable spade-work as regards uncovering the nature of the development of the work's recurrent motifs, so that I do not need to go into great detail concerning, for example, the intact world of the child or the limitations of lovers, both of which are briefly evoked in the Eighth Elegy. My main task in this respect is to examine Rilke's juxtaposition of human and animal existence. Another advantage is that you have already been introduced to, or reacquainted with, the throbbing dialectic within the individual elegies and the previous seven overall. It is essential to assimilate each individual elegy, retaining and recalling the resonances of the other elegies as one proceeds. Accordingly, the Eighth Elegy, the most pessimistic of the ten, must be evaluated within the total context of the sequence and not as an isolated poem. Viewed thus, the Eighth Elegy, grim as it is in its insistence on the limitations of our ability to respond authentically to the world around us, is not totally defeatist.

Before I move into the poem, I should like to say something, however, about the peculiar nature of the poetic language which the mature Rilke evolved in the context of European Modernism. The *Duineser Elegien* were published, after all, in the same year as T.S.Eliot's *The Waste Land* and James Joyce's *Ulysses*, in 1923, the *annus mirabilis* of European Modernism. From very early on in his career as a poet Rilke was intensely aware of the difficulty of the poet's 'raid on the inarticulate'[1]. This awareness increased constantly as he fashioned the various poetic styles of the collections of poetry which precede the *Duineser Elegien*. Under this pressure Rilke was driven, at times, to write some questionably overwrought lines of poetry, whereas, on the other hand, he was guilty in his more relaxed moments of writing some extremely slack, epigonal lines in the late nineteenth-century sentimental vein. But between these extreme lapses Rilke undeniably produced some of the most magnificently inventive poetry in

European literature as a whole. Given the vast amount of poetry he wrote, such lapses were inevitable. The reputation of most modern lyric poets rests largely on a very small *oeuvre*. Among major twentieth-century European poets, I can only think of Yeats who approaches Rilke as regards the creation of such an extensive corpus of high-quality poetry.

One particular poetic procedure which sets Rilke apart from his fellow modernist poets is his frequent use of the simile – a word-concordance of Rilke's work would have very large entry for the word 'wie'. Gottfried Benn, the arch-modernist poet, was extremely scornful toward poets who cultivated the simile. In a lecture he gave at the University of Marburg in 1951, entitled *Probleme der Lyrik*, he granted little room for the simile in modern poetry:

Wie, oder wie wenn, oder es ist, als ob, das sind Hilfskonstruktionen, meistens Leerlauf.

How, or how if, or it is as if, are makeshift constructions, mainly just empty words.

As a modernist Benn objects to the use of the simile because it distances:

Dies Wie ist immer ein Bruch in der Vision, es holt heran, es vergleicht, es ist keine primäre Setzung.[2]

This 'how' is always a break in the vision, it brings in, it compares, it is not something that was there in the first place.

It does not embody the object or concept itself as a metaphorical version does, but distances the reader from it. The successful metaphor is an illuminating poetic implosion; the simile has, as it were, a fuse, the 'wie', which necessarily means a time-lag before it takes effect. If a poet wants his words to have immediacy, he must avoid over-using the simile. Rilke could invent some extremely original and telling similes, but he did tend to cultivate this device to excess and in his quest for modernistic similes produced some muddled juxtapositions on occasion. That he was conscious of the possible shortcomings of the simile is evident in his *Neue Gedichte*, where he sometimes throws in his hand as a poet and appeals to previous painters in order to achieve the particular effect he desires. Thus in the sonnet 'Der Apfelgarten', he writes: 'Unter Bäumen wie von Dürer...' ('Under trees like Dürer's') and in 'Die Flamingos': 'In Spiegelbildern wie von Fragonard...' ('In mirror images like Fragonard's'). Here the reader's knowledge of Dürer and Fragonard must fill in what Rilke will not attempt to do with words. The truly inventive modernist poet, Trakl or Benn for example, does not do this, but eschews such adventitious aids. Trakl 'painted' his own poems and never invoked the names of Franz Marc and Egon Schiele who, had they lived longer, would have been his ideal illustrators.

Another factor to be taken into account when evaluating the extent of Rilke's achievement as regards poetic linguistic invention in the *Duineser Elegien* is his use of discursive poetic thought. This is what sets the Elegies somewhat apart from the *Neue Gedichte* and the *Sonette an Orpheus* which flank it. Hans Egon Holthusen, writing of the poetic language of the mature Rilke, claims:

In Rilke's poems there is no contrast between image and plain statement, but all has become imagery.

And he goes on to quote Rilke's friend, Rudolf Kassner, as follows:

With Keats or D. G. Rossetti metaphors are like red-letter days in the calendar; but in Rilke all is as it were printed in red, and there is no difference between 'words' and 'images'.[3]

This is certainly true of the *Neue Gedichte* and the *Sonette an Orpheus*, but does it hold for the *Duineser Elegien*? Not overall, I fear, for here Rilke faces the problem of the poet who wishes to break free from the confining density of imagist poetry in order to speak discursively and present a sustained pattern of ideas. T.S. Eliot faced this problem when he came to write his *Four Quartets,* and his difficulty was recognized by George Orwell when he reviewed three of them, 'Burnt Norton', 'East Coker' and 'The Dry Salvages'. Overall Orwell felt the *Four Quartets* to be decidedly less original and striking than *The Waste Land* and Eliot's earlier poetry in general, Eliot's submission to Anglo-Catholicism having deflected him in the direction of discursive religious poetry to the detriment of his poetic invention. Orwell rather caustically quotes the lines:

> *The rest*
> *Is prayer, observance, discipline, thought and action.*

And he adds:

Perhaps what we need is prayer, observance etc., but you do not make a line of poetry by stringing those words together.[4]

Now the situation is not that extreme with Rilke, but there is from time to time in the *Duineser Elegien* an unavoidable reining in on brilliant, innovatory poetic language to something more muted and less impressive. The conclusion of the Eighth Elegy is a case in point.

Rilke's move towards discursive poetry was dictated by his assumption of the role of poet-priest in his late period, a role with its inherent difficulties. We know that the *Duineser Elegien* were partly engendered by Rilke's reading of the 'Hymnen' of Klopstock and Hölderlin and it was not for nothing that the princess Marie von Turn und Taxis-Hohenlohe addressed Rilke at that time as 'Dottore Serafico'. From the late seventeenth century onwards German literature has produced more poet-priests than any other European literature — Kuhlmann, Klopstock, Novalis, Hölderlin, and in our own century Stefan George and Rilke. They differ from closely related 'religious' poets like Mallarmé or Dylan Thomas in that they created a very extensive, private religious mythology and with it they legislated for mankind in general. Apart from Blake and possibly Yeats, our literature is largely without such poets. The German poet-priests I have listed are, of course, poets of very different sensibilities and wrote in different situations, but they do share certain problems which are inextricable from their role as poet-priest. Addressing mankind and legislating for it, they inevitably tended towards the generic in their poetic pronouncements; they write of 'die Blumen', 'die Pflanzen', 'die Tiere' and often evoke landscape in an ideal, non-specific manner. This can lead to an aura of vagueness and diffusiveness in their poetry. Rilke in his *Neue Gedichte* had visualised certain animals, artistic artefacts and places and brilliantly reproduced them in their specificness and uniqueness. His task in the *Duineser Elegien* meant that he was forced away from such an approach towards the generic, with its attendant disadvantages which he was not always able to avoid. On occasion Rilke was, however, able to turn this generic approach to great poetic advantage as is the case in the very first line of the Eighth Elegy:

MIT allen Augen sieht die Kreatur
das Offene.

With all its eyes the creature-world sees
the open.

This short statement has a tremendous density: the totality of the creature-world beholds with all its eyes the totality of what is before it. This is an unleashing of the generic approach that is quite overpowering — a host of creatures with countless eyes apprehending the open universe. This is much more effective than if Rilke had written:

MIT ***beiden*** *Augen sieht das Tier*
das Offene.

With ***both*** *its eyes the creature-world sees*
the open.

Only after this powerful introduction does Rilke reduce the super-generic 'Kreatur' to the less generic 'Tier' in the fifth line. 'Kreatur' has an all-inclusiveness which neither 'Tier' nor its plural 'Tiere' possess.

'Das Offene' is the by now familiar Rilkean concept of the universe as a timeless continuity of life and death. Rilke wrote of it in his famous letter to Witold von Huléwicz of the thirteenth of November, 1925: 'In that mighty *open* realm all people *are* — one cannot say "simultaneously" for it is precisely the disappearance of time which determines that they *are.*'[5]

Note too, that Rilke writes '...sieht die Kreatur das Offene' and not 'ins Offene' which would separate and displace 'die Kreatur' from it somewhat. Now the Ninth Elegy will go on to show that humans can inhabit and assimilate 'das Offene' when they adopt the existential attitude for which Rilke is pleading, but the Eighth Elegy has first to clear the ground for such a possibility and the negative criticism of our limitations is swiftly embarked upon. The celebratory note of the first line is quickly dispelled when human beings are placed against 'das Offene':

Nur unsre Augen sind
wie umgekehrt und ganz um sie gestellt
als Fallen, rings um ihren freien Ausgang.

But our eyes are

as though reversed and set around it
like snares, all around its path to freedom.

Our eyes are reversed, for we are self-regarding and do not assimilate 'das Offene'. This notion of reversal comes to dominate the Eighth Elegy. Line seven presents the forced reversal of the child by adults away from 'das Offene' and in the final section of the poem we are described as being 'umgedreht' and always looking backwards.

Rilke's critique of our sensory perception is even more severe. Not only are our eyes 'umgekehrt', but they are also traps set out around the path of the 'Kreatur' to freedom, 'rings um ihren freien Ausgang'. They limit, encircle and present possible hazards for the creature-world in general. But we can have an inkling of 'das Offene' from animals, as lines five and six state:

Was draußen ist, wir wissens aus des Tiers
Antlitz allein;

What is outside, we know from the animal's
countenance alone.

The emphasized '*ist*' stresses the authentic being of 'das Offene', a procedure frequently used by the mature Rilke when he came up against the boundaries of language. Notice how he ennobles the animal by using the word, 'Antlitz', instead of the more mundane 'Gesicht', countenance as opposed to face. This ennobling of the animal takes us back beyond the first line of the poem to its dedicatee, Rudolf Kassner, to whom Rilke had been introduced in the spring of 1910 by the Princess Marie von Thurn und Taxis-Hohenlohe. Only two of the ten elegies have individual dedications — the Fifth and the Eighth — and these dedications are of especial significance. That of the Eighth Elegy is important with regard to the seemingly atavistic and regressive elements present in Rilke's focus on the animal-world and its superiority in some respects over human beings. Rilke had many conversations with Kassner and the latter later published two essays on Rilke, in 1926 and 1935 respectively, in which he refers to the Eighth Elegy and views it as being explicitly directed against his own ideas about human salvation. These are of a very idiosyncratic, mystical slant and deal with the development of the self in a Christ-dominated, temporal world. Kassner saw Rilke's celebration of the animal as atavistic, but I am of the opinion, however, that a close scrutiny of the poem will show that this is not quite so.

The Eighth Elegy laments our alienation from 'das Offene' as a result of the limitations of our minds and the ensuing intellectual constructions we have imposed on the world around us. This is a long-standing lament. It has its philosophical origins in the simile of the cave in *The Republic* of Plato. It obsessed Kant and depressed Kleist in whose essay, *Über das Marionettentheater*, an animal, a bear, is praised for its lack of self-consciousness which results in authentic being, namely, 'Grazie'. This is very close to Rilke's approach to the animal world, and so is Kleist's view of the puppet to that of Rilke's in the Fourth Elegy. It is noteworthy here that in December 1913 Rilke read his way through the whole of Kleist's work. This positive presentation of the animal dominates the first half of the Eighth Elegy and it becomes clear that Rilke, despite ennobling the animal, seemingly at the human being's expense, is somewhat removed from the atavism of which Kassner accused him and in which some of his illustrious contemporaries sometimes indulged. For example, Eliot's 'The Love Song of J. Alfred Prufrock' contains the lines:

I should have been a pair of ragged claws
Scuttling across the floor of silent seas.

Or the opening of Gottfried Benn's *Gesänge*:

O daß wir unsere Ururahnen wären,
Ein Klümpchen Schleim in einem warmen Moor.[6]

O that we were our primeval ancestors,
A little lump of slime in a warm bog.

This is real atavism, seeking oblivion in the earliest form of evolution, the furthest possible escape from the course of the intellect. Rilke is proposing, on the other hand, something positive, namely, a true awareness of 'das Offene' which could lead to its proper assimilation on the part of human beings and give them a firmer existential footing. This is only implied in the Eighth Elegy, but the Ninth and Tenth Elegies develop the implication. The animal's awareness of 'das Offene' is, then, a model for us and it is a model that can be surpassed. But there are difficulties to be surmounted first. These begin in childhood, as lines six to ten tell us:

denn schon das frühe Kind
wenden wir um und zwingens, daß es rückwärts
Gestaltung sehe, nicht das Offene, das
im Tiergesicht so tief ist. Frei von Tod.
***Ihn** sehen wir allein;*

For we already turn the small child
around and compel it to look backwards
and see formed nature, not the open that
is so deep in the animal's face. Free from death;
*we only see **that;***

The child was able to participate in 'das Offene', but is quickly and forcefully alienated from it by the rude intervention of adults. The word 'rückwärts' matches up to the eyes that are 'umgekehrt' in line three. The animal, on the other hand, knows nothing of its ultimate death. In the Fourth Elegy Rilke had written in this vein of lions unaware of their ultimate 'Ohnmacht', and lines ten to thirteen develop this idea of the animals being 'frei von Tod':

das freie Tier
hat seinen Untergang stets hinter sich
und vor sich Gott, und wenn es geht, so gehts
in Ewigkeit, so wie die Brunnen gehen.

the free animal
has its decline always behind itself
and before it God, and when it moves, it moves
in eternity, just as springs flow.

'Gott' here is just another word for 'das Offene', as is 'Ewigkeit' in line thirteen and 'den reinen Raum', 'Nirgends ohne Nicht' and 'das Reine, Unüberwachte' in the following lines. The previously quoted section contains the first flush of poetry in what until now has been a somewhat austere series of statements. Rhythmically it makes a subtle effect, in particular 'so wíe die Brúnnen géhen' which conveys the lithe gait of a quadruped, and very effective, too, is the bold triple use of the simple verb 'gehen' to evoke the continuity of the eternal progress of the animal. But when the simile is visualized there is a clash of images: springs flow, animals walk. The movement is essentialy a different one. Taken as a whole it is also a tired simile. Already Eichendorff had written many lines like: 'Hörst du nicht die

Quellen gehen...' and it was to become a familiar motif in late nineteenth-century Austrian *Heimatdichtung*. Rilke has lapsed somewhat here.

The critique of our limitations continues:

***Wir** haben nie, nicht einen einzigen Tag,*
den reinen Raum vor uns, in den die Blumen
unendlich aufgehn. Immer ist es Welt
und niemals Nirgends ohne Nicht: das Reine,
Unüberwachte, das man atmet und
*unendlich **weiß** und nicht begehrt.*

***We** have never, not for a single day,*
pure space before us, into which the flowers
open up infinitely. It is always world
and never the nowhere without no: the pure,
the unguarded realm which one breathes and
*infinitely **knows** and does not desire.*

This laments our inability to assimilate the world as an infinite, ongoing process into which (note the accusative case here, emphasizing growth and reciprocal relationships between the flowers and 'das Offene'), 'die Blumen unendlich aufgehen'. We merely see the phenomenon, 'Welt' which is cognate with 'Gestaltung' in line eight. The opposite of these two is the noumenon, 'Nirgends ohne Nicht', a desperate, paradoxical negation for something that is basically unsayable. Mystics have always used such desperate negations and paradoxical term when talking about the Godhead. Böhme coined the word 'Ungrund' for the very source of the divine, but Rilke is using his own double negation for the world *he* inhabits. And '[das] Unüberwachte' is surely Rilke's rejection of a transcendental deity.

Then Rilke begins to explore the possibilities of a breakthrough to 'das Offene' by considering the situations of the child, the dying man and the lovers. Of these I think the situation of the child is the most important for him. There are those lovely tender lines about the intact world of the child towards the end of the Fourth Elegy, and he had already broached the theme in the sixth line of this Eighth Elegy. The epiphany of 'das Offene' can be assimilated in childhood, before adult demands break the spell:

Als Kind
verliert sich eins im Stilln an dies und wird
*gerüttelt. Oder jener stirbt und **ists**.*

As a child
one loses oneself in silence to this and is
jolted out of it. Or someone dies and ***is*** *it.*

The moment and place is that of the Fourth Elegy:

im Zwischenraume zwischen Welt und Spielzeug,
an einer Stelle, die seit Anbeginn
gegründet war für einen reinen Vorgang.

in the borderland between world and toy,
in a spot that had been ordained
from the very first for an innocent event.

The child is not allowed to remain in this state of eternity for it must invariably grow up and be swallowed up by the temporal world, a process which adults with their over-zealous sense of instruction will hasten. Here he was undoubtedly influenced by Hölderlin whose view of childhood was very close to Rilke's own. It is presented in the third letter of his novel *Hyperion*:

Ja! ein göttlich Wesen ist das Kind, solang es nicht in die Chamäleonsfarbe der Menschen getaucht ist.

Es ist ganz, was es ist, und darum ist es so schön.

Der Zwang des Gesetzes und des Schicksals betastet es nicht; im Kind ist Freiheit allein.

In ihm ist Frieden; es ist noch mit sich selber nicht zerfallen. Reichtum ist in ihm; es kennt sein Herz, die Dürftigkeit des Lebens nicht. Es ist unsterblich, denn es weiß vom Tode nichts.

Aber das können die Menschen nicht leiden. Das Göttliche muß werden, wie ihrer einer, muß erfahren, daß sie auch da sind, und eh' es die Natur aus seinem Paradiese treibt, so schmeicheln und schleppen die Menschen es heraus, auf das Feld des Fluchs, daß es, wie sie, im Schweiße des Angsichtes sich abarbeite.

Yes! A child is a divine being as long as it is not dipped in the chameleon colouring of human beings.

It is entirely what it is, and therefore it is so beautiful.

The compulsion of the law and fate does not touch it; only in the child is there freedom.

In it is peace; it has not lost its sense of harmony with itself. It has riches; it knows its heart and not the inadequacy of life. It is immortal, for it knows nothing of death.

But people cannot tolerate that. What is divine must become like them, must learn that they are also there, and before nature expels it from its paradise, so people cajole it and drag it out into the accursed world, so that it, like them, must labour away in the sweat of its brow.

Both Hölderlin and Rilke knew how important it was for them as lyric poets to re-kindle the child's sense of wonder at the world. Mallarmé, too, wrote regretfully: 'L'enfant abdique son extase'. But both Rilke and Hölderlin were realistic enough to accept that the child must necessarily move out of that world of wonder in a natural and unavoidable process, from the pleasure-principle to the reality-principle, as Freud put it. What they both knew, however, in addition was that the aware lyric poet can retain or regain some of that sense of wonder and put it to good use in his poetry, something that the child can rarely do and of which the animal is totally incapable.

The dying man has brief glimpses of 'das Offene' and then becomes part of it on his death. The situation of the lovers is familiar to us from the Third Elegy: they block each other's view of 'das Offene' which they briefly glimpse almost inadvertently, before they are soon confronted by 'Welt'.

Then we are given in lines twenty-nine to thirty-one a pithy formulation of our plight:

Denn nah am Tod sieht man den Tod nicht mehr
Und starrt ***hinaus,*** *vielleicht mit großem Tierblick.*
Liebende, wäre nicht der andere, der
die Sicht verstellt, sind nah daran und staunen...
Wie aus Versehn ist ihnen aufgetan
hinter dem andern... Aber über ihn
kommt keiner fort, und wieder wird ihm Welt.
Der Schöpfung immer zugewendet, sehn
wir nur auf ihr die Spiegelung des Frein,
von uns verdunkelt.

For near to death one no longer sees death
and stares ***out,*** *perhaps with the creature's wide eye.*
Lovers, were not the other there,
blocking out the light, are close to this and marvel...
As if in error they have opened to them
what is behind the other... But no-one can
elude him, and the world crowds in again.
Constantly turned towards creation,
we see on it only a mirroring of what is free,
obscured by us.

This is very close to the imagery used in Plato's simile of the cave. Ordinary mortals are like prisoners chained up in a cave and thus they only see the shadows or reflections of objects outside on the inner wall of the cave. They never see the noumenon itself. Equally Rilke sees us as perceiving only a mirroring of what really is, 'des Frein' on the surface of 'die Schöpfung', 'Welt' or 'Gestaltung', as he variously calls it.

Plato did not believe, however, that all human beings are necessarily confined forever in this state of ignorance regarding the true nature of things. The philosopher can ascend from illusion to pure knowledge, and when he has achieved this, he is required to return to the cave in order to enlighten his fellow mortals.[7] Likewise Rilke in his nature phase conceived his task as a poet along similar lines. It was to rescue and recreate reality in his poetry for those who wished to regain contact with authentic living. This is not made explicit in the Eighth Elegy, but it is implicit in a very subtle way. Were this not so, Rilke could never have gone on to write the Ninth and Tenth Elegies and the *Sonette an Orpheus*. Here it is important to stress the complex interplay between 'wir' and 'ich' in the *Duineser Elegien* as a whole. Rilke's 'ich' does not function openly once in the Eighth Elegy, but it is at times perceptible behind the lamenting 'wir' that dominates the poem. A breakthrough is tacitly envisaged, despite the fact that Rilke is including himself in the 'wir' of limited possibilities most of the time, but the breakthrough was to come only after the Eighth Elegy had been completed. For the moment our inadequacies still have to be recounted, and lines thirty-one and thirty-two once more confront insecure mortals with the secure animal:

Oder daß ein Tier,
ein stummes, aufschaut, ruhig durch uns durch.

Or that an animal,
a mute creature, looks up calmly right through us.

Such is our existential insubstantiality that the animal looks right through us. It does not even *question* our existence any longer as was the case with 'die findigen Tiere' in the First Elegy. Rilke's judgment has become that severe by 1922. Note, however, that the animal is 'stumm', whereas we speak and those privileged enough can turn the world into poetry by means of language, as Rilke did. In 1906 Paula Modersohn-Becker started an oil painting of Rilke's head and shoulders that remained unfinished. The most remarkable thing about it is her portrayal of Rilke's mouth which becomes the focal point of the portrait, stressing Rilke's poetic articulateness. And Rudolf Kassner was to make much the same point when he wrote: 'Rilkes Gesicht hörte im Mund auf, mündete im Mund, war hier Mündung.' ('Rilke's face stopped at the mouth, converged on the mouth, was in effect mouth')[8]. It is this creative articulateness which gives us, for Rilke, ontological preeminence over the animals, despite our insecurity.

Even so our situation is always one of being blocked off by an opposite:

Dieses heißt Schicksal: gegenüber sein
und nichts als das und immer gegenüber.

This is fate: being opposite
and nothing but that and always being opposite.

Again Hölderlin springs to mind. For him the gods and children were 'schicksallos', as opposed to adult mortals who were bound up by it. As he puts in the famous 'Schicksalslied' which Hyperion sings towards the end of the novel which bears his name:

Schicksallos, wie der schlafende
Säugling, atmen die Himmlischen.

Free from fate, like the slumbering
infant, breathe the heavenly beings.

The remainder of the poem deals with the dark lot of mortals and it has been viewed as being darkly pessimistic and uncompromising, but it is only so if it is read in isolation. Read in its context, the novel, *Hyperion*, this is not quite so, for Hyperion sings it there to strengthen himself, as he tells us. He accepts suffering because it gives his life an intensity it would otherwise not have. Fate and suffering elicit the highest achievements from mortals, as Hyperion's eighth letter had triumphantly declaimed:

Des Herzens Woge schäumte nicht so schön empor und würde Geist, wenn nicht der alte stumme Fels, das Schicksal, ihr entgegenstände.

The heart's wave would not foam up so beautifully and become spirit, if that old mute rock, fate, did not oppose it.

If this attitude is not adopted, there can only be regression, a retreat back into the womb, a defeatist withdrawal from life. Hölderlin, quoting from Sophocles, placed this gloomy alternative at the head of the second part of *Hyperion*: 'Not to have been born is by far the best; but if you live, the next best is quickly to return whence you came.' (*Oedipus at Colonus*, ll. 1224-7)

There are exact correspondences with Rilke here. The Eighth Elegy, like the 'Schicksalslied', must not be read in isolation; it fulfils much the same function in the elegies as a whole as Hölderlin's poem does in his novel. And, strikingly, they both present the same antithetical possible stance towards 'Schicksal', heroic affirmation and acceptance of it or a regressive retreat away from it. In the Eighth Elegy, Rilke moves towards the former attitude in the course of his scrutiny of human and animal existence; the human being at his most evolved can make sense of 'Schicksal', which is after all, as Rilke honestly admits, something which *always* confronts him. This begins to emerge in the following lines:

Wäre Bewußtsein unsrer Art in dem
sicheren Tier, das uns entgegenzieht
in anderer Richtung —, riß es uns herum
mit seinem Wandel. Doch sein Sein ist ihm
unendlich, ungefaßt, und ohne Blick
auf seinen Zustand, rein, so wie sein Ausblick.
Und wo wir Zukunft sehn, dort sieht es Alles
und sich in Allem und geheilt für immer.

If there were consciousness, such as we have,
in the secure animal that moves towards us
in another direction —, it would drag around us
with it in its progress. But its being is
Unending, not fixed, and without a look
on its state, pure, like its look forward.
And where we see future, it sees there all things
And itself in all things and healed forever.

Here is hypothetically stated that, if the secure animal possessed our consciousness, it would pull us around and drag us with it in the right existential direction. Seen thus, the animal would be a super-being, but it is only a hypothesis, for the animal, secure as it is, is limited in a way by this security without consciousness, whereas we, hampered as we are by our consciousness, nevertheless possess this faculty which properly used can alleviate our stark confrontation with 'Schicksal'. This is another advantage we have over the animals, just as our articulateness is.

Gradually in the course of this elegy Rilke is showing that the world of the animal is not so intact after all. To his lament for man he adds qualified lament for animals, particularly for those animals who are more evolved, for they, Rilke claims, possess memory and can recall the earlier, better security of the time when they were in the womb, as lines forty-three to fifty-one have it.

Und doch ist in dem wachsam warmen Tier
Gewicht und Sorge einer großen Schwermut.
Denn ihm auch haftet immer an, was uns
oft überwältigt, — die Erinnerung,
als sei schon einmal das, wonach man drängt,
näher gewesen, treuer und sein Anschluß
unendlich zärtlich. Hier ist alles Abstand,
und dort wars Atem. Nach der ersten Heimat
ist ihm die zweite zwitterig und windig.

And yet there is in the warm, alert animal
the heaviness and care of a great sorrow.
For something always clings to it, which
often overwhelms us —, memory,
as though what we urge towards was
once nearer, truer and its connection
with us infinitely tender. Here it is all separation
and there it was breath. After the first home
the second seems not one thing or the other and doubtful.

The 'doch' in line forty-three is the turning-point of the poem, a hinge at its centre, joining praise for the animal to lament for it. Those animals who have memory are not all that secure as a result of being expelled from the womb. Only small creatures like gnats have womb-like security in the world because they have known no other womb. They do not experience 'Abstand', a sense of separation from an original state of oneness, as lines fifty-two to fifty-five convey:

O Seligkeit der kleinen Kreatur,
*die immer **bleibt** im Schooße, der sie austrug;*
*o Glück der Mücke, die noch **innen** hüpft,*
selbst wenn sie Hochzeit hat; denn Schooß ist alles.

*O bliss of the **tiny** creature*
*that always **remains** inside the womb that brought it forth.*

O happiness of the gnat that still leaps ***within***
even when it procreates; for womb is all.

The phrase 'noch *innen* hüpft' means that they are moving up and down *within* the womb which 'das Offene' composes for them. The continuation 'selbst wenn sie Hochzeit hat' echoes the German folk-song, 'Die Vögel wollten Hochzeit machen', being a euphemism for the act of procreation. Even in the act of procreation the gnat is still secure within a womb. This is the utmost security, total 'Geborgenheit' ('denn Schooß ist alles') as opposed to 'Ausgesetztsein' or, to use Rilke's word, 'Abstand'. Rilke's powers of visual perception cannot be faulted here: a gnat does move up and down ('hüpft') very quickly in a small space in the air.

This notion of the protecting womb is now further developed with regard to birds:

Und sieh die halbe Sicherheit des Vogels,
der beinah beides weiß aus seinem Ursprung,
als wär er eine Seele der Etrusker,
aus einem Toten, den ein Raum empfing,
doch mit der ruhenden Figur als Deckel.

And look at the half security of the bird,
almost aware of both from its origin,
as though it were the soul of an Etruscan,
of a dead man, enclosed within a space
yet with the figure in repose as a lid.

The bird first comes into the world enclosed in an egg delivered from its mother's womb, and then it is hatched in a warm nest covered by its mother which forms a kind of second womb not quite as reassuring as the original one.[9] This is why the bird has only 'halbe Sicherheit'. Rilke's processes of thought are complex here as he draws on the symbolic aspects of an Etruscan tomb to exlain the situation of the bird. The Etruscans placed the dead body of a person in a sarcophagus and a sculpture of that person on the lid, so that it was within a space, 'ein Raum' and also representedd as a resting figure 'als Deckel'. The bird is at first in a space within its mother and then outside as an expelled egg. On the wall of the tomb the departed soul was often depicted as a bird taking off in flight.

We come now to one of the most extreme cases of insecurity in the world of the 'Kreatur', namely, the bat, a mammal which is expelled from the womb without the protection of an egg around it and then has to fly exposed through the air:

Und wie bestürzt ist eins, das fliegen muß
und stammt aus einem Schooß. Wie vor sich selbst
erschreckt, durchzuckts die Luft, wie wenn ein Sprung
durch eine Tasse geht. So reißt die Spur
der Fledermaus durchs Porzellan des Abends.

And how dismayed is the womb-born thing
that has to fly. As though afraid of itself,
it zig-zags the air like when a crack
goes through a cup. So the trace
of the bat flaws the porcelain of the evening sky.

The bat zig-zags in panic through the air, experiencing an extreme lack of security. Its state of 'Ausgesetztsein' stands at the opposite pole to the total 'Geborgenheit' of the gnat. The pre-echoes of Heidegger are obvious here, and Heidegger is said to have remarked that his philosophy was an unfolding in thought of what Rilke had already expressed in poetry.[10] If this is so, then the Eighth Elegy must surely have been Heidegger's starting-point in this respect. The quality of poetic invention is superb here. The flight of the bat, apparently panic-stricken (visually, while not factually, correct) is masterfully conveyed by the jagged rhythms of 'wie vor sich selbst/erschreckt' and the harsh elision of 'durchzuckts'. And it is all the more striking for being set against the visually beautiful 'Porzellan des Abends' which is in turn cracked (the contracted 'durchs' is crucially effective here), as it were, by the flight of the bat. I have one reservation, however. The simile clashes with the beautiful metaphor: a crack in a cup is static, whereas the trace of the bat disappears with the movement of the bat. The lines would be better without the simile. Rilke, having investigated the fears of the birds and animals, now returns to us with a line break in verse sixty-six:

Und wir: Zuschauer, immer, überall,
dem allen zugewandt und nie hinaus!

And we: Onlookers, always, everywhere,
turned toward all that and never transcending it.

We, (the 'wir' is heavily stressed to convey our lamentable plight) are merely spectators, imprisoned in the finite world which is too much for us anyway. All we do is to attempt to put it in order, an impossible task:

Uns überfüllts. Wir ordnens. Es zerfällt.
Wir ordnens wieder und zerfallen selbst.

It overwhelms us. We order it. It disintegrates.
We order it again and disintegrate ourselves.

A lifetime of ordering and categorizing, ending in the final disintegration of the person doing it, is reduced to two short, succinct lines, whose very concision conveys the hopelessly pathetic nature of the enterprise.

The final section begins with a hollow rhetorical question:

Wer hat uns also umgedreht, daß wir,
was wir auch tun, in jener Haltung sind
von einem, welcher fortgeht?

Who has turned us around like this, so that,
do what we may, we are in the stance
of someone who is leaving?

The 'umgedreht' is the ultimate development of 'umgekehrt' and 'rückwärts' from the earlier part of the elegy. I say the question is a hollow one, because at this late stage in his life Rilke was too anti-Christian to discuss this situation in terms of the Fall. He was no longer on speaking terms with God as he was in his *Stundenbuch* of 1905, when he wore the poetic mask of a questioning monk. Now he is honest enough to present human life as a constant process of departure without any appeal of substance to a higher authority. We are always looking backwards, always departing and never moving unselfconciously forward like the animal. The first decades of the twentieth century produced a great number of valedictory works. The final movement of Mahler's Ninth Symphony, for example, which tellingly quotes from Beethoven's 'Lebewohl' sonata (opus 81a), and 'Der Abschied' from *Das Lied von der Erde*, but these works of farewell are largely those of a man who sensed his life was soon to end, whereas with Rilke there is a much more radical presentation of 'Abschied' — *every* moment of our lives is a moment of departure.

This final section of the Elegy is unremarkable in terms of modernistic poetic diction and invention. These lines could have been written any time in the second half of the nineteenth century, but they do have a superb, halting, valedictory poise, mainly achieved by the three verbs at the end of the penultimate line and the regular, drum-beat stresses of the last line of the poem:

Wie er auf
dem letzten Hügel, der ihm ganz sein Tal
noch einmal zeigt, sich wendet, anhält, weilt —,
so leben wir und nehmen immer Abschied.

Like him, who
on the last hill that shows him all of his valley
once more, turns, halts, tarries —,
so we live, forever taking our leave.

I have said that these lines are unremarkable from the modernist standpoint, and so they are compared with most of the imagery in the previous part of the poem. Perhaps T.S. Eliot ought to have the last word here. Warning against the excesses of symbolist poetry, he once wrote: 'If you aim only at the poetry in poetry, there is no poetry either'[11]. Subdued passages are necessary to set off the poetic highlights elsewhere in a poem.

As I said at the start, Rilke's 'raid on the inarticulate' resulted at times in lines of arguable value as poetry, but what is indisputable is that from *Die Aufzeichnungen des Malte Laurids Brigge* onwards Rilke rigorously adhered to the existential function of the modernist poet-priest. The *Duineser Elegien* are concerned deep down with the most serious justification of his role as a poet in the twentieth century. It was a demanding task showing that he could overcome Nietzschean censure of the poet being a deluded fool and a mere actor without substance. To do this Rilke had to affirm life, both in its beauty and its angst, and tranform this affirmation into poety. The Eighth Elegy is mainly concerned with the angst, and it would have been dishonest of Rilke not to have presented human life in such terms. On completing *Die Aufzeichnungen des Malte Laurids Brigge* Rilke wrote that after such a work all kinds of poetry were possible. He could easily have said the same again on completing the Eighth Elegy which is close in mood to that earlier prose-work. Rilke, like some of his contemporaries, saw this rigorous task as a kind of self-imposed martyrdom. Schönberg was once introduced to someone in his exile in Hollywood who asked him why he had written such terrible music, and Schönberg replied that no one else wanted to be Arnold Schönberg so he had to take the job on. Malte, too, has much the same attitude when he maintains that he, Malte, five storeys high in a Parisian slum tenement, has to register the angst of twentieth-century life, because no one else was willing to do it. And here, in the Eighth Elegy, Rilke felt compelled to present in dark poetry various forms of existential insecurity. It is against this that the affirmation and achievement of his later poetry has to be measured.

---

[1] Eliot, 'East Coker', l. 179.

[2] Gottfried Benn, *Probleme der Lyrik* (Wiesbaden, 1951), p. 16.

[3] Hans Egon Holthusen, *Rainer Maria Rilke A Study of his Later Poetry*, translated by J.P. Stern, (Cambridge 1952), p. 12.

[4] George Orwell, *The Collected Essays, Journalism and Letters*, Volume 2, *My Country Right or Left 1940-1943*, edited by Sonia Orwell and Ian Angus (Harmondsworth, 1970), p. 278.

[5] From the translation by K.G.Knight, Romano Guardini, *Rilke's Duino Elegies*, pp. 211-212.

[6] *Trunkene Flut* (Wiesbaden, 1949), p. 33.

[7] See *The Republic*, Part VII, Book 7.

8 Hans Egon Holthusen, *Rainer Maria Rilke in Selbstzeugnissen und Bilddokumenten* (Reinbek 1958), p. 65. A reproduction of Paula Modersohn-Becker's unfinished oil portrait of Rilke is to be found on p. 64.

[9] Rilke derived these ideas from Lou Andreas-Salomé's *Drei Briefe an einen Knaben* and acknowledged his debt to her in a letter written on 20 February 1914 (DE, I, 101; also 102, 105). See also Angela Livingstone, *Lou Andreas-Salomé* (London, 1984), pp. 222-3.

[10] The point is discussed by Erich Heller, *The Disinherited Mind* (London, 1957), pp. 164-5.

[11] *After Strange Gods. A Primer of Modern Heresy* (London, 1934), p. 12.

ELEGY NINE

Karen Leeder

The Ninth Elegy grows directly out of the two preceding elegies, with which its argument and imagery are intimately connected. Above all it takes up once again the tone of the Seventh Elegy, composed only two days before, and should be read with that close link in mind. Here again the poetic mission to bear witness to the world and thus to immortalise it in invisible inwardness is affirmed. Because of this the Ninth is generally thought of as the great epiphany of the Elegies. It marks the point where the poetic voice stops defining itself in relation to the realm of the Angels and turns instead definitively to the realm of the here and now, the moment when Rilke comes closest to uttering an absolute affirmation of the supreme task of existence, and in particular of poetry. It is a common for critics to debate which of those concerns are pre-eminent for Rilke: the poet or the man (DE, II, 210-224). Let me pre-empt my conclusion by saying straight away that, for me, both of these things co-exist in his work.

Certainly, the movement towards a fundamental saying of the world is very powerful. However, it would be wrong, in tracing the positive poetic trajectory of the Elegy, to obscure the undertone of doubt, despair and inadequacy which accompanies it. It has already been pointed out that the elegy form itself allows for impulses of regret, celebration and affirmation to exist simultaneously. The structure of the *Duino Elegies* dramatises a long struggle in which changes of direction, hesitations, contradictions and reconciliations are given form, whilst never, finally, cancelling each other out. In the Ninth Elegy the same structure pertains in miniature and a similar simultaneity of impulses demands to be taken seriously. Like many of the Elegies it tends to invite a linear interpretation, because it makes use of the rhetoric of rational argument and employs prominent signals to mark that movement: 'why?', 'because' 'and so', 'therefore'. The temptation is compounded because the language so clearly gestures beyond itself towards values external to the poem and rooted in philosophy or a theology of sorts. Nevertheless it is a mistake to attempt to construe a coherent system of belief, or even a reliable aesthetic programme, out of this Elegy. Even if the poem borrows the language of rational argument, its true power lies in moments of poetic insight and its true persuasion is emotional.

WARUM, wenn es angeht, also die Frist des Daseins
hinzubringen, als Lorbeer, ein wenig dunkler als alles
andere Grün, mit kleinen Wellen an jedem
Blattrand (wie eines Windes Lächeln) —: warum dann
Menschliches müssen — und, Schicksal vermeidend,
sich sehnen nach Schicksal?...

WHY, when this brief interval of being might be spent
as a laurel, slightly darker than all
other greens, with tiny waves on the edge
of each leaf (like the smile of a breeze) —: why then
have to be human and, shrinking from Fate,
still yearn for it too?...

'Warum' (why): the Ninth Elegy begins with a question. It is the first in a sequence of questions and answers which give the elegy its shape and dynamic. That one word is the first question, the one which has animated the history of mankind's philosophical enquiry, the one which animates the poetic enquiry of Rilke's Elegies. But it does not stand alone: the construction is delayed, the tension spread across five lines. By the time the 'why' has been repeated and the question completed, it has become at once more refined, more specific and more urgent. Now it is not simply the reason for earthly existence which is sought, but rather the reason why we are fated to suffer a particular quality of existence — human existence. These first five and a half lines appear to go back to the first period of work on the Elegies in Duino in March 1912. When Rilke came across them again amongst his papers in 1915, he could not remember writing them but found himself 'devastated' ('erschüttert') by them (DE, I, 128).

The full force of the question can only be understood against the background of the previous elegies, in which mankind's self-consciousness appears only to leave him exposed, alienated, divided and existentially at odds with the rest of creation. In the Eighth Elegy this disjunction is contrasted with the animals who move securely through creation in their intimate and undivided consciousness. Here in the Ninth Rilke goes further. Now, it is the unity and integrity of the organic world which is offered as an alternative to the brief span of our fractured existence. In the reference to the laurel, however, Rilke adds an extra and specific dimension. The laurel encourages us to think of the legend of the nymph Daphne, who escaped the amorous pursuit of Apollo by being transformed by the earth-mother into a laurel bush. In longing to enjoy existence as a laurel (it is not a simile — not *like* a laurel) the lyric subject appears to be seeking respite from sexuality and from a descent into human fate. Yet the symbol is more complicated than it at first might seem. Apollo is the god of enlightenment, art and music: the laurel is sacred to him, and it is the laurel which traditionally crowns the poet. Already Rilke is introducing the notions of transformation and poetry, key ideas which will be fused together later in the Elegy.

It is not only the mythological connotations of the laurel bush that Rilke exploits, but also its physical aspect. Laurel is an evergreen plant, therefore not marked by time. It is described as being of a more sombre hue than other greens (ll. 2-3). This perhaps refers primarily to the colour of the leaves. But grammatically it is the very being of the laurel which is identified as dark green, evoking an association with darkness, profundity, even death. It is difficult to tell where the smile (l. 4) comes from. Perhaps the curved edges of its leaves suggest it, or perhaps their peaceful stirring in the wind. In all these respects, however, the laurel appears to comprehend all one might aspire to in existence: unity, unconsciousness, openness to the natural world, poetry, permanence. Why if such an existence is possible on earth, does mankind suffer something so completely different?

The line breaks as if to pause after the immense implications of that question. At first the answers are a kind of evasion: a list of repeated negatives, as if the lyric subject were running through a catalogue of possibilities. 'Happiness' (l. 7) would not be temptation enough to compel us to choose the human state. The German word 'Glück' is an amalgam of luck, joy, happiness and fortune, and is resistant to adequate translation. Whatever it appears to promise is superficial and cannot be counted on to last, hence the rhetoric of material advantage, of commerce (l. 8).

dieser voreilige Vorteil eines nahen Verlusts.

its premature profit the prelude to imminent loss.

As swiftly and effortlessly as 'Glück' announces its arrival, so it departs. Rilke emphasises the slipperiness of its promises in the slippery alliteration and assonance of the line and in the play on the word 'Vorteil' (advantage, profit). Moving on it seems human existence cannot be motivated by curiosity (l. 9) either, nor by the opportunity it affords to 'practise the heart'. This is unclear again, but perhaps suggests a capacity for emotion or love that would also exist, it is claimed, in the laurel. Presumably we are meant to think of the presence and spirit of Daphne within the bush. Later in the Elegy it becomes clear that Rilke posits desires and needs — those qualities which we would otherwise associate with human life — within all things.

However, these negations still do not offer the answer to the first question. After the elaborate evasions, the 'Aber' of line 11 announces an answer which comes quite simply at first.

Aber weil Hiersein viel ist, und weil uns scheinbar
alles das Hiesige braucht, dieses Schwindende, das
seltsam uns angeht. Uns, die Schwindendsten. ***Ein*** *Mal*
jedes, nur ***ein*** *Mal.* ***Ein*** *Mal und nichtmehr. Und wir auch*
ein *Mal. Nie wieder. Aber dieses*
ein *Mal gewesen zu sein, wenn auch nur* ***ein*** *Mal:*
irdisch *gewesen zu sein, scheint nicht widerrufbar.*

But because being here means much, and because all
that is here, all that is fleeting, seems to need us,
and concerns us strangely. Us, the most fleeting of all. ***Once***
for each thing, only ***once****.* ***Once*** *and no more. And the same for us,*
only ***once****. Never again. But having been*
this ***once****, though only* ***once****:*
having been ***earthly****, seems irrevocable.*

The emphasis on being mortal, being here, on earth, recalls the triumphant affirmation of line 39 in the Seventh Elegy: 'Hiersein ist herrlich' ('To be here is glorious'). It is immediately echoed in 'Hiesige' (l. 12), and 'hier' (l. 32 and l. 43). 'Hier', in the sense that Rilke uses it, is what one would call in English the 'here and now'. These lines offer a first formulation and validation of the supreme usefulness of human existence in that here and now. The fact that mankind is transient, and is also aware of that transience, is both a torment and a singular gift. Precisely because we participate in both consciousness and the physical world of objects, we have a unique sensibility for the fleeting world whose fate we are doomed to share. This is why creation is said to 'need' us and to concern us, call out to us even ('angehen' contains both senses), in strange (as yet) perhaps unintelligible, ways. The next few lines (ll. 13-17) are wonderfully poised. We hear a bitter lament for the 'once and only' of passing time. Yet, quite tentatively as yet (the repetition of 'scheinbar' and 'scheint' is striking), the worth of the transient is also attested. The desire for permanence which haunted the earlier elegies is now rejected and replaced by the dignity and intensity of finite existence. '*Irdisch*' (earthly), announced prominently at the start of line 17, is a key word which points forward to the significance of the earth later in the Elegy. It can also mean mundane or mortal, as opposed to transcendent or divine. That part of it is perhaps in the background here, but should not be forgotten. In the celebrated letter to his Polish translator Witold Hulewicz, Rilke uses the same word as a talisman against Christian interpretations of his Elegies, insisting that the process of transformation be conducted 'in einem rein irdischen, tief irdischen, selig irdischen Bewußtsein' (within a purely terrestrial, profoundly, blessedly terrestrial consciousness) (DE, I, 20).

However, a kind of transformation (or translation if you like) is at work in this passage, even if it is not religious in the conventional sense. In the extraordinary repetition and urgency of these lines (the words 'ein Mal' are repeated six times in four lines) the poet transforms what was a desperate lament for the finite nature of existence into something else again. This repetition becomes a kind of echo, which, literally, cannot be 'revoked' (l. 17) and which resounds through the elegy. In the 'saying' of the poetry itself the fleetingness of human life assumes a kind of stability and permanence. Thus the capacity for poetic transformation has already been demonstrated in these lines, before the Elegy has named it or identified it as the ultimate potential of man. However much it is doubted, it will not be revoked.

In the fourth and longest section of the Elegy (ll. 18-42), having seen the purpose of existence, humankind rushes to achieve it.

Und so drängen wir uns und wollen es leisten,
wollens enthalten in unsern einfachen Händen,
im überfüllteren Blick und im sprachlosen Herzen.
Wollen es werden. — Wem es geben? Am liebsten
alles behalten für immer... Ach, in den andern Bezug,
wehe, was nimmt man hinüber? Nicht das Anschaun, das hier
langsam erlernte, und kein hier Ereignetes. Keins.
Also die Schmerzen. Also vor allem das Schwersein,
also der Liebe lange Erfahrung, — also

lauter Unsägliches. Aber später,
unter den Sternen, was solls: ***die*** *sind* ***besser*** *unsäglich.*

And so we urge ourselves on, trying to accomplish it,
seeking to contain it in our simple hands,
in our overcrowded gaze and in our speechless heart.
Trying to become it. To give it to whom? We'd rather
hold on to it all for ever... Ah, but — alas — what can we take
over into the other relation? Not the art of seeing,
which is learned so slowly here, and no event of the world. Not one.
Take then the pain, above all else, take the huge weight of being
and the long experience of love, — take what is truly
unsayable. But later, under the stars,
what's the use. ***They*** *are* ***better*** *unsayable.*

Even the rhythm and repetition underline the frantic willingness of man to put his realization into practice. Lines 19-21 describe a steady escalation in the intensity of man's attempts to grasp existence — in the hands, the eyes, in the heart, and finally by identification with it. At each turn, however, the simple organs of apprehension are hopelessly overstretched. Any attempt at acquisition, any hope of hoarding existence or even passing it on, proves fruitless. At this point (l. 22) the train of thought seems to break off. Some stages in the argument appear to be missing and need to be construed by the reader. Perhaps, now that the lyric subject has dedicated himself to here and now, he is asking himself what it would be appropriate to offer the Angel. Perhaps he is wondering what will outlive him when he dies. Neither the Angel nor death are mentioned by name; the 'other dimension' (l. 23) is identified only by the stars. The pause in the middle of line 22 enacts the despairing recognition that nothing which belongs to this physical world can be taken over (trans-lated) into the other realm. Human effort is checked by the force of the unsayable. What could not survive or be tolerated within it is, however, clear enough. Anything which has been conditioned by time or space: 'Anschaun' (l. 23), the contemplation laboriously mastered during the course of the Elegies themselves; 'Ereignetes' (l. 24), the events which have befallen us in the physical world, cannot make the transition.

Unsayable things, the feelings of love or sorrow that have left their imprint on our soul, at first offer themselves as alternative possibilities. But the colloquial outburst 'what's the use' (l. 28) reveals the frustration as the lyric subject is brought up short by the absoluteness and the intensity of that other dimension. The grammar of that last line is opaque. The emphatic use of italics suggests that 'die' refers to the stars. Rendering 'besser' into English is more difficult. Are the stars more deeply unsayable, better at the unsayable, or better off unsayable? The force of the whole must surely be that anything unsayable that we attempt to rescue from the here and now will already be comprehended and superseded in the superlative realm beyond. However, the oddity of the phrase is important. Here, as elsewhere, the italics are used as a kind of condensation and suspension of meanings. Poetically they make manifest the strain that is put on language if it is called upon to bear witness to the realm of the unsayable.

Here the argument appears to break off once again. At first sight it is difficult to make a connection between the anecdote which follows about a traveller in the mountains, and the more abstract argument which has preceded it. The shift from the discursive mode to something new is signalled in the self-conscious inversion (l. 29). In fact these lines serve as a metaphorical amplification — a 'translation' — of what has already been argued out.

Bringt doch der Wanderer auch vom Hange des Bergrands
nicht eine Hand voll Erde ins Tal, die Allen unsägliche, sondern
ein erworbenes Wort, reines, den gelben und blaun
Enzian.

For the traveller does not return from the mountain to the valley
with a handful of earth, unsayable to others, but instead
a word, hard-won, pure, the yellow and blue
gentian.

The image fuses landscape and language in the same way as the celebrated poem 'Ausgesetzt auf den Bergen des Herzens' (SW, II, 94-5) which could usefully be set alongside these lines. In order to do justice to the metaphorical implications of the image, one has to keep different levels of meaning simultaneously in mind. The wayfarer returning from the mountain does not bring back a handful of earth as evidence of what he has experienced. Its essence could not be translated between the two realms and what it contained would remain closed and finally unsayable to those below. Later in the Elegy (l. 37) the earth itself will be described as 'verschwiegen' (silent, secretive). Everything that the handful of earth could express is, however, made manifest and thus 'said' in the flower. The gentian belongs to the world of the here and now: it blossoms and dies — is transient. Yet the mountain slope, the earth, need the gentian as their talisman, for in its short blossoming it bears witness to its own world in a form which those in the valley can understand. Just as the gentian is the pure florescence of the earth and the mountain, so too the word 'gentian' is a pure word. But one should not lose sight of the traveller in all this. He is also needed, in order to risk the extremities of experience, away from the safety of the valley, and in order to bring back a word to render them comprehensible. The traveller (and here we may read 'poet') has wrung a word out of the extremes of the unsayable. One must also take one further step back in order to read these beautiful lines in their fullest sense. Taken as a whole they are themselves a highly visual metaphor for rendering the unsayable into the realm of the sayable. The mountain and flower act as the equivalents for intangible things; they make them manifest. As a whole the metaphor enacts that translation from the heights of unsayable experience into language comprehensible and lasting, that is into poetry.

In this image Rilke has all but answered his first question, which demanded a purpose of our human existence. It is to act as the translator of pure spirit. But as yet this answer is itself metaphorical, poetic. When he continues, however, though with a faltering tone (note the 'perhaps' and the interrogative), it is to draw the conclusions of the metaphor for his own existence. If, in its short blossoming, the gentian 'says' the world it belongs to, perhaps it is also our purpose to 'say' the modest things of the world we inhabit (l. 32).

Sind wir vielleicht ***hier****, um zu sagen: Haus,*
Brücke, Brunnen, Tor, Krug, Obstbaum, Fenster, —
höchstens: Säule, Turm.... aber zu ***sagen****, verstehs,*
oh zu sagen ***so****, wie selber die Dinge niemals*
innig meinten zu sein.

Are we perhaps ***here*** *to say: House,*
Bridge, Fountain, Gate, Jug, Fruit-tree, Window, —
at most, Column, Tower... but to ***say*** *them — you understand —*
oh to say them ***more intensely*** *than the things themselves*
ever dreamed they could be?

The transition from poetic language to the language of argument (ll. 32-36) is a clumsy one. The faltering assertion that our purpose on the earth might be to say the word 'house' or 'jug' seems at first more than faintly ridiculous. Of course, for Rilke, this is not a simple saying; it is one which will offer those things a higher, more intense, and more permanent existence than even they could yearn for (l. 35). Yet, following on from the lucidity of the lines before, one does sense the strain of apprehension in the italics and the apparently arbitrary clustering of nouns. On a first reading, these nouns give the impression that they must be symbols, incantations of a sort (there are nine of them, in the Ninth Elegy). In fact these things have in common that they are all modest things, objects of the really existing world, all of them artifacts of a kind. This is not the place to elucidate the symbolic value of each of these objects in Rilke's work as a whole. That has been done elsewhere and does not perhaps take us much further in understanding their meaning here.[1] More immediately significant here is the fact that they are all meaningful to us in our ordinary lives, but also subject to time and decay. At this point it is not possible to make much more of them. It is with a new accentuation and new urgency that the poem continues.

Ist nicht die heimliche List
dieser verschwiegenen Erde, wenn sie die Liebenden drängt,
daß sich in ihrem Gefühl jedes und jedes entzückt?
Schwelle: was ists für zwei
Liebende, daß sie die eigne ältere Schwelle der Tür
ein wenig verbrauchen, auch sie, nach den vielen vorher
und vor den Künftigen...., leicht.

Is it not the secret purpose
of this sly earth when she urges the lovers on,
that all things should delight in the feelings they feel.
Threshold: what is it for two lovers,
that they too should wear away the ancient
threshold of their door a little, after so many before them
and before so many to come...., lightly.

Now the authority of the lovers is sought in the processes of transformation. They have already appeared in Elegy Two, accredited with some kind of transformative power. Although there, as in the First Elegy, they ran the risk of obscuring each other's view of the open, they are now re-affirmed as productive models of transformation, even if incomplete ones. Urged on by the agency of the earth, the lovers have the power to transform the physical world around them, just as the poet's language does. When they look upon things with their intensified gaze, they invest those things with meaning. At once the things are rescued from anonymity and chaos, and partake of the radiance of the lovers' feelings. The harmony is underlined in the poem by the lilting modulation of 'ei' and 'ie' sounds, until it is brought up sharp with Rilke's coinage 'sich entzückt' (enter into raptures). The threshold (l. 39) then appears as another example of the modest human artifacts which were listed in the previous lines. It appears with a colon, as if it is about to be defined or interpreted. No interpretation is offered, however; rather an account of the process of transition into meaning. Presumably because the threshold of the door separating the lovers is worn away as they come to meet, it derives an emotional significance in connection with them. As its physical form is rubbed away it supersedes its own concrete existence and is raised to a sphere where it may be recognised and expressed in its innermost essence. We sense that Rilke has not chosen the threshold at random. If we have followed the logic of the Elegy so far, many such objects in the physical world must press on the human consciousness with the desire to be recognised and changed into symbols within. The threshold is one of these, but it is also a symbol of the passage from one realm to the next. It is not clear whether the transforming energies of the lovers are quite the same as those invoked previously on behalf of the poet. The translation enacted by them certainly seems a spontaneous and easy one — 'leicht' (l. 43), compared to the strains of 'saying'. But unless at this point we read their ecstatic recognition of an object as a metaphorical kind of 'saying', we can only assume that it is of a different order.

The next two sections return to the transformative powers of saying with a new energy -- marked by the confident exhortations of the piece (l. 44, l. 53, l. 55-6, l. 58 and l. 60). This is a very different tone from the early part of the text. The energy has been gathered through that painstaking and sometimes tortuous process of argument and is suddenly unleashed (l. 43).

> ***Hier*** *ist des* ***Säglichen*** *Zeit,* ***hier*** *seine Heimat.*
> *Sprich und bekenn.*
>
> ***Here*** *is the time for the* ***sayable;*** ***here*** *is its home.*
> *Speak and bear witness!*

This is the turning point of the poem. In rhythmic, almost hieratic tones the lyric subject demands that the poet bear witness, speak the fleeting physical world and rescue it from oblivion. The urgency of the poetic task is almost immediately underscored by reference to the increased threat which faces the world we might experience. The next lines, which surely reflect Rilke's own anxious apprehension of the age of the Modern, are obscure. They seem to be written in a kind of short-hand. Perhaps it is only by adducing evidence from elsewhere, in particular from the Seventh Elegy (ll. 50-57) and the letter to Hulėwicz of 1925, that sense can be made of them.

In the letter Rilke argues that in times past people interacted with singular objects that were known to them and had personal meaning for them. Over the centuries a special significance accrued to such things, which was recorded in an image and existed in our consciousness and in poetry. In the modern world, which is increasingly governed by the forces of industry, of mass-production for example, objects are defined by their functionality rather than their individual qualities. They leave no lasting trace within us. They vanish. He regrets the passing of those things which had been invested with the imagination and intimacy of our forbears. They have been ousted by an influx of 'leere gleichgültige Dinge, Schein-Dinge, *Lebens-Attrappen*' (empty indifferent things, imitation things, shams) issuing from America, the cradle of technological progress (DE, I, 321). In the Elegy the same sort of feeling becomes condensed and subtly changed. Here the world is filled with directionless activity. This is underlined by the prominent energy of the verbs 'Tun' (do), 'verdrängen' (drive out), 'zerspringen' (burst open) and the pace of the lines. This energy is, however, arbitrary because it has no preserving image which will transform it. In the midst of this brutal agitation an 'imageless act' (l. 46) is all that remains. The defining limits placed on it by mankind, its 'crusts' (l. 47), are constantly burst through, exceeded and redundant, as the inner activity strives to redefine itself in a more intense way. The image is potent if not immediately clear. The semblance of signification which we foist upon such things in order to 'define' them, can perhaps be likened to the superficial fixity of the 'gedeutete[n] Welt' (interpreted world) of the First Elegy (l. 13). Once this link has been made, it becomes clear that Rilke is not only, or even primarily, concerned with the transience of things. His main concern here is the place of art in the age of technology.

In the midst of the menace, however, come four lines of extraordinary clarity and vision, lines marked off from the rest of the text by their brevity and by the dactylic rhythm (forming a hidden elegiac couplet).

Zwischen den Hämmern besteht
unser Herz, wie die Zunge
zwischen den Zähnen, die doch,
dennoch, die preisende bleibt.

Between the hammers our heart
endures, like the tongue
between the teeth, which still,
even so, continues to praise.

Following hard on an image of the disjunction of the modern world, as these lines do, the hammers immediately invoke the degraded and degrading world of industry. Indeed Rilke uses similar images in his *Sonette an Orpheus*. The lines would seem then to evoke the embattled existence of the transforming heart amidst the chaos of the modern. The force of the simile (l. 50) is to imply a comparable relation between the tongue (animator of speech) and the teeth (agents of destruction). Both 'besteht', meaning exist or endure, and the breathy repetition of 'doch, / dennoch' (despite everything) would seem to underline that determined 'saying against the odds'. The poetic logic is convincing until one considers the mechanics of human speech.[2] Elegy Ten offers a possibility of rethinking the first half of the simile. There the beating of the heart is identified as a hammering (l. 3). The tongue, as the organ of the sayable, is dependent on the teeth in order to be able to articulate, but must preserve its existence apart from the teeth, which could at any moment shut and silence it. The heart, as the organ of the inner world, which will become later in the Elegy the invisible heart (l. 66), is dependent on the beating of the physical heart. In both cases the transformative organ is reliant on reality, the outside world, but must assert its existence in order to preserve the possibility of transcending it.

How do these lines relate to what has gone before? In the triumphant 'praising' of the tongue they vouch for the energy of poetic 'saying' in the midst of threat. Once again they also confirm that this is a possibility which is open to mankind as a result of his duality: he belongs to the physical world and, at the same time, aspires beyond it. In a sense they perform the resonant 'contradiction' of poetry — what the poet Hilde Domin, quoting these lines, called its fundamental 'Dennoch' (DE, III, 290-1). These lines are among the most memorable and significant of the Elegies as a whole. They recall the 'strip of land, fertile, of our own, / between river and rock' of Elegy Two (ll. 74-6). The poet's tongue and the poetic word are a fertile possibility between barrenness and flux, between objects and consciousness, between saying and silence. This is the fragile and utopian power of poetry, once more made manifest in poetic form.

Having arrived at this point, the true task of humanity can be articulated along with its relation to the angelic realm.

Preise dem Engel die Welt, nicht die unsägliche. ***Ihm***
kannst du nicht großtun mit herrlich Erfühltem; im Weltall,
wo er fühlender fühlt, bist du ein Neuling. Drum zeig
ihm das Einfache, das, von Geschlecht zu Geschlechtern gestaltet,
als ein Unsriges lebt, neben der Hand und im Blick.
Sag ihm die Dinge. Er wird staunender stehn; wie du standest
bei dem Seiler im Rom, oder beim Töpfer am Nil.
Zeig ihm, wie glücklich ein Ding sein kann, wie schuldlos und unser,
wie selbst das klagende Leid rein zur Gestalt sich entschließt,
dient als ein Ding, oder stirbt in ein Ding —, und jenseits
selig der Geige entgeht.

Praise this world to the Angel, not the unsayable. ***He***
cannot be impressed with the world of splendid sensation; in the universe
where he feels more feelingly, you are a novice. So show
him a simple thing, fashioned from generation to generation,
so that it lives on as ours — near the hand, in the gaze.
Tell him of things. He will stand more amazed; just as you stood
by the rope-maker in Rome, by the potter on the banks of the Nile.
Show him how happy a thing can be, how guiltless and ours,
how even the lamentations of grief might purely settle on a form,
serve as a thing, or die into a thing — and escape, blissfully,
beyond the violin.

These lines pick up the thread of argument from lines 22-28, when the lyric subject realized that he had nothing to offer of the world or the unsayable to the super-conscious realm of the Angels. The superlative sensibility of the angelic realm is made apparent in the marvellous intensification 'fühlender fühlt', picked up in 'Erfühltem' (l. 54). Instead, man can offer his own powers of transformation. The simple artifacts of our world, which are being or have been transformed in our souls, are things fit to bring before the Angel. These things are truly 'ours' (l. 60), not because we have grasped them rashly and acquisitively, as in lines 19-22, but because they have slowly acquired inner significance for us over generations (and here we understand the significance of the objects invoked in lines 32-4). Just as the onlooker is amazed at the way a craftsman gives form to an object (ll. 58-9), so too the Angel will be amazed at the human ingenuity to form aesthetic significance beyond the physical.[3] Even grief — an ultimate of the unsayable — can be transposed by a violin and transmuted into musical form. This image (l. 63) recalls the violin which offered itself to the lyric subject in the First Elegy and the music which rises from the lament of Linus. Both hint ultimately at the legend of Orpheus and his music born of grieving. Unsayable grief can be transformed into music and rendered sayable, beautiful and lasting. Conspicuous musicality is also a feature of these lines. It is created by their alliterations, assonances, repetitions and rhythmic quality. *In nuce* we have here the movement of elegy itself which informs the whole cycle. Grief, mourning, and remembrance find form in the music of poetry.

The final part of this section (ll. 63-7) echoes the second section of the Elegy (ll. 10-16). It is by virtue of our compound transience that we are in a position to give utterance to those things which are themselves voiceless but 'live from their vanishing' (a telling paradox). They entrust their fate to us, who are 'the most transient' of all (the echo of ll. 12-13 is clear). When we convert them into inner significance we offer them a refuge, what Heller calls an 'invisible ark of inwardness' (DE, II, 227). We do not save them physically, of course. The pots and ropes (l. 59) are not themselves salvaged from the impermanence of existence. Instead they lose their outward trappings within us and become pure. They are salvaged in an inner sustaining image which must be translated into an outward form to become sayable. The violin did it for grief. For the pots the essential translator is the poem itself.

Finally the Elegy seeks the origin of our desire to transform and to redeem.

Erde, ist es nicht dies, was du willst: ***unsichtbar***
in uns erstehn? — Ist es dein Traum nicht,
einmal unsichtbar zu sein? — Erde! unsichtbar!
Was, wenn Verwandlung nicht, ist dein drängender Auftrag?
Erde, du liebe, ich will. Oh glaub, es bedürfte
nicht deiner Frühlinge mehr, mich dir zu gewinnen —, ***einer,***
ach, ein einziger ist schon dem Blute zu viel.
Namenlos bin ich zu dir entschlossen, von weit her.
Immer warst du im Recht, und dein heiliger Einfall
ist der vertrauliche Tod.

Earth, is it not this that you want — to arise
***invisibly** within us. Is it not your dream*
to be one day invisible? Earth! invisible!
What is your urgent command, if not transformation?
Earth, my dearest, I will. Oh, believe me, your
springtimes are no longer needed to win me; ***one***
— ah even a single one — is too much for my blood.
Before all naming I was yours — from the first.
You were always right, and your holy inspiration
is our intimate, Death.

It is the silent mandate of the earth which works on us as it did on the lovers or in the unsayable earth of the mountain. The earth demands to be rescued from its own silence and from the impermanence of time. Now the intensely anthropomorphic energies of the text fall into place: the 'needing' (l. 12), the 'cunning' (l. 36), the 'understanding' (l. 64) and the 'trust' (l. 65), which are attributed to the earth and the things of the earth, are all part of a desperate bid for survival. Even the springtimes which were already at work on the lyric subject in the First Elegy are part of the call of the earth. There they seemed to announce a lover (ll. 32-3). Here it is with the initial coyness and then the simplicity of a lover that the earth is now directly addressed. In tender rhythmic words the lyric subject confirms his acquiesence in the task before him. Indeed he recognises that, even before he could name, understand, or identify that task, he was devoted to his work for the earth.

Fascinating in this confession of love and obedience is the prominence of the physical: the intensity of the springtimes as they work on his blood, the repetition of 'Erde' (earth), the 'einer', 'ein einziger' (one, a single one) which must inevitably recall the repeated 'ein Mal' (once) of earlier in the poem. Growing out of that physicality, however, is the world of the transformed, the invisible (DE, II, 112-128). They are caught together in the marvellous chiastic structure of 'Erde! unsichtbar!' (Earth! invisible!). The space between them is the place of transformation, the invisible heart. But that it is indeed the heart, not apparently the word, highlights a slippage from the rhetoric of 'saying' and the 'unsayable' to that of the visible and invisible in the course of the Elegy. It creates a problem for the reader. On the one hand it seems to confirm the place of the lovers in the elegy, which had at first seemed hard to understand. On the other hand, the role of the poet as privileged translator of things, a role which has been underlined in the many references to saying, words, silences, and translation itself, is put in doubt. Is the capacity for transformation in fact to be found within all who exist and see and feel with a pure heart?

The problem is not, I think, ever absolutely decided one way or the other in Rilke. There are a number of clues, however, which can help us to understand the sense of this Elegy. It is said that the earth seeks to 'rise up' within us in invisible form (ll. 68-9). The word used here, 'erstehen', is caught with extra emphasis on the run-over line and inevitably brings to mind 'auferstehen' (resurrect). Rilke uses this more loaded version in the Huléwicz letter when describing man's duty to transform (DE, I, 321). It joins with 'Ein Rettendes' (l. 65) (power of salvation: literally 'a saving thing') and 'heilig' (l. 76) (holy) in suggesting religious connotations for the transformative act. The object dies to the real world and is born again into a new more intense life within the imaginary space of the 'other relation'. But how does the thing accede to this space? From the Elegy so far it could be supposed that two methods were possible: the mute transformation of the heart and the exulting voice of the poet. Only one of these, however, retains its effectiveness past the ultimate transformation of death. It is necessary to examine this before the distinction can be understood.

Death has been a constant threatening presence in the Elegies. It is the preoccupation with death that exiles mankind from the blissful unconsciousness of the animal world and gives fearful delimitation to our brief span of existence. Yet here in a final, delayed revelation it appears as benevolent, familiar, part of the holy inspiration which animates all things.[4] It is almost as if the whole Elegy has been spent in finding courage to confront it. In the First Elegy we had been warned that it was our sense of death as something other that obscured our true understanding of life (ll. 80-1). Rather than perceiving our flimsy borders between the two states, the Angels go among the living and dead and cannot tell one from the other. This same thought is expressed in another form in the Huléwicz letter (DE, I, 319).

Der Tod ist die uns abgekehrte, von uns unbeschienene *Seite des Lebens* [...] es *gibt weder ein Diesseits noch Jenseits, sondern die große Einheit...*

Death is the *side of life* which is not turned towards us, nor do we shed any light upon it [...] *there is neither a here and now nor a beyond but the great unity...*

In the Ninth Elegy this sense of the great unity of life and death is accepted. Death is no longer perceived as a negation of life nor as a limitation. Through our new-won intimacy with the earth we are able accept the celebration of life and death as one. The final strophe moves to a confident assertion of this new understanding of existence. It begins with a moving simplicity: the simple 'I am' of an existence at peace with itself and its mortality.

Siehe, ich lebe. Woraus? Weder Kindheit noch Zukunft
werden weniger..... Überzähliges Dasein
entspringt mir im Herzen.

Behold, I am living. On what? Neither childhood nor future
diminish..... Being without number
springs up in my heart.

Yet it is only when the substance of that existence is questioned that the full extent of what has been won is announced. The 'woraus' (literally 'out of what') is not far from the 'why' which initiated the elegy. How differently it is answered here! A unique potentiality is claimed, a place between times, not encroaching on either past or future — a perfectly stable moment which has escaped the linear flow of time. And that welling up of being within the heart is faithful to the plenitude and superabundance of earthly existence. It springs forth without limits, surpassing all acquisition or calculation. The Elegy started by asking why we must suffer the brief span of tortured mortal existence; it ends by celebrating death in life with the advent of incalculable being.

Given what I said earlier about the dynamic of affirmation and negation which motivates the elegy, my conclusion might seem unnecessarily up-beat. Perhaps I have been carried away by the breathless excitement which animates the poem. It is infectious, and the sudden moments of quickened perception which drive the text along are strategically placed to keep the pace. But it is also worth emphasising the things which work against that drive: the pauses, hesitations, ellipses, the oscillation between doubt and certainty, the rawness of humankind's existential 'exposure'. Certainly the presence of these moments endorses the veracity of the struggle towards poetic affirmation. But they are also more than that. Just as the Elegy demands that death be comprehended in our perception of life, so these moments of hesitation must be comprehended in any reading of the Elegy itself.[5] In the same light one should also register the failures of the poetry, the strains, abstractions or examples of confused syntax that occur when the rhetoric of argument attempts to come to terms precisely with that which goes beyond it: the unsayable. These must stand alongside those crystalline moments when the translation is complete and Rilke allows poetry, rather than argument, to speak.

These final observations bring me back to the question which I left unresolved earlier. That is the relative merits of the different forms of transformation which are offered in the Elegy. Death, of course, is another model of transformation which snatches things from a visible world into an invisible one beyond. While I would not argue that the several realms into which transformation takes place are identical, one could argue that the 'other relation', the invisible inwardness of the heart, the 'beyond' of death, and the place of superabundant being all gesture towards the space of the poem. The magnificent affirmation of line 43 which collapses time and space into endless simultaneity could also be read in this way: '*Hier* ist des *Säglichen* Zeit, *hier* seine Heimat' (as above), ultimately that 'hier' is the space of the Ninth Elegy itself.

In the hierarchy of transforming consciousness poetry must be supreme in that it is language in which all the modes of transformation become explicit. Although heroes, lovers, and the youthful dead, in their different ways, accede to this other relation, only the poetic voice can truly give it lasting utterance. Even Rilke's Angels are projections of the transforming poetic consciousness — although idealized ones. In a world without God, a world no longer underpinned by transcendental beliefs, they are, to borrow the words of Wallace Stevens, 'the supreme fiction' –– to which humankind, and particularly the poet, aspires.[6] But they are also ultimate representations of a peculiarly modern human need to guarantee significance though our own consciousness. This is both a desperate and a monumental undertaking. It offers within it the possibility of superlative poetry. Stephen Spender has pinpointed how the tension between the fragility of mankind's place in the universe and the immensity of his poetic aspiration gives the Elegies as a whole their extraordinary dynamic: 'Rilke's truth in its negative aspect rests on the tragic inadequacy of humanity to attain consciousness in its situation as the sole consciousness in the universe. On the positive side his poem provides us with an extraordinary vision of what such consciousness might be.'[7] This is perhaps nowhere more the case than in the Ninth Elegy.

---

[1] See Jacob Steiner, *Rilkes Duineser Elegien*, pp. 218-224.

---

[2] op. cit., pp. 232-3.

[3] These examples are both drawn from Rilke's own experience recorded in a letter to Alfred Schaer, 26 February 1924 (DE, I, 307-8).

[4] Death is dealt with by Schwarz (DE, II, 33-7), and briefly by Guardini (DE, II, 83-5). Probably the most illuminating treatment of this subject is the chapter 'Rilke and Death's Demand' in Maurice Blanchot, *The Space of Literature*, translated by Ann Smock (Lincoln, London, 1982), pp. 121-59.

[5] Paul de Man identifies this kind of reversal and recuperation as a structural principle of Rilke's work in *Allegories of Reading*, p. 50.

[6] Kathleen L. Komar, *Transcending Angels*, offers an extended comparison between Stevens' fiction of 'the necessary angel' and Rilke's angels.

[7] 'Rilke and Eliot', in Ernst S. Warren, R. Frank Barton and Dick Maurer (eds), *Rilke: The Alchemy of Alienation* (Lawrence, 1980), p. 61.

ELEGY TEN

In memoriam
Leslie Seiffert, 1934-90

Roger Paulin

It is a natural reaction to see in Elegy Ten a kind of summation of the ideas and images of the whole cycle. The themes that we have been tracing do of course recur: angels, flowers, lovers, mythologies. And themes and motifs that dominate Rilke's whole poetic oeuvre find a voice, the image of the night sky, for instance.[1] But the sombre grandeur of this elegy comes from the theme of death that dominates it from start to finish, coming as it does on the heels of that affirmation of the here and now, the only existence we have, that was first introduced in Elegies Six and Seven and then reinforced in the sixfold '*ein* Mal' of Elegy Nine. Not only is Elegy Ten the longest; it introduces in its well over 100 lines several seemingly disjunct sequences that only move towards a thematic resolution when we are fifty verses into the text. In its lament for the dead, but in the fierce prophetic indignation at the loss of touch with the culture of pain and bereftness and death, it has echoes of Elegy Five. As there, what makes it both difficult and at the same time moving, is this juxtaposition of disparate moods, encapsulated in a mythology that takes us from 'Klagen' to 'Leid-Stadt' to 'Ur-Leid'. The tone ranges from Hölderlinian sonority to the occasional foreshadowing of *The Waste Land*. An analogy from the fine arts also springs to mind. In 1912, the year of the cycle's conception (and of the first fifteen verses of our elegy), an exhibition was held in Cologne by the *Sonderbund*, of the most significant works of the modern art movements.[2] The examples ranged from Renoir and Monet and Liebermann to Picasso and Braque to Delaunay and Severini. Cheek by jowl one saw traditions and positions confront and challenge each other. (Seeing the repeat exhibition in 1962 was one of my lasting formative experiences.) The analogy does not work entirely. At most it reminds us that while Rilke stands at the threshold of the most radical formal experiment our century has known, he also looks back to and is firmly rooted in traditions that inform and shape the nineteenth century (Rilke's angels, for instance, also link him with the previous century).[3] But he does bring home to us the essential and timeless link between poetry and myth, that is, saying in human terms the expressible about the ultimately inexpressible mysteries of life and death, and of the timeless role of the poet set aside to recount human response to those mysteries. In our poem we have two magic plants, one at the beginning and one at the end. For where would the poetry of proclamation and of lament, such as this is, be without its priests and their arcana?

As I said, one might expect of this elegy some kind of summation, some statement of achievement, some climactic message or some conspectual view. This would be a fair expectation after what may have appeared to have been a cyclical motion through nine different phases and modes of experience, now to become ten. There are numerous hints in letters from the period in which the Elegies were taking shape, that the search for meaning in 'das Hiersein' (DE, I, 131), 'das Hiesige' (ibid., 162), essential for the *Neue Gedichte* and *Malte Laurids Brigge*, had not been abandoned. As he writes in 1915 to Princess Marie von Thurn und Taxis, it is in the human that we find consolation. And to this end:

> *es müßte nur unser Auge eine Spur schauender, unser Ohr empfangender sein, der Geschmack einer Frucht müßte uns vollständiger eingehen, wir müßten mehr Geruch aushalten, und im Berühren und Angerührtsein geistesgegenwärtiger und weniger vergeßlich sein —: um sofort aus unseren Erfahrungen Tröstungen aufzunehmen, die überzeugender, überwiegender, wahrer wären als alles Leid, das uns erschüttern kann. (DE, I, 129)*

> *only our eyes would need to be a shade more seeing, our ear more receptive, we ought to take in more fully the taste of a fruit, we ought to be more aware of our sense of smell, and in touching and being touched more sharp-witted and less forgetful —: to gain from our experiences consolations straightway, that would be more convincing, all-encompassing and true than all the suffering that can shake and undermine us.*

Yet the breaking off of the Elegies in 1912 and their resumption after not quite ten years, in 1921-22, tells us that this process of lyrical perception and apprehension is beset from the outset with doubts and velleities. The 'ineffable', the 'unspeakable', the 'un-sayable' in the realm of the angels, is overcome only gradually in the resigned contentment with relationships in the here and now, and in the resumption of poetic confidence that accompanies it.

Instead of looking for some kind of grand climax in Elegy Ten, we might reverse the process and note instead that the cycle is referential within itself in ways that make us read back and forward. We are always finding premonitions and preformulations of images and motifs that find their definitive utterance in one or more of the elegies. Thus the audience of the dead in Numbers Four and Five, 'die unendlich Toten', as our elegy (l. 105) will call them, beyond recall but ever-present around us, are a more accurate point of reference in Number Ten than the invocation at its opening of the angels. At most, that address will serve as a reminder that Elegy Ten owes its first fifteen verses to the initial burst of inspiration in Duino in 1912. And yet the elegy will take up, already in its second verse, what must be the central theme of grand poetry — and *stilus altus* this poetry is, make no mistake — that of singing: 'aufsingen' and 'zustimmen' (l. 2). We have already had 'ansingen' in Elegy One. Now, 'aufsingen' and 'zustimmen' are what *we* do and what the *angels* do respectively. So already in the first draft of 1912, as it were, Rilke had expressed the idea that, while we cannot have a dialogue with the absolute and the ineffable, we can have a kind of antiphonal song, we singing of our experience, they of theirs — not in an equal contest, of course, but in an awareness that we see what is visible, they all that is invisible. This notion, expressed in a late letter, we can apply by extension to the central image and theme of Elegy Ten: life and death. They represent two spheres of equal validity, the one merely the side of the other turned away from us for the moment, the one for the time being not cast in light ('des Lebens abgekehrte Hälfte' DE, I, 283). And in the unity of life and death, in this awareness, the angels have their dwelling.

But how can we *sing* all of this? When Rilke had completed the Elegies, his immediate reaction was in the language of religious, even hieratic utterance: 'Aber nun *ists*. Ist. Ist. Amen' (DE, I, 236), 'sehr, sehr sehr herrlich. Wunder. Gnade.' (ibid., 237). This biblical and almost liturgical language is both helpful and misleading. For we must not forget that the composition of the Elegies coincides with one of the greatest literary events of the early twentieth century: the first issue of the complete works of Hölderlin, by Norbert von Hellingrath in 1912-14[4]. This suddenly made certain kinds of poetic diction problematic. It sat in judgment on the nineteenth century that had so often been satisfied with the epigonal and the nearly good. I believe that Rilke is momentarily caught up in this event. There are clear echoes of *Brod und Wein* in Elegy One (and elsewhere). The very adaptation of the elegiac couplet is part of this. So too the kenosis, the emptying of oneself in the service of speaking and being spoken through; but also the more than occasional and distinctly unnerving changes of tone from the gnomic to the rhetorically expansive that we know in Hellingrath's term, as applied to Hölderlin, as 'harte Fügung'. But Hölderlin and his models, Pindar, the Psalmist and the prophets, are inimitable: where Rilke in other poetry between 1912-14 does in fact slip into the Hölderlinian mode, he falls very flat indeed. For in the years 1912-22 there can be can no creating of a private mythology or religion. True, the early twentieth century is littered with the wrecks of such attempts, the great unreadables, Mombert, Däubler, even the late Stefan George. And so 'sehr, sehr sehr herrlich, Wunder. Gnade' is an expression also of the poet's humility at having succeeded in sustaining — even against the awesome presence of a Hölderlin — his own style and his own utterance.

As if to remind us that we are in the last statement of a cycle of *elegies*, Rilke in Number Ten unfolds the lexis of the elegiac: Harm, Schmerz, Leid, Klage, Ur-Leid, Zorn, Tränen, Wehmut, Trauer. The two key words of the poem seem to be 'Leid' and 'Klage': one the experienced feeling, the *dolor*, the pain and suffering at the ultimate loss in death; the other, again crucial for the poet, its utterance, its sound and articulation, the *planctus*, the lament. I would go so far as to say: the 'lamentation', for this elegy is also a 'Klagelied', Luther's word for Jeremiah's complaint (and it is the same word that in German poetics was once used for the later 'Elegie'). But while this elegy reproduces the cadences of the elegiac couplet, there is no anxious attempt (as in Seven) at metrical correctness, only the framework, structure or tone of elegiac utterance. Yet if this elegy is one thing, it is certainly not a mere disquisition on the passing of all things. Its tone is not that of 'Weltschmerz': we have left that ontological 'Katzenjammer' behind in the nineteenth century where it belongs. No, here Rilke attempts to see beyond loss and transience in order to perceive some sense, in a way to turn the tables on death (John Donne's 'for thou are not so', if you like, but not quite) and to integrate death into a scheme whose totality we mortals of course never grasp (the angels do) and whose two sides we cannot experience simultaneously.

Athough it is fair to say that the theme of death is omnipresent in Rilke's oeuvre, it is also worthy of note that his thinking on the subject was intensified during the years of composition of the elegies. It was his concern, as he expressed it in a letter of 1915, to see death as that which is experienced (that is, it happens to us all) and yet which in its reality cannot be experienced. We are always conscious of it, yet never really admit it, as 'das gefährliche Glas unseres Glücks, aus dem wir jeden Augenblick können vergossen werden' (DE, I, 135) ('the perilous glass of our happiness from which we can be poured at any moment'). For all that, as a later letter stresses, death is not a contrary principle. Its inner essence is in reality more conscious of life, 'lebenswissender' (DE, I, 162) than our most vital moments of life. We must make it our task therefore to win death's confidence, to learn daily of it, through seizing, as Rilke says, the fruit of the here and now and biting into it ('die ergriffene und aufgebissene Frucht des Hiesigen' DE, I, 204)). Indeed a letter of 1923 will state categorically that death is the ultimate affirmer ('Ja-Sager'), it alone says 'Yes' to eternity: 'Er, der Tod (ich beschwöre Sie, es zu glauben!) ist der eigentliche Ja-Sager. Er sagt *nur*: Ja. Vor der Ewigkeit' (DE, I, 284). In Elegy Ten, Rilke the poet is placing himself in a new relationship to death, as life fades, and a newer, paradoxically brighter, existence seems to beckon (although that, too, is ultimately 'unsäglich'). In terms of his thanatology, however, he is also aligning himself with a strand that goes well back into the nineteenth century, say, to Ludwig Feuerbach, whistling very loud in the dark indeed and stating that my death is the fulfilment of all that I have lived for, all my human relationships are completed in it — for there is nothing beyond.[5] More significantly, perhaps, Rilke associates himself with the Tolstoy of *The Death of Ivan Ilyich* (DE, I, 137). There we read of a life of squalid untruth, of unreality, finding a final purpose in the recognising of death as no more than the voice that declares that life to have been untrue or unfulfilled. That voice ceases, is silent, is at an end, as physical life comes to an end. More tellingly, we think of Freud's injunction of 1916, 'man muß an ihn [den Tod] glauben'[6], or of Ludwig Wittgenstein's 'Bejahung des Todes'[7], that affirmation of death through which we both acknowledge and also overcome its pervasive influence on life.

But these, necessarily sketchy, preliminaries will not take us further than the threshold of the poem. There needs to be one more preliminary, if the poem is not to withhold from us another dimension that is crucial for its understanding: the poem as myth. It is, as I stressed before, not a twentieth-century attempt at yet another private mythology, along the lines that Hölderlin had so wonderfully and tragically plotted a century before. Nor is it the renewal of myth in the way we see Yeats or Eliot or Pound doing, as say in the theme of poetic metamorphosis that Charles Tomlinson chose for the theme of his Clark Lectures some years ago[8]. Instead, Rilke is giving a mythopoeic dimension to the world of the heart, of human feeling, (the angels escape the realm of human sensation and emotion) and then in the whole range of experiences of the human heart that are subsumed under the key words of the poem, 'Klage' and 'Leid'. It is not a world of cogent mythological equivalents, nor is it some kind of allegory where equivalents and correspondences slot neatly into place (DE, II, 251). For all that, we enter into a world that has its own terms of reference, its own structures and hierarchies, its own beginning and its own end.

DASS ich dereinst, an dem Ausgang der grimmigen Einsicht,
Jubel und Ruhm aufsinge zustimmenden Engeln.
Daß von den klar geschlagenen Hämmern des Herzens
keiner versage an weichen, zweifelnden oder
reißenden Saiten. Daß mich mein strömendes Antlitz
glänzender mache; daß das unscheinbare Weinen
blühe. O wie werdet ihr dann, Nächte, mir lieb sein,
gehärmte. Daß ich euch knieender nicht, untröstliche Schwestern,
hinnahm, nicht in euer gelöstes
Haar mich gelöster ergab. Wir, Vergeuder der Schmerzen.
Wie wir sie absehn voraus, in die traurige Dauer,
ob sie nicht enden vielleicht. Sie aber sind ja
unser winterwähriges Laub, unser dunkeles Sinngrün,
***eine** der Zeiten des heimlichen Jahres —, nicht nur*
Zeit —, sind Stelle, Siedelung, Lager, Boden, Wohnort.

MAY the time come when, at the end of my terrible vision,
I raise up my song of praise and delight to the voice of the angels.
And may the clear blows from the heart's hammers
not strike dully on strings that are soft, doubting
or brittle. And may my tear-streaming cheeks
shine all the more brightly; and the weeping in secret
bloom. Oh how dear you will be to me then, you nights
of sorrow. Would I had knelt even lower, to accept you, disconsolate sisters,
given more of myself in touching
your hair that was untied in mourning. We, who are wastrels of sorrows.
We see them approach, into the endless sadness,
hoping perhaps they will end. But they are
our leaves through the winter, our dark green of remembrance,
one of the times of the inward year — not merely
time —, are our place, settlement, encampment, ground, habitation.

The poem opens with a five-fold repetition (l. 1-6) of the word 'daß', suggesting in its optative 'may' or 'o that' the rhetorical structure of supplication or prayer or even of affirmation. We note, however, that they are all unfulfilled statements, the first four referring to future achievement, the fifth looking back to what was not done, and in its turn leading over to the *sententia* 'Wir, Vergeuder der Schmerzen' (l. 10), then the long and sustained poetic metaphor on the nature of those sorrows of which we are so prodigal. This by now familiar structure of 'if we were to', 'if we but could' forms a kind of prooemion or prologue that is echoed and perhaps answered by the final colophon of the poem ('But if they could... then this' ll. 107ff.), followed by the metaphor and the rounding-off statement of general application. Set in between these 'unfulfilled' sections are the sustained narrative, the mythopoeic passages that trace the transition from life to death, from the 'Leid-Stadt' to the 'Klage-Land' to the 'Berge des Ur-Leids'.

In this series of invocations or petitions, the poet begins with the awareness that perhaps only the moment of death, some day ('dereinst'), at the moment of full recognition (when he emerges from the 'grimmige Einsicht'), will be the fitting moment to sing the angels ('aufsingen'), receiving not only their nodding approval ('zustimmenden' — a double meaning in the German —) but the harmony and concinnity, where poetic and angelic voice are part of the same process, 'auf-' *and* 'zu-', as one reaches out in song and the other picks up the theme of the other voice. Indeed this image of singing is carried over to that of the hammers of the piano on the strings and becomes one of performance: may they all be tuned and taut. Song or melody leads over to weeping and the first indication that the act of singing or invoking is also a poetic act of charity. For the coming alive and affirmation of the nights of lamentation is a new awareness: human acts, as Elegy Seven reminded us, are not only worthy when they produce tower or pylon, but also the qualities of 'Innerlichkeit', mercy and pity. Thus the grief-stricken nights (l. 8) of weeping become the first of those elegiac mythical creations — the sisters whom I did not (*past* tense now) recognize for what they were (did not kneel before, whose hair untied for the rite of mourning I did not touch), unaware as I was that 'Schmerz' is not only inextricably bound up with existence, but actually has substance, more substance perhaps than a life that is limited only by 'Glück'. That knowledge and consciousness is then transferred into a supremely beautiful poetic line: 'Sie aber sind ja/ Unser winterwähriges Laub, unser dunkeles Sinngrün' (l. 12-13). Here the metre and rhythm of a near-hexameter is utilised to bring out both the possessives 'unser' but also the images of evergreen growth — with a hidden touch in that 'Sinngrün' that needs a brief gloss. For one might read 'Sinngrün' as a bold compound metaphor, playing on 'Sinn' as sense, or even on the verb 'sinnen', contemplation or reflection. That association would be legitimate. Yet 'Sinngrün' or 'Singrün' (from 'sin-', long past, long ago) is the plant that in German is also called 'Wintergrün' or 'Immergrün', that grows on the graves of the dead — and in English is the humble periwinkle, vinca minor. It is also one of the magic plants[9] that remind us of the primitive links between divination and poetry. Not only that: grief and sorrow are part of the 'inner year' of human experience, that is 'heimlich' (l. 14), both familiar (related to 'homely') and secret or hidden. And from the botanical, Rilke switches images to ones (six in all) of human habitation, the 'Wohnort' (l. 15) the 'Sitz im Leben', where we dwell, keeping the double association that we have in English for the word 'dwell', for both the physical necessities of existence and for the inner life. Both 'Sinngrün' and 'Wohnort' are, metrically speaking, spondees, a feature of this elegy, with their equal stress on both syllables. In this they are quite different from the distichs of German classical verse, where the Greek or Latin spondee is normally rendered by a trochee. Thus many of the key words of the poem, the most elegiac of the cycle, have a stately accentuation in both sense and sound ('Leid-Stadt', 'Leidland', 'Ur-Leid').

Freilich, wehe, wie fremd sind die Gassen der Leid-Stadt,
wo in der falschen, aus Übertönung gemachten
Stille, stark, aus der Gußform des Leeren der Ausguß
prahlt: der vergoldete Lärm, das platzende Denkmal.
O, wie spurlos zerträte ein Engel ihnen der Trostmarkt,
den die Kirche begrenzt, ihre fertig gekaufte:
reinlich und zu und enttäuscht wie ein Postamt am Sonntag.
Draußen aber kräuseln sich immer die Ränder von Jahrmarkt.
Schaukeln der Freiheit! Taucher und Gaukler des Eifers!
Und des behübschten Glücks figürliche Schießstatt,
wo es zappelt von Ziel und sich blechern benimmt,
wenn ein Geschickterer trifft. Von Beifall zu Zufall
taumelt er weiter; denn Buden jeglicher Neugier
werben, trommeln und plärrn. Für Erwachsene aber
ist noch besonders zu sehn, wie das Geld sich vermehrt, anatomisch,
nicht zur Belustigung nur: der Geschlechtsteil des Gelds,
alles, das Ganze, der Vorgang —, das unterrichtet und macht
fruchtbar.........

Alas, though, how alien the streets of Grief City,
where in the counterfeit silence, made of a surfeit of noise,
blatantly struts the form that is cast in the mould
of emptiness: the tinselly din, the statue burst open.
O, how an angel would trample to nothing their Cure-All Fair,
with the church hard by, the one bought to order:
tidy and shut and forlorn like the Post on a Sunday.
But outside curl around still the amusement park's edges.
Swings of Freedom! Acrobats of Enthusiasm!
And prettified happiness' shooting gallery, befigured,
targets all jostling , each jangling the other,
when a good marksman scores. From claps to chance-taking
on his way then he lurches; for sideshows are there for the curious,
their barkers hailing and drumming. Adults Only!
Special attraction! The reproduction of money (anatomical details),
not just for amusement: money's organs of gender,
the whole lot, nothing left out —, what they get up to — a lesson and
brings you results ....

The poem now breaks off abruptly from the fifteen verses that came to Rilke in 1912. He had drafted quite a different continuation in 1913 (DE, I, 90f., SW, III, 64ff.), with a sustained nature image following on from 'winterwähriges Laubwerk' (the 1913 variant of 'Sinngrün'). In 1922, however, nature was first to be alienated before being given a function in the wider scheme of the poem. That disjunction comes also in the marked and abrupt incongruity of 'alas, though' the fairly colloquial 'Freilich' (l. 16) and the high-style 'wehe', the elegiac word that runs through the whole cycle. From nature's cycle, and a secure place of dwelling, we move to the 'Leid-Stadt', a place where there is no dwelling, and a long, sustained catalogue of all that is cheap and counterfeit and vulgar. This city of grief, this Pandaemonium, has two aspects. First, there is a section where the very strident awfulness produces a paradoxical kind of silence, a failure to say ('aus Übertönung gemachte Stille' l. 17f.), where words like 'Lärm', 'prahlt' and 'vergoldet' set the tone. Note 'der vergoldete Lärm', like 'sich blechern benimmt' lower down, with their bold transference of senses, as if the poet in his outrage cannot find the connecting links of meaning. Is it a real city, like one of those 'Plätze in Paris' from Elegy Five where Madame Lamort holds sway? Certainly the drumming and general commotion is the same. Or is it, as some commentators have suggested (Gadamer, Guardini) actually the city graveyard, the necropolis, with its false pomp, a living proof of how outwardness has triumphed over inwardness, of how even the church — in Rilke's fierce joke ('wie ein Postamt am Sonntag') — forms one of the sides of the 'Trostmarkt' (l. 20) and is thus taken over by commerce and brokerage. The angels — the last time, incidentally, that we encounter them in the cycle and here in a kind of apocalyptic or eschatological role — not knowing any distinction between the inner and the outer life, would crush this under foot, without trace, recalling Expressionist images like Ludwig Meidner's imploding cities or Georg Heym's visions of destruction. But already we hear the sounds of 'roll up, all the fun of the fair!' In Elegy Nine, human achievement was measured in terms of the craftsman's art. Here, everything is dominated by frauds, mountebanks and hucksters. Rilke's Vanity Fair takes us from sideshows of 'Freedom!' to 'Enthusiasm!' to 'Glück!' The images become jangled and kaleidoscopically jumbled as the things to be won in the shooting-galleries, and the shooters themselves, change sides, as it were (the jumping for joy of the marksman is transferred to the targets and prizes themselves). But 'you haven't seen anything yet'. Adults Only, anatomical waxwork displays that lay bare, with the lovelessness of the sexologist's manual, the sex-act of money, money that makes this world go round. If, as I suggested, this prophetic wrath reminds us of the Expressionists' visions of destruction, their clean sweep through material values, it is also where Rilke comes closest to *The Waste Land*. Yet we should not forget that, all along, he has not abandoned his approximation to classical elegiac verse, and in l. 34 that tone begins to reassert itself.

....Oh aber gleich darüber hinaus,
hinter der letzten Planke, beklebt mit Plakaten des »Todlos«,
jenes bitteren Biers, das den Trinkenden süß scheint,
wenn sie immer dazu frische Zerstreuungen kaun...,
gleich im Rücken der Planke, gleich dahinter, ists ***wirklich****.*
Kinder spielen, und Liebende halten einander, — abseits,
ernst, im ärmlichen Gras, und Hunde haben Natur.
Weiter noch zieht es den Jüngling; vielleicht, daß er eine junge
Klage liebt..... Hinter ihr her kommt er in Wiesen. Sie sagt:
— Weit. Wir wohnen dort draußen.....
Wo? Und der Jüngling
folgt. Ihn rührt ihre Haltung. Die Schulter, der Hals —, vielleicht
ist sie von herrlicher Herkunft. Aber er läßt sie, kehrt um,
wendet sich, winkt... Was solls? Sie ist eine Klage.

....O but further beyond,
past the last billboards, stuck over with posters for 'Deathless',
that bitter beer that seems sweet to the drinkers
only as long as they chew fresh distractions to go with it....
Past the boards, just beyond, there, things are real.
Children are playing, lovers embracing, — away from the others,
pensive, on a few blades of grass, and dogs — do as dogs do.
The boy is drawn further on; perhaps he's in love with a young
Lament. And he follows after her over the meadows. She says:
-- Far. We live away out there.
Where? And the boy
follows, touched by her walk, her shoulder, her neck —, perhaps
she's of noble descent. But he leaves her, turns round,
about once again, waves ... What's the point? She's a Lament,

But, ('Oh, aber') outside, beyond the last paling fence, there is the first vestige of reality ('*wirklich*', Rilke's italics). Note the fences plastered with advertisements for that 'unreal' ale 'Todlos' (l. 35), for the denial of death is, in the terms of this elegy, a denial of any meaningful existence. But how real, despite the underlining of '*wirklich*', is this bleak space outside the city? At most we could say that here there is some freedom — for children, lovers, and dogs — some demonstration of feeling, but it isn't much. But it is also a final glance, almost over our shoulders, at three of the important strands and symbolic figures in the landscape of the whole cycle: children, imperilled in their innocence by death; lovers, who so seldom achieve a true meeting of souls; and animals, who do not share our sense of death.

Although there is no break in the poetry, in that Rilke does not introduce a space such as he will do later on, the poetry now enters a new sphere. It leaves for good that world where all is counterfeit or half-fulfilled. But before we enter into the new realm, we the readers should not forget with what poetic virtuosity Rilke has castigated that false and tinselly world, keeping a kind of prophetic anger sustained in the long near-distichs and displaying his full powers of virtuosity in the images of city and funfair. This is one side of the lament that this poem entails, the lamentation over the great city.

But now we have '*den* Jüngling' (my italics), unprepared, presumably one of the young people or lovers, for whom the few blades of grass provided a place for their feelings. As in the great set-piece dream sequences in Romantic novels (and as in dreams themselves), the transition into another sphere of consciousness is imperceptible, It would seem that the realm of 'Klage' is but an extension of the so-called 'real' world. We must forget the reminiscences of Homer or Virgil or Dante — or even of Rilke's two great poems *Orpheus. Eurydike. Hermes* and *Alkestis*. For here there is no descent into the shades, no passing through waters. And yet for all that we seem to be in some kind of transitional realm between the city of suffering and the finality of death. Here live 'Klagen', the expression and manifestation of pain both suffered and articulated. But in this space, their country, there is paradoxically more light and beauty than in the city that has been left behind. The boy, who follows the 'Klage', is presumably still alive, not yet ready to reflect on the ultimate futility of existence in the 'Leid-Stadt', and certainly not yet ready to engage in a dialogue. He turns back ('Was solls').

Nur die jungen Toten, im ersten Zustand
zeitlosen Gleichmuts, dem der Entwöhnung,
folgen ihr liebend. Mädchen
wartet sie ab und befreundet sie. Zeigt ihnen leise,
was sie an sich hat. Perlen des Leids und die feinen
Schleier der Duldung. — Mit Jünglingen geht sie
schweigend.

Only the young dead, unheeding,
untouched by time, taking slow leave of life,
follow her, loving. The girls
she waits for and offers them friendship. Shows them gently
what she is wearing. Pearls of Sorrow and the fine-woven
veils of Forbearance. — With boys she walks
in silence alongside them.

Only the young dead have this capacity, as they start their journey towards the land of silence. We have to ask ourselves a question at the outset of this journey. Leaving aside any notion of allegory, is 'Klage', the articulation of grief, its poetic expression even, that which accompanies the dead until they are, in the real sense, fully dead? For at the end of the journey there can be no sound, all is 'tonlos' (l. 106). The passage from life to death is made clear by the words 'ersten Zustand' and 'Entwöhnung' (l. 47f.): the Lament instructs and takes under her wing the young dead and shows them things that life knew little of, 'Duldung und Leid' (l. 49f.) as garments of beauty. We note in passing that it is the young maidens among the dead who are initiated into these secrets, an extension of those 'Frühentrückten' of Elegy One who no longer need us, the living. But it is in fact the boy who is led by an older Lament into the land of the dead. She tells him — and us — of the landscape and history, the reality of expressed suffering, in a sequence of poetry that, appropriately, is remarkable for its expansion of line and its sonority and dignity.

Aber dort, wo sie wohnen, im Tal, der Älteren eine, der Klagen,
nimmt sich des Jünglinges an, wenn er fragt: — Wir waren,
sagt sie, ein Großes Geschlecht, einmal, wir Klagen. Die Väter
trieben den Bergbau dort in dem großen Gebirg; bei Menschen
findest du manchmal ein Stück geschliffenes Ur-Leid
oder, aus altem Vulkan, schlackig versteinerten Zorn.
Ja, das stammte von dort. Einst waren wir reich. —

But there, where they live, in the valley, one of the older Laments
answers kindly the boy as he asks: —We were,
she says, a Mighty Nation, once, we Laments. Our fathers
dug out the mines there in the high range of mountains; men
sometimes will show you an ancient fragment of Suffering, polished,
or, out of a crater, Wrath, molten, rock-hardened.
Yes, we took it from there. Once we were rich. —

This world of the Laments we must sketch briefly. It is a *real* and also a *mythical* landscape. It reflects a hierarchical order in the affairs of men and in nature, where all the elements shown and explained to the boy are extensions of the rites surrounding the dead. These are the Laments that were once part of the rites of passage and departure. Rilke describes them in his *Requiem. Für eine Freundin* (1908) as 'Klagefrauen', whose duty is 'Klagen nachholen' (SW I, 653), serving the function we know in all cultures, from the Celts to the Polynesians, to keen the dirges in the elaborate and circumstantial channelling of grief into an accessible ritual. This, as the older Klage explains, was what once ruled this country: 'Wir waren, /sagt sie, ein Großes Geschlecht, einmal, wir Klagen' (l. 56f.) Where once there was delving and digging of the passions, the bringing up out of the depths of 'Ur-Leid' and 'Zorn' — those familiar with German Romanticism will recognize the potent symbols of mining as self-discovery[10] — we have archaeology. Now, there are just a few pyroclastic fragments, and silence (the loss of that 'aufsingen' in lament).

Und sie leitet ihn leicht durch die weite Landschaft der Klagen,
zeigt ihm die Säulen der Tempel oder die Trümmer
jener Burgen, von wo Klage-Fürsten das Land

einstens weise beherrscht. Zeigt ihm die hohen
Tränenbäume und Felder blühender Wehmut,
(Lebendige kennen sie nur als sanftes Blattwerk);
zeigt ihm die Tiere der Trauer, weidend, — und manchmal
schreckt ein Vogel und zieht, flach ihnen fliegend durchs Aufschaun,
weithin das schriftliche Bild seines vereinsamten Schreis. —
Abends führt sie ihn hin zu den Gräbern der Alten
aus dem Klage-Geschlecht, den Sibyllen und Warn-Herrn.
Naht aber Nacht, so wandeln sie leiser, und bald
mondets empor, das über Alles
wachende Grab-Mal. Brüderlich jenem am Nil,
der erhabene Sphinx —: der verschwiegenen Kammer
Antlitz.
Und sie staunen dem krönlichen Haupt, das für immer,
schweigend, der Menschen Gesicht
auf die Waage der Sterne gelegt.

And with ease she guides him through the Laments' wide expanses,
shows him the columns of temples or the ruins of
fortresses, where the Laments' princes
once held wise sway. Shows him the tall
tear-trees and fields of Doleful in blossom
(known to the living only when it's still in first leaf);
shows him the creatures of sadness, grazing — sometimes
a bird starts, and unfolds, flying low as they gaze upwards,
the pattern of letters made by her cry in the loneness . —
At evening she leads him to the tombs of the patriarchs
of the race of Laments, the sybils and sages.
At nightfall their footstep is softer, and shortly,
bright as the moonlight, looms up
the tomb standing watch over all,
brother to that on the Nile, the lofty Sphinx:
face of the chamber hidden in silence.
And they take in with wonder the regal-crowned head, that forever,
not speaking, laid the face of man
on the scales of the stars.

But the landscape also informs of a once wise order and rule — 'einstens' (l. 65) — now represented by a kind of Baalbek or Palmyra. The land itself, is, however, still fertile with plants and herds, unlike the counterfeit and sterile 'Trostmarkt' and 'Leid-Stadt' that now seems so far behind. Note that 'Wehmut' — I have rendered it as Doleful — thrives here and flowers; here the ever-green, the symbol and emblem of mourning, actually bursts into flower. We hear, too, from l. 62 onwards, how the verse sustains this account by assonating the many 'ei-' sounds: 'Und sie l*ei*tet ihn l*ei*cht durch die w*ei*te Landschaft der Klagen', '*ei*nstens w*ei*se beherrscht. Z*ei*gt ihm die hohen'.

Two words stand out in the account that follows: 'Aufschaun' (l. 69) and 'Schaun' (l. 82). They, and the word 'zeigen' (l. 62,64) that recurs in the poem's colophon (l. 107), indicate a strand of seeing and showing and signifying and indicating that is part of the elegiac process, part of the 'aufsingen'. But it is also the sign of a set of extraordinary poetic images that signify not just the poetic way of seeing, but the enhanced vision that is granted to the dead and which (in the final image of the poem),were they able, they would grant to us. Thus the bird (l. 68f.) that suddenly starts up before our eyes transfers the sound of its cry to a set of written characters; the optical and the aural are no longer in separate compartments of perception. So, too, with the image of the sphinx (76f.) and the owl.

We have one or two details to clear up before we attempt that image. It is night (note that wonderfully Hölderlinian 'mondets empor' l. 73); we are led down to the figures of the doubly dead, who are dead in the realm of death and exist only as monuments to the dead. It isn't Egypt, but clearly we are in a valley of tombs where a culture similar to Egypt's once held sway (DE, I, 322), and we remember that no other culture gives death a greater significance in its cosmogony. From now on, only the moon and the stars shine down on the land of the dead. The bold verb 'mondets empor' expresses the effect of seeing the most majestic death monument of all, in the moonlight: the sphinx — 'erhaben', 'krönlich', the lord of all being in this land, where 'Klage' has its supreme place in the hierarchy of emotions. The sphinx contains a burial chamber which is hidden and inaccessible but which through 'Schaun' can be seen on the face of the sphinx, and that face, expressing human features, has taken on such a significance that it has, in Rilke's image (l. 77f), been placed on the balances of the stars (a double meaning, 'Waage' denoting a pair of scales and also Libra), has become like Orion or Castor and Pollux, a named constellation. And the scales of the stars might be taken to signify the equipoise and harmony between life and death that is achieved in this sphere between the two states.

Nicht erfaßt es sein Blick, im Frühtod
schwindelnd. Aber ihr Schaun,
hinter dem Pschent-Rand hervor, scheucht es die Eule. Und sie,
streifend im langsamen Abstrich die Wange entlang,
jene der reifesten Rundung,

zeichnet weich in das neue
Totengehör, über ein doppelt
aufgeschlagenes Blatt, den unbeschreiblichen Umriß.

His gaze cannot grasp it, so early dead,
unsteady. But their beholding,
over the top of the diadem, scares out the owl. It,
slow in its flying, barely touching the cheek,
where it rounds at its fullest,
softly it draws into the new
dead's hearing, on both halves of the paper,
folded in two, the outline that hand cannot trace.

The boy, newly dead, cannot take in the awesomeness of this monument. But 'ihr Schaun' (her looking or their looking — it could be both, l. 82) brings out from behind the 'Pschent' — a grandly exotic word for the crown of Upper and Lower Egypt — an owl. Rilke in 1911, lying in the moonlight in front of the sphinx, had seen just this (DE, I, 97). The newly dead — and by implication we who mourn the young dead — need some idea of the dimension of this state, through 'Schaun'. The owl flies along the cheek of the sphinx, the finest contour ('die reifeste Rundung') into which the human face has been formed; it traces in the ear of the dead that contour, records it acoustically 'über ein doppelt aufgeschlagenes Blatt' (l. 87). As if taking a sheet of paper and folding it double to indicate the two sides, the owl, non-articulate, but tracing with its wing, and the ear, receiving the written character with the new 'Totengehör' (l. 87), make clear that our senses in death extend beyond any earthly physical capacity.

Und höher, die Sterne. Neue. Die Sterne des Leidlands.
Langsam nennt sie die Klage: — Hier,
siehe: den ***Reiter****, den* ***Stab****, und das vollere Sternbild*
nennen sie: ***Fruchtkranz****. Dann, weiter, dem Pol zu:*
Wiege; Weg; Das Brennende Buch; Puppe; Fenster.
Aber im südlichen Himmel, rein wie im Innern
*einer gesegneten Hand, das klar erglänzende »****M****«,*
das die Mütter bedeutet......—

Doch der Tote muß fort, und schweigend bringt ihn die ältere
Klage bis an die Talschlucht,
wo es schimmert im Mondschein:
die Quelle der Freude. In Ehrfurcht
nennt sie sie, sagt: — Bei den Menschen
ist sie ein tragender Strom. —

And higher, the stars. New ones. The stars of the Land of Suffering.
The Lament names them slowly: — Here,
*behold: the **Rider**, the **Staff**, and the cluster of stars*
*they call **Garland of Fruits**. Then further on, nearer the **Pole**:*
***Cradle; Path; The Burning Book; Puppet; Window**.*
But in the southern skies, pure like the palm of a
*hand that is blessed, '**M**' burning clearly and brightly,*
standing for Mothers......—

But the dead boy must depart, and in silence the older
Lament brings him as far as the gorge of the valley,
where there gleams in the moonlight
the spring of joy. In hushed tone
she names it and says: — Among men
it is a mighty river. —

And so the Lament now shows the boy the constellations in the heavens. They are all to be taken as symbols of different processes of transition ('Wiege', 'Weg', 'Stab', 'Reiter') or of fruition and achievement ('Fruchtkranz'), of vision beyond oneself ('Fenster'), of hope and renewal ('Puppe', both in the sense of Elegy Four and in the meaning of chrysalis). Horses and riders in the stars fascinated him in other contexts ('Heißt kein Sternbild »*Reiter*?«' ask the *Sonette an Orpheus* I, xi, and a late poem of 1924 likens falling stars to horses, SW, I, 737). The burning book might seem to be *the* poetic icon, in the German one letter away from the burning bush ('not consumed'), giving light and being incandescent in itself. Rilke is, of course, playing on existing names of constellations, like 'Puppis', or stars, like 'Vega' ('Wega' in German), adding a few of his own, equally concrete and exotic. They culminate in that '*M*', lighting up the whole of the southern sky, a good luck sign in palmistry, but reminding us that mothers, in the terms of these elegies (especially Elegy Six), are also destined to lose what they have borne. Speech now has no further function — 'schweigend' l. 96 — as the Lament brings the boy through the last stages of his journey towards silence. She has imparted her wisdom to him — and in a sense the poet, through the poetic act, is imparting it to those who mourn the young dead. The mourning learn that the dead have the 'sense' of their dying explained to them in the wisdom of the 'Klagekulturen' that are unfolded before them (not, we note, through a theogony that makes of death a mystery or a terror). The 'Quelle der Freude' (l. 99) suggests perhaps that there is an inner link between grief and joy; it is that which may spring up again in those who are left behind 'bei den Menschen' (l. 100) in mourning.

Stehn am Fuß des Gebirgs.
Und da umarmt sie ihn, weinend.

Einsam steigt er dahin, in die Berge der Ur-Leids.
Und nicht einmal sein Schritt klingt aus dem tonlosen Los.

*

They halt at the foot of the mountains.
And there she embraces him, weeping.

Alone he makes his way up into the mountains of Once-Suffering.
Not even the ring of his steps is heard, his lot is silence.

*

The poetry becomes more laconic and poignant as the language of lament gives way to silence: 'stehn am Fuß des Gebirgs' (l. 103), 'da umarmt sie ihn' (l. 104), 'Einsam steigt er dahin' (l. 105). We learn nothing of the nature of the 'Ur-Leid' (l. 105); only he will experience that in the loneliness of death. He is no longer accessible to lament or even language. When laments are silent, when the 'Klage' is no longer with the young dead, he is dead in the sense that he belongs to those whose loss we can now bear, or to those who we know are in the land of silence and forgetfulness ('das tonlose Los' of l. 105).

Aber erweckten sie uns, die unendlich Toten, ein Gleichnis,
siehe, sie zeigten vielleicht auf die Kätzchen der leeren
Hasel, die hängenden, oder
meinten den Regen, der fällt auf dunkles Erdreich im Frühjahr. —

Und wir, die an ***steigendes*** *Glück*
denken, empfänden die Rührung,
die uns beinah bestürzt,
wenn ein Glückliches ***fällt.***

But were they to waken for us, the endlessly dead, a symbol,
behold, they would point to the catkins on the bare
hazel, hanging downwards, or
have us believe in the rain that falls on the dark soil in springtime. —

And we, who think of happiness
rising, our hearts would be moved
more than perhaps we could bear,
when a happy thing falls.

There Rilke will not leave us, in total silence, with no words, no sound. We come back to that 'would that', 'would but' of the elegy's opening that told us what, but for our inadequacy, would be the true purpose and function of the poetic act. They, 'die unendlich Toten' (l. 107), are beyond articulation, but were they able, they would give us this likeness. It is a double image, one of the hanging catkins on the hazel bush, and of the spring rain on the ground ('Erdreich' l. 110 suggesting perhaps already dug for cultivation). Rilke was not always secure in his botany, despite the many flower and plant images in his poetry, not least in this cycle. The conceit of the fig tree in Elegy Six is not encouraging. In fact, Rilke orginally wanted the willow catkin to express the image of hanging and falling (DE, I, 269), but, as anyone knows, it does not hang down. The alteration is significant, not just for getting the facts right, but for assuring the integrity of the text, for the 'Ding' must be congruent if it is also to be charged with meaning. Botany aside, and Rilke's intention with the image aside, we note that he has chanced on an image that may go beyond his original first association: the hanging catkins of the male flower. But then it is unlikely that he 'chanced' on anything. These flowers are in themselves not fertile, they cannot produce fruit on their own, but they are the promise of it. Similarly, the rain is not the fertility itself, but it brings about the process of fruition and plenitude. Was he thinking of the hazel's other associations, as one of the first of the bushes of the hedgerows to show blossom? It is a magic plant,[11] revered in many religions, but notably the Germanic, and for that reason it is the twig used for the water-diviner's rod. The German for that rod is 'Wünschelrute', itself the title of one of the shortest, but most telling poems in the language, informing of the power of poetry to open up the secrets of the things around us, 'die Dinge'. It is Eichendorff's little poem:

Schläft ein Lied in allen Dingen,
Die da träumen fort und fort,
Und die Welt hebt an zu singen,
Triffst du nur das Zauberwort.[12]

The catkin and the rain, which fall, are the symbols of this final colophon of verses. But does not hope *spring* eternal in the human breast, does not our heart *leap* up when we behold, and is this poem not prefaced with the poet's action upwards in that verb '*auf*singen'? No, we experience 'Rührung' (l. 113), implying being touched by the emotions, — to our surprise ('Bestürzung' l. 114) — when hopes of happiness are dashed, when, in the terms of the poem, a young life is unfulfilled; but we come by the same token to the realisation that the so-called unfulfilled life may have its own happiness. That is perhaps one aspect. The other is the awareness that the sadness produced by falling is overcome in the hope of life that emerges from it. Rilke himself claimed that this should not be taken to imply a cyclical movement, some kind of mere biological organic process[13]; instead, the gesture of falling in itself brings happiness. We might, however, feel justified in setting his view aside. There is the evidence of another poem, from the year 1922, with the same imagery, where rain and earth, respectively, represent the processes of death and mourning (DE, I, 218). And the elegies urge us to a resolution by the very fact of their being a cycle, but not to any easy or mundane conclusion, neatly tied up and of an easy consistency for all readers. Instead, there is the awareness that poetry mediates, but in an interreaction of language and symbol that is never direct. We search therefore for indications of resolution, perhaps in terms of that 'Quelle der Freude' (l. 100) that the Lament mentions in awe ('in Ehrfurcht'). But it can be no coincidence that both the poem and the whole cycle end on the word '*fällt*' (Rilke's italics). The elegiac verse can also be read in a way that is different from the printed image, where the lines tail off into a colophon (and a colophon was originally the printer's signature; here it is the poet's). Run the third-last and the fourth-last lines together and the last two, and you will find a couplet that bears some resemblance to the elegiac distich (it's actually closer to two pentameters). Any correctly turned distich will end on a strong beat — it has to — but only the great elegy will end on a strong beat *and* a word that sums up the whole of what has gone before. Hölderlin's *Brod und Wein*, that some might see as the very greatest elegy in the language, does it with the final word 'schläft'. Rilke's, certainly one of the greatest, achieves it with the word '*fällt*'.

---

1 See Rainer Maria Rilke, *Gedichte an die Nacht*. Auswahl und Nachwort von Anthony Stephens, Bibliothek Suhrkamp, 519 (Frankfurt am Main, 1957).

2 Cf. the catalogue *Europäische Kunst 1912. Zum 50. Jahrestag der Aus-*

---

stellung des 'Sonderbundes westdeutscher Kunstfreunde und Künstler in Köln'. Wallraf-Richartz-Museum (Cologne, 1962).

3 Cf. *Engel. Texte aus der Weltliteratur*, ed. Anne Marie Fröhlich, Manesse Bibliothek der Weltliteratur (Zurich, 1991).

4 Hölderlin, *Sämtliche Werke*. Historisch-kritische Ausgabe, ed. Norbert von Hellingrath, assist. Friedrich Seebass and Ludwig von Pigenot, 6 vols (Berlin, 1913-23).

5 Ludwig Feuerbach, *Todesgedanken*, in *Sämmtliche Werke*, ed. Wilhelm Bolin and Friedrich Jodl, 10 vols (Stuttgart, 1903-11), I, 20. '[Der Tod] ist nur die Erscheinung des Actes des inneren Ablösens, Trennens und Scheidens, die Bewahrheitung Deiner Liebe, die Verkündigung, die Du während Deines ganzen Lebens im Stillen bethätigt hast, dass Du ohne und ausser dem geliebten Gegenstand Nichts bist'.

6 Sigmund Freud, 'Unser Verhältnis zum Tode', in *Zeitgemäßes über Krieg und Tod, Studienausgabe* (Frankfurt/Main, 1969-79), X, 344

7 Brian McGuinness, *Wittgenstein: A Life. Young Ludwig, 1889-1921* (London, 1988), p.158.

8 Charles Tomlinson, *Poetry and Metamorphosis* (Cambridge, 1983).

9 *Handwörterbuch des deutschen Aberglaubens*, ed. E. Hoffmann-Kray, assist. Hanns Bächtold-Stäuble, 10 vols (Berlin and Leipzig, 1927-42), IV, 673-6; Robert Graves, *The White Goddess. A Historical Grammar of Poetic Myth* (London, 1981), p.323.

10 Thedore Ziolkowski, *German Romanticism and Its Institutions* (Princeton, 1990), pp.18-63.

11 *Handwörterbuch des deutschen Aberglaubens* (as in note 9), III,1527-42.

12 Joseph von Eichendorff, *Neue Gesamtausgabe der Werke und Schriften*, ed. Gerhard Baumann and Siegfried Grosse, 4 vols. (Stuttgart, 1957), I, 112.

13 According to Katharina Kippenberg. Rainer Maria Rilke, *Duineser Elegien. Die Sonette an Orpheus*. Mit den Erläuterungen von Katharina Kippenberg, Manesse Bibliothek der Weltliteratur (Zurich, 1951), p.172. Thus Rilke would seem to stand in marked contrast to the thinking of Wilhelm Fliess, with whose views on life and death he was familiar (DE, I, 137f.). Cf. 'Der Tod schafft nach einer bewundernswürdigen Ordnung Raum für das erwachende Leben'. Wilhelm Fliess, *Vom Leben und vom Tod. Biologische Vorträge* (Jena, 1924), p. 93.

DUINESER ELEGIEN

AUS DEM BESITZ DER FÜRSTIN
MARIE VON THURN UND TAXIS-HOHENLOHE

DUINO ELEGIES

THE PROPERTY OF PRINCESS
MARIE VON THURN UND TAXIS-HOHENLOHE

DIE ERSTE ELEGIE

WER, wenn ich schriee, hörte mich denn aus der Engel
Ordnungen? und gesetzt selbst, es nähme
einer mich plötzlich ans Herz: ich verginge von seinem
stärkeren Dasein. Denn das Schöne ist nichts
als des Schrecklichen Anfang, den wir noch grade ertragen,
und wir bewundern es so, weil es gelassen verschmäht,
uns zu zerstören. Ein jeder Engel ist schrecklich.
Und so verhalt ich mich denn und verschlucke den Lockruf
dunkelen Schluchzens. Ach, wen vermögen
wir denn zu brauchen? Engel nicht, Menschen nicht,
und die findigen Tiere merken es schon,
daß wir nicht sehr verläßlich zu Haus sind
in der gedeuteten Welt. Es bleibt uns vielleicht
irgend ein Baum an dem Abhang, daß wir ihn täglich
wiedersähen; es bleibt uns die Straße von gestern
und das verzogene Treusein einer Gewohnheit,
der es bei uns gefiel, und so blieb sie und ging nicht.
O und die Nacht, die Nacht, wenn der Wind voller Weltraum
uns am Angesicht zehrt —, wem bliebe sie nicht, die ersehnte,
sanft enttäuschende, welche dem einzelnen Herzen
mühsam bevorsteht. Ist sie den Liebenden leichter?
ach, sie verdecken sich nur mit einander ihr Los.
Weißt du's *noch* nicht? Wirf aus den Armen die Leere
zu den Räumen hinzu, die wir atmen; vielleicht daß die Vögel
die erweiterte Luft fühlen mit innigerm Flug.

Ja, die Frühlinge brauchten dich wohl. Es muteten manche
Sterne dir zu, daß du sie spürtest. Es hob
sich eine Woge heran im Vergangenen, oder
da du vorüberkamst am geöffneten Fenster,
gab eine Geige sich hin. Das alles war Auftrag.
Aber bewältigtest du's? Warst du nicht immer
noch von Erwartung zerstreut, als kündigte alles
eine Geliebte dir an? (Wo willst du sie bergen,
da doch die großen fremden Gedanken bei dir
aus und ein gehn und öfters bleiben bei Nacht.)
Sehnt es dich aber, so singe die Liebenden; lange
noch nicht unsterblich genug ist ihr berühmtes Gefühl.
Jene, du neidest sie fast, Verlassenen, die du
so viel liebender fandst als die Gestillten. Beginn
immer von neuem die nie zu erreichende Preisung;
denk: es erhält sich der Held, selbst der Untergang war ihm
nur ein Vorwand, zu sein: seine letzte Geburt.

THE FIRST ELEGY

WHO, if I cried out, would hear me among the ranks
of the angels? and even if one of them suddenly
clasped me to his heart, I should die of his
stronger being. For beauty is nothing
but the very beginning of terror we're only just able to bear,
and its wonder for us is that it casually spares us
instead of destroying. Each one of the angels is terrible.
And so I hold back, stifle the luring-call
of my dark sobbing. Alas, who then is left
we can ask for help? Not angels, not people,
and the quick-witted animals knew long ago
that we are not quite securely at home
in the interpreted world. Perhaps all we have
is some tree on a slope, one that we see every day,
or yesterday's street where we walked,
and the spoilt faithfulness of a habit
that liked being with us, stayed on and never left.
O and the night, the night, when the wind, swelled with cosmic space,
comes to devour our faces — night is there for us all, longed for
and gently disappointing, and for the lonely heart
a travail always in prospect. Is night easier for lovers?
each is only a shield for the other to hide from their fate.
Haven't you, even yet, learned this? Throw that emptiness out of your arms
out to the spaces we breathe; it may be the birds
will feel the air widened, and fly with more grace.

Yes, Spring has needed you. And many a star
meant you to notice its presence. Towards you
a wave rose up from a long-ago sea, or
out of an open window as you went by
a violin made its surrender. All this was a task laid upon you.
But did you perform it? Were you not always
distracted, expecting it all to announce
new love, a new sweetheart? (And where could you keep her,
when you know you have all those great strange thoughts
constantly coming and going and quite often staying the night.)
But, if this is your longing, then sing of the lovers; there's need
to make the fame of their feeling much more undying.
Those you have envied, or almost; the forsaken, those
you thought had so much more love than the happy. Begin
again and again the praise that can never be perfect;
think: the hero lives on, even his death was for him
only a pretext for life: his last birth.

Aber die Liebenden nimmt die erschöpfte Natur
in sich zurück, als wären nicht zweimal die Kräfte,
dieses zu leisten. Hast du der Gaspara Stampa
denn genügend gedacht, daß irgend ein Mädchen,
dem der Geliebte entging, am gesteigerten Beispiel
dieser Liebenden fühlt: daß ich würde wie sie?
Sollen nicht endlich uns diese ältesten Schmerzen
fruchtbarer werden? Ist es nicht Zeit, daß wir liebend
uns vom Geliebten befrein und es bebend bestehn :
wie der Pfeil die Sehne besteht, um gesammelt im Absprung
mehr zu sein als er selbst. Denn Bleiben ist nirgends.

Stimmen, Stimmen. Höre, mein Herz, wie sonst nur
Heilige hörten: daß sie der riesige Ruf
aufhob vom Boden; sie aber knieten,
Unmögliche, weiter und achtetens nicht:
So waren sie hörend. Nicht, das du *Gottes* ertrügest
die Stimme, bei weitem. Aber das Wehende höre,
die ununterbrochene Nachricht, die aus Stille sich bildet.
Es rauscht jetzt von jenen jungen Toten zu dir.
Wo immer du eintratst, redete nicht in Kirchen
zu Rom und Neapel ruhig ihr Schicksal dich an?
Oder es trug eine Inschrift sich erhaben dir auf,
wie neulich die Tafel in Santa Maria Formosa.
Was sie mir wollen? leise soll ich des Unrechts
Anschein abtun, der ihrer Geister
reine Bewegung manchmal ein wenig behindert.

Freilich ist es seltsam, die Erde nicht mehr zu bewohnen,
kaum erlernte Gebräuche nicht mehr zu üben,
Rosen, und andern eigens versprechenden Dingen
nicht die Bedeutung menschlicher Zukunft zu geben;
das, was man war in unendlich ängstlichen Händen,
nicht mehr zu sein, und selbst den eigenen Namen
wegzulassen wie ein zerbrochenes Spielzeug.
Seltsam, die Wünsche nicht weiterzuwünschen. Seltsam,
alles, was sich bezog, so lose im Raume
flattern zu sehen. Und das Totsein ist mühsam
und voller Nachholn, daß man allmählich ein wenig
Ewigkeit spürt. — Aber Lebendige machen
alle den Fehler, daß sie zu stark unterscheiden.
Engel (sagt man) wüßten oft nicht, ob sie unter
Lebenden gehn oder Toten. Die ewige Strömung
reißt durch beide Bereiche alle Alter
immer mit sich und übertönt sie in beiden.

But Nature, exhausted, takes lovers back into herself
as if she hadn't the strength to bring forth more than once
that creation. Have you given your thoughts
to Gaspara Stampa enough — and how any young girl
who is left by her lover, may think of that grander example
and say: let me be as she was?
Shouldn't these oldest of sufferings
be more of use to us now? Isn't it time that in love
we learned to be free of our lover and, trembling, endure it,
as the arrow endures the bowstring, and then, centred for flight
becomes *more* than itself. For there's no standing still.

Voices, voices. Listen, my heart, as, till now,
only saints listened: so that the thundering summons
raised them up from the ground; but they stayed in their kneeling position
impossibly, kneeling in air, and oblivious:
that's how they listened. Not that you would be able to bear
the voice of God. But hear on the whispering air
the news that the silence creates, never ceasing.
Now the faint sound comes from the young dead to your ears.
Wherever you entered a church, did you not hear
in Rome or in Naples, the soft voice of their destiny speaking to you?
Or an inscription stood proud in your sight
like that tablet just lately in Santa Maria Formosa.
What do they want of me? That I should efface the seeming injustice
Whose traces make heavy, at times,
their spirits' lightness of movement.

True, it is strange not to inhabit the earth any more
no longer to practice the customs so lately acquired,
not to perceive, in roses and other things laden with promise
a meaning for what is to come, for a human future;
no longer to be the self that we were, in tirelessly
careful hands, and even abandon
our own given names as if they were toys that are broken.
Strange, not to desire our desires any more. Strange
to see all the pattern of things blown about in space
fluttering, separate. It's hard work, being dead,
and having to try to collect, to catch up, until very slowly
a little eternity dawns. — But the living all make
the same error, they draw lines too hard and fast.
Angels, (it's said) are often unable to tell
if they move among living or dead. The eternal river
swiftly carries all the ages through the two kingdoms
for ever, and outroars their voices in both.

Schließlich brauchen sie uns nicht mehr, die Früheentrückten,
man entwöhnt sich des Irdischen sanft, wie man den Brüsten
milde der Mutter entwächst. Aber wir, die so große
Geheimnisse brauchen, denen aus Trauer so oft
seliger Fortschritt entspringt —: *könnten* wir sein ohne sie?
Ist die Sage umsonst, daß einst in der Klage um Linos
wagende erste Musik dürre Erstarrung durchdrang;
daß erst im erschrockenen Raum, dem ein beinah göttlicher Jüngling
plötzlich für immer enttrat, das Leere in jene
Schwingung geriet, die uns jetzt hinreißt und tröstet und hilft.

DIE ZWEITE ELEGIE

JEDER Engel ist schrecklich. Und dennoch, weh mir,
ansing ich euch, fast tödliche Vögel der Seele,
wissend um euch. Wohin sind die Tage Tobiae,
da der Strahlendsten einer stand an der einfachen Haustür,
zur Reise ein wenig verkleidet und schon nicht mehr furchtbar;
(Jüngling dem Jüngling, wie er neugierig hinaussah).
Träte der Erzengel jetzt, der gefährliche, hinter den Sternen
eines Schrittes nur nieder und herwärts: hochauf-
schlagend erschlüg uns das eigene Herz. Wer seid ihr?

Frühe Geglückte, ihr Verwöhnten der Schöpfung,
Höhenzüge, morgenrötliche Grate
aller Erschaffung, — Pollen der blühenden Gottheit,
Gelenke des Lichtes, Gänge, Treppen, Throne,
Räume aus Wesen, Schilde aus Wonne, Tumulte
stürmisch entzückten Gefühls und plötzlich, einzeln,
Spiegel: die die entströmte eigene Schönheit
wiederschöpfen zurück in das eigene Antlitz.

Denn wir, wo wir fühlen, verflüchtigen; ach wir
atmen uns aus und dahin; von Holzglut zu Holzglut
geben wir schwächern Geruch. Da sagt uns wohl einer:
ja, du gehst mir ins Blut, dieses Zimmer, der Frühling
füllt sich mit dir... Was hilfts, er kann uns nicht halten,
wir schwinden in ihm und um ihn. Und jene, die schön sind,
o wer hält sie zurück? Unaufhörlich steht Anschein
auf in ihrem Gesicht und geht fort. Wie Tau von dem Frühgras
hebt sich das Unsre von uns, wie die Hitze von einem
heißen Gericht. O Lächeln, wohin? O Aufschaun:
neue, warme, entgehende Welle des Herzens —;
weh mir: wir *sinds* doch. Schmeckt denn der Weltraum,
in den wir uns lösen, nach uns? Fangen die Engel

They who have died too soon, in the end they don't need us,
they are weaned from the Earth as we gently
are weaned from the breasts of our mother. But for us,
whose need is for greatness and mystery, whose mourning so often
brings blessing and progress —; how *could* we exist without them?
It can't be in vain that the legend of mourning for Linus
tells how music first dared then to steal through bleak numbness,
so that in the shocked space he, almost godlike,
had left so abruptly for ever, the void
first quivered with sound that now enchants and consoles us und helps.

THE SECOND ELEGY

EVERY angel is terrible. And still, alas,
I sing to you, near-deadly birds of the soul,
In knowledge of you. Where have they gone, the days of Tobias,
When one of those radiant beings stood at a simple threshold,
A little disguised for the journey and no longer terrifying
(a youth to the youth, as he peered out inquisitively).
Should now the archangel, full of danger, step from behind the stars
Just one pace downwards and toward us: outbeating
itself our own heart would destroy us. Who are you?

Early-happy ones, the world's fond favourites,
Majestic heights, ridges of all creation
touched by the dawn, pollen of blossoming Godhead,
junctures of light, passages, stairways, thrones,
spaces of being, shields of bliss, tumults
of feeling in storms of delight and suddenly, singly,
mirrors: each pouring its own beauty
back into its own countenance.

For we, in our feelings, evaporate; alas we
breathe ourselves out and away; from ember to ember
yielding a fainter tang. Someone, it is true, may say:
yes, you are in my blood, this room, this springtime
is full of you... What's the use? He cannot hold us,
we vanish within him and around him. And those who have beauty,
who can restrain them? Ceaselessly appearance
begins in their faces and goes forth. Like dew from the morning grass
what's ours leaves us, like the heat rising
from a hot dish. O what becomes of a smile? Of a gaze:
new, warm, ephemeral wave of the heart —;
Woe is me: this is what we *are*. Does the cosmic space
into which we dissolve, perhaps bear our taste? Do the angels

wirklich nur Ihriges auf, ihnen Entströmtes,
oder ist manchmal, wie aus Versehen, ein wenig
unseres Wesens dabei? Sind wir in ihre
Züge soviel nur gemischt wie das Vage in die Gesichter
schwangerer Frauen? Sie merken es nicht in dem Wirbel
ihrer Rückkehr zu sich. (Wie sollten sie's merken.)

Liebende könnten, verstünden sie's, in der Nachtluft
wunderlich reden. Denn es scheint, daß uns alles
verheimlicht. Siehe, die Bäume *sind*; die Häuser,
die wir bewohnen, bestehn noch. Wir nur
ziehen allem vorbei wie ein luftiger Austausch.
Und alles ist einig, uns zu verschweigen, halb als
Schande vielleicht und halb als unsägliche Hoffnung.

Liebende, euch, ihr ineinander Genügten,
frag ich nach uns. Ihr greift euch. Habt Ihr Beweise?
Seht, mir geschiehts, daß meine Hände einander
inne werden oder daß mein gebrauchtes
Gesicht in ihnen sich schont. Das giebt mir ein wenig
Empfindung. Doch wer wagte darum schon zu *sein*?
Ihr aber, die ihr im Entzücken des anderen
zunehmt, bis er euch überwältigt
anfleht: nicht *mehr* —; die ihr unter den Händen
euch reichlicher werdet wie Traubenjahre;
die ihr manchmal vergeht, nur weil der andre
ganz überhandnimmt: euch frage ich nach uns. Ich weiß,
ihr berührt euch so selig, weil die Liebkosung verhält,
weil die Stelle nicht schwindet, die ihr, Zärtliche,
zudeckt; weil ihr darunter das reine
Dauern verspürt. So versprecht ihr euch Ewigkeit fast
von der Umarmung. Und doch, wenn ihr der ersten
Blicke Schrecken besteht und die Sehnsucht am Fenster,
und den ersten gemeinsamen Gang , *ein* Mal durch den Garten:
Liebende, *seid* ihrs dann noch? Wenn ihr einer dem andern
euch an den Mund hebt und ansetzt —: Getränk an Getränk:
o wie entgeht dann der Trinkende seltsam der Handlung.

Erstaunte euch nicht auf attischen Stelen die Vorsicht
menschlicher Geste? war nicht Liebe und Abschied
so leicht auf die Schultern gelegt, als wär es aus anderm
Stoffe gemacht als bei uns? Gedenkt euch der Hände,
wie sie drucklos beruhen, obwohl in den Torsen die Kraft steht.
Diese Beherrschten wußten damit: so weit sind wirs,
dieses ist unser, uns *so* zu berühren; stärker

really only gather in what is theirs, what they give off,
or is there sometimes, as if by mistake, a little
of our own being there too? Are we mixed in with their
features, like the vagueness into the faces
of pregnant women? They do not notice it in the whirlwind
of their return to themselves. (How could they notice it.)

Lovers, if they only knew how, might speak wondrously
in the night air. For it seems that everything
conceals us. See, the trees *are*; the houses
in which we live still stand where they were. We alone
pass by all this like air changing places with air.
And all things conspire to silence us, half
in shame and half in inexpressible hope.

Lovers, you who are satisfied in one another,
I ask about us. You hold each other. But do you have proof?
See, sometimes it happens to me that my hands
grow aware of each other, or that my used-up face
finds refuge in them. This gives me a little
sensation. But who from this alone would presume to be?
You, though, increasing in the other's rapture
till he, overwhelmed, implores you:
no *more* —; in each others hands
growing more abundant for one another like vintage years,
perishing sometimes, only because the other
flourished too vigorously: you I ask about us. I know
why there is such bliss in your touch: because your caress is
sustaining,
because the place does not vanish which, so gently,
you cover; because beneath it you sense
pure permanence. And so you promise each other eternity, almost,
from an embrace. And yet, if you endure
those first frightened glances and the longing at the window,
and the first walk, *once* through the garden together:
Lovers, *are* you still lovers? When you
raise each other to your lips —: drink against drink:
O how strangely the drinker eludes the drinking.

Did not the circumspection of human gestures on attic stelae
surprise you? Were not love and parting
laid so gently upon their shoulders, as if made
of different stuff than with us? Remember the hands,
how they rest without pressure, though there is strength in the torsos.
Thus controlled, they knew: this is what we are,
this much is ours, to touch each other *thus*; the gods

stemmen die Götter uns an. Doch dies ist Sache der Götter.

Fänden auch wir ein reines, verhaltenes, schmales
Menschliches, einen unseren Streifen Fruchtlands
zwischen Strom und Gestein. Denn das eigene Herz übersteigt uns
noch immer wie jene. Und wir können ihm nicht mehr
nachschaun in Bilder, die es besänftigen, noch in
göttliche Körper, in denen es größer sich mäßigt.

DIE DRITTE ELEGIE

EINES ist, die Geliebte zu singen. Ein anderes, wehe,
jenen verborgenen schuldigen Fluß-Gott des Bluts.
Den sie von weitem erkennt, ihren Jüngling, was weiß er
selbst von dem Herren der Lust, der aus dem Einsamen oft,
ehe das Mädchen noch linderte, oft auch als wäre sie nicht,
ach, von welchem Unkenntlichen triefend, das Gotthaupt
aufhob, aufrufend die Nacht zu unendlichem Aufruhr.
O des Blutes Neptun, o sein furchtbarer Dreizack.
O der dunkele Wind seiner Brust aus gewundener Muschel.
Horch, wie die Nacht sich muldet und höhlt. Ihr Sterne,
stammt nicht von euch des Liebenden Lust zu dem Antlitz
seiner Geliebten? Hat er die innige Einsicht
in ihr reines Gesicht nicht aus dem reinen Gestirn?

Du nicht hast ihm, wehe, nicht seine Mutter
hat ihm die Bogen der Braun so zur Erwartung gespannt.
Nicht an dir, ihn fühlendes Mädchen, an dir nicht
bog seine Lippe sich zum fruchtbarern Ausdruck.
Meinst du wirklich, ihn hätte dein leichter Auftritt
also erschüttert, du, die wandelt wie Frühwind?
Zwar du erschrakst ihm das Herz; doch ältere Schrecken
stürzten in ihn bei dem berührenden Anstoß.
Ruf ihn... du rufst ihn nicht ganz aus dunkelem Umgang.
Freilich, er *will*, er entspringt; erleichtert gewöhnt er
sich in dein heimliches Herz und nimmt und beginnt sich.
Aber begann er sich je?
Mutter, *du* machtest ihn klein, du warst, die ihn anfing;
dir war er neu, du beugtest über die neuen
Augen die freundliche Welt und wehrtest der fremden.
Wo, ach, hin sind die Jahre, da du ihm einfach
mit der schlanken Gestalt wallendes Chaos vertratst?
Vieles verbargst du ihm so; das nächtlich-verdächtige Zimmer
machtest du harmlos, aus deinem Herzen voll Zuflucht
mischtest du menschlichern Raum seinem Nacht-Raum hinzu.

bear upon us more fiercely. But that is the concern of the gods.

Could we but find a simple, sheltered, small
human place, a strip of land, fertile of our own.
between river and rock. For our own heart exceeds us
as theirs did of old. And we can no longer gaze
after it, forming images in which it is calmed, or
godlike bodies in which it finds a larger restraint.

THE THIRD ELEGY

ONE thing it is to sing the beloved. Another, alas,
that hidden guilty river-god of the blood.
That one she knows from afar, her young man, what does he know
himself of the lord of pleasure, who often from within his lonely being,
before the girl could soothe him, often as if she did not exist, dripping
from what unknowable depths, raised the god-head,
arousing the night to infinite turmoil?
Oh, Neptune of the blood, oh, his terrible trident.
Oh, the dark wind of his breast out of the convolute shell,
Hark, how the night takes on hollows and curves. You stars,
do you not impart the lover's delight in the face
of the beloved ? Does not his wrapt contemplation
of her pure face derive from the pure stars?

Not you, alas, nor was it his mother
who stretched the bow of his brows to such expectation.
It was not you, girl, that felt him, not you
who caused his lip to curve into more fruitful expression.
Do you really suppose it was your gentle approach
that stirred him so deeply, you who move as light as the morning breeze?
True, it was you who struck fear in his heart; but more ancient terrors
assailed him as he stirred to your touch.
Call him... you will never quite call him away from those sombre
companions.
Of course, it's his wish, he escapes; relieved, he accustoms himself to
your intimate heart and takes and begins himself.
But did he ever begin himself?
Mother, you made him small, it was you who started him;
for you he was new, you inclined to his new
eyes the friendly world and shielded him from the world that was strange.
Where, oh where have the years gone when you simply
with your slender figure stood before surging chaos?
Many things thus you concealed from him; the menacing room at night
you made feel safe, and your heart full of refuge
added a realm more human to his realm of night.

Nicht in die Finsternis, nein, in dein näheres Dasein
hast du das Nachtlicht gestellt, und es schien wie aus Freundschaft.
Nirgends ein Knistern, das du nicht lächelnd erklärtest,
so als wüßtest du längst, *wann* sich die Diele benimmt...
Und er horchte und linderte sich. So vieles vermochte
zärtlich dein Aufstehn; hinter den Schrank trat
hoch im Mantel sein Schicksal, und in die Falten des Vorhangs
paßte, die leicht sich verschob, seine unruhige Zukunft.

Und er selbst, wie er lag, der Erleichterte, unter
schläfernden Lidern deiner leichten Gestaltung
Süße lösend in den gekosteten Vorschlaf —:
schien ein Gehüteter... Aber *innen*: wer wehrte,
hinderte innen in ihm die Fluten der Herkunft?
Ach, da *war* keine Vorsicht im Schlafenden; schlafend,
aber träumend, aber in Fiebern: wie er sich ein-ließ.
Er, der Neue, Scheuende, wie er verstrickt war,
mit des innern Geschehns weiterschlagenden Ranken
schon zu Mustern verschlungen, zu würgendem Wachstum, zu tierhaft
jagenden Formen. Wie er sich hingab — . Liebte.
Liebte sein Inneres, seines Inneren Wildnis,
diesen Urwald in ihm, auf dessen stummem Gestürztsein
lichtgrün sein Herz stand. Liebte. Verließ es, ging die
eigenen Wurzeln hinaus in gewaltigen Ursprung,
wo seine kleine Geburt schon überlebt war. Liebend
stieg er hinab in das ältere Blut, in die Schluchten,
wo das Furchtbare lag, noch satt von den Vätern. Und jedes
Schreckliche kannte ihn, blinzelte, war wie verständigt.
Ja, das Entsetzliche lächelte... Selten
hast du so zärtlich gelächelt, Mutter. Wie sollte
er es nicht lieben, da es ihm lächelte. *Vor* dir
hat ers geliebt, denn, da du ihn trugst schon,
war es im Wasser gelöst, das den Keimenden leicht macht.

Siehe, wir lieben nicht, wie die Blumen, aus einem
einzigen Jahr; uns steigt, wo wir lieben,
unvordenklicher Saft in die Arme. O Mädchen,
dies: daß wir liebten *in* uns, nicht Eines, ein Künftiges, sondern
das zahllos Brauende; nicht ein einzelnes Kind,
sondern die Väter, die wie Trümmer Gebirgs
uns im Grunde beruhn; sondern das trockene Flußbett
einstiger Mütter — ; sondern die ganze
lautlose Landschaft unter dem wolkigen oder
reinen Verhängnis —: *dies* kam dir, Mädchen, zuvor.

No, it was not into the darkness but into your innermost being
that you placed the night-light, so that it seemed to glow with friendship.
There was no creak you could not explain with a smile,
as if you had always known *when* the floorboards would move... And he
listened and felt soothed. That much
your consoling presence could do; from behind the wardrobe stepped forth
his tall cloaked destiny, and into the folds of the curtain
fitted, gently swaying, his restless future.

And he himself, as he lay, unburdened, under
drowsy eyelids shaped by your gentle touch,
absorbing sweetness into the first taste of sleep,
seemed well protected... But *within*: who could resist,
prevent the floods of origin within him? Alas, within the sleeping boy
there was no restraint; sleeping,
but dreaming, but febrile: how deep was his downfall.
He, so new, shying away, how he became entangled,
with ever-encroaching tendrils of inward processes
twisted to patterns, to throttling growths, into forms
straining with animal energies. What self-abandon —. Loved. Loved his
inner self, his inner jungle,
the primeval forest inside him, upon whose silent overthrownness
his heart stood bathed in green light. Loved. Left it, went through his
own roots into primitive origin,
where his little birth was already outlived. Loving,
he descended into the more ancient blood, into ravines
where terror lurked, still gorged with his fathers. And every
dread knew who he was, winked, knowingly.
Yes, what was baleful smiled... Rarely
have you smiled so tenderly, mother. How should
he not love it, when it smiled at him. Long *before* you
he loved it, for even as you were carrying him
it was dissolved in the waters that sustain the germ of the child.

Look, we do not love, like flowers in one
single year; where we love, there rises
immemorial sap in our arms. Girl,
this is what matters: that we loved in ourselves, not simply one
object, something to come, but
unceasing ferment; not just a single child,
but the fathers lying within our depths
like fragments of a mountain range; the dried-up river-bed
of former mothers; the whole
soundless landscape beneath our cloudy or
clear destiny —: *this*, girl, was there before you.

Und du selber, was weißt du —, du locktest
Vorzeit empor in dem Liebenden. Welche Gefühle
wühlten herauf aus entwandelten Wesen. Welche
Frauen haßten dich da. Was für finstere Männer
regtest du auf im Geäder des Jünglings? Tote
Kinder wollten zu dir... O leise, leise,
tu ein liebes vor ihm, ein verläßliches Tagwerk, — führ ihn
nah an den Garten heran, gieb ihm der Nächte
Übergewicht......
                Verhalt ihn......

DIE VIERTE ELEGIE

O Bäume Lebens, o wann winterlich?
Wir sind nicht einig. Sind nicht wie die Zug-
vögel verständigt. Überholt und spät,
so drängen wir uns plötzlich Winden auf
und fallen ein auf teilnahmslosen Teich.
Blühn und verdorrn ist uns zugleich bewußt.
Und irgendwo gehn Löwen noch und wissen,
solang sie herrlich sind, von keiner Ohnmacht.

Uns aber, wo wir Eines meinen, ganz,
ist schon des andern Aufwand fühlbar. Feindschaft
ist uns das Nächste. Treten Liebende
nicht immerfort an Ränder, eins im andern,
die sich versprachen Weite, Jagd und Heimat.
  Da wird für eines Augenblickes Zeichnung
ein Grund von Gegenteil bereitet, mühsam,
daß wir sie sähen; denn man ist sehr deutlich
mit uns. Wir kennen den Kontur
des Fühlens nicht: nur, was ihn formt von außen.
  Wer saß nicht bang vor seines Herzens Vorhang?
Der schlug sich auf: die Szenerie war Abschied.
Leicht zu verstehen. Der bekannte Garten,
und schwankte leise: dann erst kam der Tänzer.
Nicht *der*. Genug! Und wenn er auch so leicht tut,
er ist verkleidet und er wird ein Bürger
und geht durch seine Küche in die Wohnung.
  Ich will nicht diese halbgefüllten Masken,
lieber die Puppe. Die ist voll. Ich will
den Balg aushalten und den Draht und ihr
Gesicht aus Aussehn. Hier. Ich bin davor.
Wenn auch die Lampen ausgehn, wenn mir auch
gesagt wird: Nichts mehr —, wenn auch von der Bühne

And you yourself, what do you know —, you stirred up
times long ago in your lover. What feelings
welled up out of beings now vanished. What
women hated you in him. What sinister men
you aroused in the young man's veins. Dead
children reached out to you... Oh, gently, gently,
carry out a loving daily task before him, a reliable task, — lead him close
to the garden, outweigh the nights
for him......
Restrain him......

THE FOURTH ELEGY

O trees of life, when is wintertime?
We're not at one. We don't have instinct
like migratory birds. Overtaken and late,
we suddenly cast ourselves upon the winds
and land on some unwelcoming pool.
Flowering and withering are known in the same moment.
And somewhere lions are still roaming and know
no weakness, while they are in their prime.

But as for us, even when we are committed to one thing, totally,
we feel the whole force of the other. Conflict
is never far away. Lovers
keep on running into barriers in the other,
where they had hoped for open country, hunting and a home.
Even for a sketch to be done in an instant
the surface must be prepared with a contrasting ground, laboriously,
so that we may see it ; because things are spelled out
quite clearly for us. We don't know the contour
of our feelings, only what forms it from outside.
Who has never sat in dread before the curtain of the heart?
Up it went. A backdrop of departure.
Easy to understand. The familiar garden,
stirring slightly. Only then did the dancer make his entrance.
Not *him*! Enough! For all his pirouettes,
he's dressed for a part, and he'll turn into an ordinary mortal
and enter his house through the kitchen.
I won't endure these half-filled masks,
I'd rather a puppet. At least it's full. I'll put up
with the stuffed skin, and the wires, and the
blankly-staring face. Here. In front.
Even if the lights go out; even if I'm told:
'That's all'; even if emptiness

das Leere herkommt mit dem grauen Luftzug,
wenn auch von meinen stillen Vorfahrn keiner
mehr mit mir dasitzt, keine Frau, sogar
der Knabe nicht mehr mit dem braunen Schielaug:
Ich bleibe dennoch. Es giebt immer Zuschaun.

Hab ich nicht recht? Du, der um mich so bitter
das Leben schmeckte, meines kostend, Vater,
den ersten trüben Aufguß meines Müssens,
da ich heranwuchs, immer wieder kostend
und, mit dem Nachgeschmack so fremder Zukunft
beschäftigt, prüftest mein beschlagnes Aufschaun, —
der du, mein Vater, seit du tot bist, oft
in meiner Hoffnung, innen in mir, Angst hast,
und Gleichmut, wie ihn Tote haben, Reiche
von Gleichmut, aufgiebst für mein bißchen Schicksal,
hab ich nicht recht? Und ihr, hab ich nicht recht,
die ihr mich liebtet für den kleinen Anfang
Liebe zu euch, von dem ich immer abkam,
weil mir der Raum in eurem Angesicht,
da ich ihn liebte, überging in Weltraum,
in dem ihr nicht mehr wart....: wenn mir zumut ist,
zu warten vor der Puppenbühne, nein,
so völlig hinzuschaun, daß, um mein Schauen
am Ende aufzuwiegen, dort als Spieler
ein Engel hinmuß, der die Bälge hochreißt.
Engel und Puppe: dann ist endlich Schauspiel.
Dann kommt zusammen, was wir immerfort
entzwein, indem wir da sind. Dann entsteht
aus unsern Jahreszeiten erst der Umkreis
des ganzen Wandelns. Über uns hinüber
spielt dann der Engel. Sieh, die Sterbenden,
sollten sie nicht vermuten, wie voll Vorwand
das alles ist, was wir hier leisten. Alles
ist nicht es selbst. O Stunden in der Kindheit,
da hinter den Figuren mehr als nur
Vergangnes war und vor uns nicht die Zukunft.
Wir wuchsen freilich und wir drängten manchmal,
bald groß zu werden, denen halb zulieb,
die andres nicht mehr hatten, als das Großsein.
Und waren doch, in unserem Alleingehn,
mit Dauerndem vergnügt und standen da
im Zwischenraume zwischen Welt und Spielzeug,
an einer Stelle, die seit Anbeginn
gegründet war für einen reinen Vorgang.

drifts from the stage in that grey draught;
even if not one of my silent ancestors
still sits with me, no woman, not even
the boy with the squint in his brown eye:
I'll stay on. One can always watch.

Aren't I right? You who on my account always found life
so bitter, as you took a sip of mine, father,
tasting again and again, as I grew up,
the first cloudy infusion of my will — you who,
troubled by the aftertaste of so strange a future,
would look searchingly into the opacity of my gaze,
father, you who, now you are dead,
are often afraid, deep within me, in my hopes,
and give up a serenity such as the dead enjoy,
kingdoms of serenity, for my modicum of fate,
aren't I right? And you,
who loved me because of my first show of love to you,
a love from which I always turned away, because the space
in your features, even as I loved it, dissolved into cosmic space,
in which you were no longer present...: aren't I right when I feel
impelled to wait in front of the puppet-stage, no,
to stare with such intensity that, in the end,
to counterweigh my gaze
an angel must be sent as actor
to jerk the stuffed skins into activity?
Angel and puppet: then at last we have a play.
Then there comes together what we always
split simply by being here. Only then do
our seasons reveal the cycle
in all these transformations. Then the angel
plays high above us. Think, shouldn't
the dying be able to intuit how everything
we accomplish is full of pretence. Nothing
is itself. Oh those hours in childhood,
when behind the figures there was more than simply
what was past, and no future stretched before us.
It's true we were growing and sometimes strove
to be grown-up quickly, half to please those
who had nothing else in life than adulthood.
And yet in our solitude we found
contentment in what endures; and we lived there,
in the borderland between world and toy,
in a spot that had been ordained
from the very first for an innocent event.

Wer zeigt ein Kind, so wie es steht? Wer stellt
es ins Gestirn und giebt das Maß des Abstands
ihm in die Hand? Wer macht den Kindertod
aus grauem Brot, das hart wird, — oder läßt
ihn drin im runden Mund, so wie den Gröps
von einem schönen Apfel?...... Mörder sind
leicht einzusehen. Aber dies: den Tod,
den ganzen Tod, noch *vor* dem Leben so
sanft zu enthalten und nicht bös zu sein,
ist unbeschreiblich.

DIE FÜNFTE ELEGIE

Frau Hertha Koenig zugeeignet

WER aber *sind* sie, sag mir, die Fahrenden, diese ein wenig
Flüchtigern noch als wir selbst, die dringend von früh an
wringt ein *wem, wem* zu Liebe
niemals zufriedener Wille? Sondern er wringt sie,
biegt sie, schlingt sie und schwingt sie,
wirft sie und fängt sie zurück; wie aus geölter,
glatterer Luft kommen sie nieder
auf dem verzehrten, von ihrem ewigen
Aufsprung dünneren Teppich, diesem verlorenen
Teppich im Weltall.
Aufgelegt wie ein Pflaster, als hätte der Vorstadt-
Himmel der Erde dort wehe getan.
Und kaum dort,
aufrecht, da und gezeigt: des Dastehns
großer Anfangsbuchstab..., schon auch, die stärksten
Männer, rollt sie wieder, zum Scherz, der immer
kommende Griff, wie August der Starke bei Tisch
einen zinnenen Teller.

Ach und um diese
Mitte, die Rose des Zuschauns:
blüht und entblättert. Um diesen
Stampfer, den Stempel, den von dem eignen
blühenden Staub getroffnen, zur Scheinfrucht
wieder der Unlust befruchteten, ihrer
niemals bewußten, — glänzend mit dünnster
Oberfläche leicht scheinlächelnden Unlust.

Da: der welke, faltige Stemmer,
der alte, der nur noch trommelt,
eingegangen in seiner gewaltigen Haut, als hätte sie früher
zwei Männer enthalten, und einer

Who can portray a child as he is? Who can place him
in his constellation, or put into his hands the measuring-rod
of distance? Who can mould a child's death
out of grey bread which grows hard? Or leave it
in the hollow of his mouth like the core
of a lovely apple?...... It's easy to see
into a murderer's mind. But this: to contain death —
death in its entirety — even before life has begun,
to contain it so gently, and not to feel resentment,
this lies beyond the power of words.

THE FIFTH ELEGY

Dedicated to Frau Hertha Koenig

BUT who *are* they, tell me, these travellers, a little
more fleeting even than we, driven from early years, wrung by a
(*whose*, for *whose* sake?)
ever unsatisfied will? Yet it wrings them,
bends them, slings them and swings them
throws them and catches them again; as out of oiled
more slippery air they come down
on the threadbare carpet, thinned by their everlasting
leaping-up, this forlorn carpet
lost in the universe.
Laid on like a plaster, as if the suburban
sky had injured the earth there.
And no sooner there,
upright, here and presented: the big capital
D of Display..., at once even the strongest
men are rolled again, in sport, by the ever-
returning grasp, as Augustus the Strong once at table
doubled a pewter plate.

Alas and around this
centre the rose of an audience:
blooms and unpetals. Around this

pestle, this pistil, caught by its own
blossoming pollen, fertilized
again to a sham-fruit of boredom, yet
never conscious, — gleaming with thinnest
surface-light sham-smiling boredom.

There, the withered, wrinkled weight-lifter,
an old man, who only drums now,
shrivelled back inside his mighty skin, as if it once
had contained *two* men, and one

läge nun schon auf dem Kirchhof, und er überlebte den andern,
taub und manchmal ein wenig
wirr, in der verwitweten Haut.

Aber der junge, der Mann, als wär er der Sohn eines Nackens
und einer Nonne: prall und strammig erfüllt
mit Muskeln und Einfalt.

Oh ihr,
die ein Leid, das noch klein war,
einst als Spielzeug bekam, in einer seiner
langen Genesungen....

Du, der mit dem Aufschlag,
wie nur Früchte ihn kennen, unreif,
täglich hundertmal abfällt vom Baum der gemeinsam
erbauten Bewegung (der, rascher als Wasser, in wenig
Minuten Lenz, Sommer und Herbst hat) —
abfällt und anprallt ans Grab:
manchmal, in halber Pause, will dir ein liebes
Antlitz entstehn hinüber zu deiner selten
zärtlichen Mutter; doch an deinen Körper verliert sich,
der es flächig verbraucht, das schüchtern
kaum versuchte Gesicht... Und wieder
klatscht der Mann in die Hand zu dem Ansprung, und eh dir
jemals ein Schmerz deutlicher wird in der Nähe des immer
trabenden Herzens, kommt das Brennen der Fußsohln
ihm, seinem Ursprung, zuvor mit ein paar dir
rasch in die Augen gejagten leiblichen Tränen.
Und dennoch, blindlings,
das Lächeln.....

Engel! o nimms, pflücks, das kleinblütige Heilkraut.
Schaff eine Vase, verwahrs! Stells unter jene, uns *noch* nicht
offenen Freuden; in lieblicher Urne
rühms mit blumiger, schwungiger Aufschrift: »*Subrisio Saltat.*«.
  Du dann, Liebliche,
du, von den reizendsten Freuden
stumm Übersprungne. Vielleicht sind
deine Fransen glücklich für dich —,
oder über den jungen
prallen Brüsten die grüne metallene Seide
fühlt sich unendlich verwöhnt und entbehrt nichts.

already lay in the churchyard, and he was outliving the other,
deaf and sometimes a little
bewildered, in his widowed skin.

But the young one, the man, as if he were the son of a neck
and a nun: taut and strapping and full
of muscles and innocence.

Oh you,
that a sorrow, small still and young
once received as a toy, in one of its
long convalescences....

You who, with the thud
that only fruit know, unripe,
daily drop hundredfold from the tree of the movement
they build up together (the tree that, faster than water, in few
minutes has spring, summer and autumn) —
drops and rebounds on the grave:
sometimes, in half-pauses, a sweet
face tries to appear to send across to your seldom
tender mother; yet on your body it's lost,
spent on the surface, that shy
scarcely attempted look... And then once more
the man claps his hands for the leap, and before even
a pang can be clearer to you in the nearness of the ever
galloping heart, the burning of your soles,
running even before its source, chasing suddenly
into your eyes a few bodily tears.
And yet, all blindly,
the smile.....

Angel! O gather it, pluck it, that small healing-herb.
Make a vase, keep its bloom! Set it among those joys not *yet*
open to us; in a charming urn
honour it with florally soaring inscription: '*Subrisio Saltat.*'.
  Then you, pretty one,
you, whom the most charming joys
dumbly leap over. Perhaps your
fringes are happy for you —,
or over your young
tight breasts the green metallic silk
feels itself endlessly spoilt and wants for nothing.

Du,
immerfort anders auf alle des Gleichgewichts schwankende Waagen
hingelegte Marktfrucht des Gleichmuts,
öffentlich unter den Schultern.

Wo, o *wo* ist der Ort — ich trag ihn im Herzen —,
wo sie noch lange nicht *konnten*, noch von einander
abfieln, wie sich bespringende, nicht recht
paarige Tiere; —
wo die Gewichte noch schwer sind;
wo noch von ihren vergeblich
wirbelnden Stäben die Teller
torkeln.....

Und plötzlich in diesem mühsamen Nirgends, plötzlich
die unsägliche Stelle, wo sich das reine Zuwenig
unbegreiflich verwandelt —, umspringt
in jenes leere Zuviel.
Wo die vielstellige Rechnung
zahlenlos aufgeht.

Plätze, o Platz in Paris, unendlicher Schauplatz,
wo die Modistin, *Madame Lamort*,
die ruhlosen Wege der Erde, endlose Bänder,
schlingt und windet und neue aus ihnen
Schleifen erfindet, Rüschen, Blumen, Kokarden, künstliche Früchte —,
alle
unwahr gefärbt, — für die billigen
Winterhüte des Schicksals.
. . . .

Engel!: Es wäre ein Platz, den wir nicht wissen, und dorten,
auf unsäglichem Teppich, zeigten die Liebenden, die's hier
bis zum Können nie bringen, ihre kühnen
hohen Figuren des Herzschwungs,
ihre Türme aus Lust, ihre
längst, wo Boden nie war, nur an einander
lehnenden Leitern, bebend, — und *könntens*,
vor den Zuschauern rings, unzähligen lautlosen Toten:
Würfen die dann ihre letzten, immer ersparten,
immer verborgenen, die wir nicht kennen, ewig
gültigen Münzen des Glücks vor das endlich
wahrhaft lächelnde Paar auf gestilltem
Teppich?

You,
never twice the same on all the faltering scale-pans of balance,
laid out market-fruit of serenity,
publicly shown among shoulders.

Where, O *where* is the place — I carry it in my heart —,
where they *could* not yet do it, by far, falling away still
from each other like animals trying to mount, not properly
ready for mating; —
where the weights are still heavy;
where the vainly twirling
plates on their stems still
reel…

And then, in this wearisome nowhere, all of a sudden,
the wordless impossible place where the pure too-little
incomprehensibly turns — leaps round
into that empty too-much.
Where the many-figured sum
works out without remainder.

Squares, O square in Paris, infinite showplace,
where the milliner *Madame Lamort*
fashions the restless paths of the earth, endless ribbons,
loops and winds them, invents from them new
bows, ruffles, flowers, cockades, artificial fruit —, all
falsely coloured, — for the cheap
winter bonnets of fate.
. . . .

Angel!: If there were a square that we do not know of, and there
on a wordless impossible carpet, the lovers who here
never can quite do it, might show their bold
high-flying feats of the heart's swing,
their towers of desire, their two
ladders that long since, where ground never was, have leaned
only on each other, trembling, — and could do it,
before the gathered spectators, the numberless unspeaking dead:
  Would they then fling their last, ever saved up,
ever hidden, that we never know of, eternally
valid coinage of bliss before the finally
truthfully smiling couple on the quieted
carpet?

DIE SECHSTE ELEGIE

FEIGENBAUM, seit wie lange schon ists mir bedeutend,
wie du die Blüte beinah ganz überschlägst
und hinein in die zeitig entschlossene Frucht,
ungerühmt, drängst dein reines Geheimnis.
Wie der Fontäne Rohr treibt dein gebognes Gezweig
abwärts den Saft und hinan: und er springt aus dem Schlaf,
fast nicht erwachend, ins Glück seiner süßesten Leistung.
Sieh: wie der Gott in den Schwan.
...... Wir aber verweilen,
ach, uns rühmt es zu blühn, und ins verspätete Innre
unserer endlichen Frucht gehn wir verraten hinein.
Wenigen steigt so stark der Andrang des Handelns,
daß sie schon anstehn und glühn in der Fülle des Herzens,
wenn die Verführung zum Blühn wie gelinderte Nachtluft
ihnen die Jugend des Munds, ihnen die Lider berührt:
Helden vielleicht und den frühe Hinüberbestimmten,
denen der gärtnernde Tod anders die Adern verbiegt.
Diese stürzen dahin: dem eigenen Lächeln
sind sie voran, wie das Rossegespann in den milden
muldigen Bildern von Karnak dem siegenden König.

Wunderlich nah ist der Held doch den jugendlich Toten. Dauern
ficht ihn nicht an. Sein Aufgang ist Dasein; beständig
nimmt er sich fort und tritt ins veränderte Sternbild
seiner steten Gefahr. Dort fänden ihn wenige. Aber
das uns finster verschweigt, das plötzlich begeisterte Schicksal
singt ihn hinein in den Sturm seiner aufrauschenden Welt.
Hör ich doch keinen wie *ihn*. Auf einmal durchgeht mich
mit der strömenden Luft sein verdunkelter Ton.

Dann, wie verbärg ich mich gern vor der Sehnsucht: O wär ich,
wär ich ein Knabe und dürft es noch werden und säße
in die künftigen Arme gestützt und läse von Simson,
wie seine Mutter erst nichts und dann alles gebar.

War er nicht Held schon in dir, o Mutter, begann nicht
dort schon, in dir, seine herrische Auswahl?
Tausende brauten im Schooß und wollten *er* sein,
aber sieh: er ergriff und ließ aus —, wählte und konnte.
Und wenn er Säulen zerstieß, so wars, da er ausbrach
aus der Welt deines Leibs in die engere Welt, wo er weiter
wählte und konnte. O Mütter der Helden, o Ursprung
reißender Ströme! Ihr Schluchten, in die sich

THE SIXTH ELEGY

FIG-TREE, for how long now have I found it significant
that you almost entirely pass over your blossoming
and urge your pure mystery, unproclaimed,
into your early-disclosed fruit.
Like the curved pipe of a fountain, your arching boughs drive the sap
downward and up again; and almost without waking
it bursts out of sleep into its sweetest achievement.
See: like the god entering the swan.
...... But for our part we linger,
alas, we are flattered into blossoming and we enter
the belated interior of our final fruit betrayed.
In only a few does the urge to action rise up so strongly
that they halt, glowing in their heart's abundance,
when, like the soft night air, the temptation to blossom
touches their youthful mouths, their eyelids:
heroes perhaps, and those destined to die young,
whose veins Death the gardener bends in a different way.
These plunge on ahead: in advance of their own smile like the team of
galloping horses before the triumphant
pharaoh in the mild hollowed reliefs of Karnak.

Wondrously near is the hero to those who die young. Permanence
does not concern him. His rise is true being; constantly
he removes himself and passes into the altered constellation
of his perpetual danger. Few would find him there. But
Fate, which is darkly silent of us, grows suddenly excited
and sings him into the storm of his upsurging world.
I hear none like him. All at once I am pierced
by his darkened sound, borne on the rushing air.

Then how gladly I would hide from the longing: O would that
I were a boy once again, with my life before me, and could sit
leaning on future arms and reading of Samson,
how his mother bore first nothing, then all.

Was he not a hero already inside you, mother? Did he not
begin his lordly selection there already in you?
Thousands seethed in the womb, wanting to be him,
but see: he took hold and let go, he chose, he could do it.
And if he sundered pillars, it was when he burst
from the world of your body into the narrower world, where again
he chose and could do it. Oh mothers of heroes, oh source
of raging torrents! You ravines into which

hoch von dem Herzrand, klagend,
schon die Mädchen gestürzt, künftig die Opfer dem Sohn.

Denn hinstürmte der Held durch Aufenthalte der Liebe,
jeder hob ihn hinaus, jeder ihn meinende Herzschlag,
abgewendet schon, stand er am Ende der Lächeln, — anders.

DIE SIEBENTE ELEGIE

WERBUNG nicht mehr, nicht Werbung, entwachsene Stimme,
sei deines Schreies Natur; zwar schrieest du rein wie der Vogel,
wenn ihn die Jahreszeit aufhebt, die steigende, beinah vergessend,
daß er ein kümmerndes Tier und nicht nur ein einzelnes Herz sei,
das sie ins Heitere wirft, in die innigen Himmel. Wie er, so
würbest du wohl, nicht minder —, daß, noch unsichtbar,
dich die Freundin erführ, die stille, in der eine Antwort
langsam erwacht und über dem Hören sich anwärmt, —
deinem erkühnten Gefühl die erglühte Gefühlin.

O und der Frühling begriffe —, da ist keine Stelle,
die nicht trüge den Ton der Verkündigung. Erst jenen kleinen
fragenden Auflaut, den, mit steigernder Stille,
weithin umschweigt ein reiner bejahender Tag.
Dann die Stufen hinan, Ruf-Stufen hinan, zum geträumten
Tempel der Zukunft —; dann den Triller, Fontäne,
die zu dem drängenden Strahl schon das Fallen zuvornimmt
im versprechlichen Spiel.... Und vor sich, den Sommer.
Nicht nur die Morgen alle des Sommers —, nicht nur
wie sie sich wandeln in Tag und strahlen vor Anfang.
Nicht nur die Tage, die zart sind um Blumen, und oben,
um die gestalteten Bäume, stark und gewaltig.
Nicht nur die Andacht dieser entfalteten Kräfte,
nicht nur die Wege, nicht nur die Wiesen im Abend,
nicht nur, nach spätem Gewitter, das atmende Klarsein,
nicht nur der nahende Schlaf und ein Ahnen, abends...
sondern die Nächte! Sondern die hohen, des Sommers,
Nächte, sondern die Sterne, die Sterne der Erde.
O einst tot sein und sie wissen unendlich,
alle die Sterne: denn wie, wie, wie sie vergessen!

Siehe, da rief ich die Liebende. Aber nicht *sie* nur
käme... Es kämen aus schwächlichen Gräbern
Mädchen und ständen... Denn, wie beschränk ich,
wie, den gerufenen Ruf? Die Versunkenen suchen
immer noch Erde. — Ihr Kinder, ein hiesig

maidens have plunged, from the highest rim of the heart, lamenting,
henceforth in sacrifice to the son.

For the hero stormed forth through the abodes of love,
each one bore him up and away, each heartbeat that was meant for him,
till he stood, at the end of the smiles, turned away, — different.

THE SEVENTH ELEGY

WOOING no more, not wooing, oh voice which has outgrown it,
be the nature of your cry; true, were you to cry as purely as the bird,
when that time of year uplifts him, that rising time, almost
forgetting
that he's a creature of care and not just a solitary heart
which is thrown into azure, into innermost heavens. Like him
you too would probably woo, no less —, so that, still invisible,
your beloved friend would sense you, that quiet friend in whom a
reply
slowly awakened, and, as it listened, grew warmer,—
the female form, flushed by your fortified feelings.

Oh, and spring would understand —, there is no place
which would not carry the tone of annunciation. First that small
questioning note which, with rising stillness,
is surrounded by the silence of a pure, affirming day.
Then up the steps, those steps of notes towards that dreamt-of
temple of the future; then the trill, like a fountain
where the falling stream awaits the rising jet
in promising play.... And ahead of that day, the summer.
Not just the mornings of summer, each one, not just
their changing to day, their gleam before sunrise.
Not just the days, so gentle to flowers below,
so mighty, so strong to the trees, fully formed, above.
Not just the worship and awe of those unfolded forces
not just the paths, not just the meadows at evening,
not just, after late evening storms, the pure breath of clearness,
not just approaching sleep and the longing of evening...
but also the nights! But also those limitless nights
of summer, but also the stars, those stars of our earth.
Oh to be finally dead and to know them forever,
all the stars; for how, how, how to forget them!

Look, I was calling the lover. But not only *she* would
come... Girls from frail graves would rise and would
stand there... For how, how could I restrict my call,
once made? Those who have sunk away still
seek our earth.— You children, one thing in this world, if truly grasped,

einmal ergriffenes Ding gälte für viele.
Glaubt nicht, Schicksal sei mehr, als das Dichte der Kindheit;
wie überholtet ihr oft den Geliebten, atmend,
atmend nach seligem Lauf, auf nichts zu, ins Freie.

Hiersein ist herrlich. Ihr wußtet es, Mädchen, *ihr* auch,
die ihr scheinbar entbehrtet, versankt —, ihr, in den ärgsten
Gassen der Städte, Schwärende, oder dem Abfall
Offene. Denn eine Stunde war jeder, vielleicht nicht
ganz eine Stunde, ein mit den Maßen der Zeit kaum
Meßliches zwischen zwei Weilen —, da sie ein Dasein
hatte. Alles. Die Adern voll Dasein.
Nur, wir vergessen so leicht, was der lachende Nachbar
uns nicht bestätigt oder beneidet. Sichtbar
wollen wirs heben, wo doch das sichtbarste Glück uns
erst zu erkennen sich giebt, wenn wir es innen verwandeln.

Nirgends, Geliebte, wird Welt sein, als innen. Unser
Leben geht hin mit Verwandlung. Und immer geringer
schwindet das Außen. Wo einmal ein dauerndes Haus war,
schlägt sich erdachtes Gebild vor, quer, zu Erdenklichem
völlig gehörig, als ständ es noch ganz im Gehirne.
Weite Speicher der Kraft schafft sich der Zeitgeist, gestaltlos
wie der spannende Drang, den er aus allem gewinnt.
Tempel kennt er nicht mehr. Diese, des Herzens, Verschwendung
sparen wir heimlicher ein. Ja, wo noch eins übersteht,
ein einst gebetetes Ding, ein gedientes, geknietes —,
hält es sich, so wie es ist, schon ins Unsichtbare hin.
Viele gewahrens nicht mehr, doch ohne den Vorteil,
daß sie's nun *innerlich* baun, mit Pfeilern und Statuen, größer!

Jede dumpfe Umkehr der Welt hat solche Enterbte,
denen das Frühere nicht und noch nicht das Nächste gehört.
Denn auch das Nächste ist weit für die Menschen. *Uns* soll
dies nicht verwirren; es stärke in uns die Bewahrung
der noch erkannten Gestalt. — Dies *stand* einmal unter Menschen,
mitten im Schicksal stands, im vernichtenden, mitten
im Nichtwissen-Wohin stand es, wie seiend, und bog
Sterne zu sich aus gesicherten Himmeln. Engel,
dir noch zeig ich es, *da*! in deinem Anschaun
steh es gerettet zuletzt, nun endlich aufrecht.
Säulen, Pylone, der Sphinx, das strebende Stemmen,
grau aus vergehender Stadt oder aus fremder, des Doms.

would stand for so many.
Do not believe that fate is more than the fulness of childhood;
how often you would run past your lover, breathless,
breathless in blissful pursuit of nothing but wide open spaces.

To be here is glorious. You girls knew that, even those of you
who seemed wanting, who sank away —, those in the foulest
streets of the cities, festering, doomed to be cast out as rubbish.
For each of you had an hour, perhaps not quite
an hour, a point between periods,
barely perceptible —, when you truly existed.
When you had everything. Your veins full of life.
But we forget so easily what is not confirmed
or envied by our laughing neighbour. We must lift it
up, visibly, when yet the most visible joy reveals itself
only when we transform it, within.

Nowhere, beloved, can there be world but within us. Our life's
course proceeds in a process of change. Yet the outside
world is ever diminished. Where once was a house built to last,
a cerebral image now rises, obliquely, still part
of the mind, still quite in the brain.
Our age creates for itself vast garners of power,
soulless, like the force and the tension it draws from all things.
We can no longer recognise temples. These, luxuries of the soul,
we save now more secretly than in the past. Nay, where one of
them still survives,
a thing that was worshipped, served, bowed down to —,
it reaches, just as it is, into the unseen world.
Many no longer perceive it, not taking advantage of
building it greater, with columns and statues, *within*!

Each sluggish turn of our world has such disinherited minds,
to whom neither past nor yet future belongs.
For even what's coming is far for mankind. This
must not confuse us; let it strengthen our memory
of forms which we still can perceive. This *stood* once amongst us,
stood at the mercy of fate, the destroyer, stood in the midst of
not-knowing-where-next, as though it were living, and drew
the firm stars from their place in the heavens. *Angel,*
let me show it to you, *there*! in your gaze
let it be finally saved, fully upright, at last.
Columns, pylons, the Sphinx, the striving upward thrust of the
minster,
grey against background of fading, or foreign, town.

War es nicht Wunder? O staune, Engel, denn *wir* sinds,
wir, o du Großer, erzähls, daß wir solches vermochten, mein Atem
reicht für die Rühmung nicht aus. So haben wir dennoch
nicht die Räume versäumt, diese gewährenden, diese
unseren Räume. (Was müssen sie fürchterlich groß sein,
da sie Jahrtausende nicht unseres Fühlns überfülln.)
Aber ein Turm war groß, nicht wahr? O Engel, er war es, —
groß, auch noch neben dir? Chartres war groß —, und Musik
reichte noch weiter hinan und überstieg uns. Doch selbst nur
eine Liebende —, oh, allein am nächtlichen Fenster....
reichte sie dir nicht ans Knie —?
Glaub *nicht*, daß ich werbe.
Engel, und würb ich dich auch! Du kommst nicht. Denn mein
Anruf ist immer voll Hinweg; wider so starke
Strömung kannst du nicht schreiten. Wie ein gestreckter
Arm ist mein Rufen. Und seine zum Greifen
oben offene Hand bleibt vor dir
offen, wie Abwehr und Warnung,
Unfaßlicher, weitauf.

DIE ACHTE ELEGIE

Rudolf Kassner zugeeignet

MIT allen Augen sieht die Kreatur
das Offene. Nur unsre Augen sind
wie umgekehrt und ganz um sie gestellt
als Fallen, rings um ihren freien Ausgang.
Was draußen *ist,* wir wissens aus des Tiers
Antlitz allein; denn schon das frühe Kind
wenden wir um und zwingens, daß es rückwärts
Gestaltung sehe, nicht das Offene, das
im Tiergesicht so tief ist. Frei von Tod.
Ihn sehen wir allein; das freie Tier
hat seinen Untergang stets hinter sich
und vor sich Gott, und wenn es geht, so gehts
in Ewigkeit, so wie die Brunnen gehen.
Wir haben nie, nicht einen einzigen Tag,
den reinen Raum vor uns, in den die Blumen
unendlich aufgehn. Immer ist es Welt
und niemals Nirgends ohne Nicht: das Reine,
Unüberwachte, das man atmet und
unendlich *weiß* und nicht begehrt. Als Kind
verliert sich eins im Stilln an dies und wird
gerüttelt. Oder jener stirbt und *ists*.
Denn nah am Tod sieht man den Tod nicht mehr

Was that not marvellous? Oh gaze in wonder, Angel, for it was *us*,
oh Great Being, us, recount that we managed such things, my breath
cannot last for the praise which is due. So we have not, despite all,
neglected earth's spaces, those welcoming spaces, our very own
spaces. (How fearfully large they must be,
if not overflowing by thousands of years of our feelings.)
But a tower was great, was it not? Oh Angel, it was,—
great, even beside you? And Chartres was great —, and music
rose further still and even surpassed us. But simply
a girl in love —, oh, alone, at an evening window...
did she not reach as far as your knee —?
Do *not* believe I am wooing,
Angel, and even if I were! You do not come. For my
call is forever full of rejection; with such a strong current
you cannot make headway. Like an arm outstretched
is my call. And my hand, outheld,
ready for grasping, is open before
you, as if warding away and warning,
Ungraspable One, far above.

THE EIGHTH ELEGY

Dedicated to Rudolf Kassner

WITH both its eyes the creature-world sees
the open. But our eyes are
as though reversed and set around it
like snares, all around its path to freedom.
What *is* outside, we know from the animal's
countenance alone. For we already turn the small child
around and compel it to look backwards
and see formed nature, not the open that
is so deep in the animal's face. Free from death;
we only see *that*, the free animal
has its decline always behind itself
and before it God, and when it moves, it moves
in eternity, just as springs flow.
We have never, not for a single day,
pure space before us, into which the flowers
open up infinitely. It is always world
and never the nowhere without no: the pure,
the unguarded realm which one breathes and
infinitely *knows* and does not desire. As a child
one loses oneself in silence to this and is
jolted out of it. Or someone dies and *is* it.
For near to death one no longer sees death

Und starrt *hinaus*, vielleicht mit großem Tierblick.
Liebende, wäre nicht der andere, der
die Sicht verstellt, sind nah daran und staunen...
Wie aus Versehn ist ihnen aufgetan
hinter dem andern... Aber über ihn
kommt keiner fort, und wieder wird ihm Welt.
Der Schöpfung immer zugewendet, sehn
wir nur auf ihr die Spiegelung des Frein,
von uns verdunkelt. Oder daß ein Tier,
ein stummes, aufschaut, ruhig durch uns durch.
Dieses heißt Schicksal: gegenüber sein
und nichts als das und immer gegenüber.

Wäre Bewußtsein unsrer Art in dem
sicheren Tier, das uns entgegenzieht
in anderer Richtung —, riß es uns herum
mit seinem Wandel. Doch sein Sein ist ihm
unendlich, ungefaßt, und ohne Blick
auf seinen Zustand, rein, so wie sein Ausblick.
Und wo wir Zukunft sehn, dort sieht es Alles
und sich in Allem und geheilt für immer.

Und doch ist in dem wachsam warmen Tier
Gewicht und Sorge einer großen Schwermut.
Denn ihm auch haftet immer an, was uns
oft überwältigt, — die Erinnerung,
als sei schon einmal das, wonach man drängt,
näher gewesen, treuer und sein Anschluß
unendlich zärtlich. Hier ist alles Abstand,
und dort wars Atem. Nach der ersten Heimat
ist ihm die zweite zwitterig und windig.
  O Seligkeit der *kleinen* Kreatur,
die immer *bleibt* im Schooße, der sie austrug;
o Glück der Mücke, die noch *innen* hüpft,
selbst wenn sie Hochzeit hat; denn Schooß ist alles.
Und sieh die halbe Sicherheit des Vogels,
der beinah beides weiß aus seinem Ursprung,
als wär er eine Seele der Etrusker,
aus einem Toten, den ein Raum empfing,
doch mit der ruhenden Figur als Deckel.
Und wie bestürzt ist eins, das fliegen muß
und stammt aus einem Schooß. Wie vor sich selbst
erschreckt, durchzuckts die Luft, wie wenn ein Sprung
durch eine Tasse geht. So reißt die Spur
der Fledermaus durchs Porzellan des Abends.

and stares *out*, perhaps with the creature's wide eye.
Lovers, were not the other there,
blocking out the light, are close to this and marvel...
As if in error they have opened to them
what is behind the other... But no-one can
elude him, and the world crowds in again.
Constantly turned towards creation,
we see on it only a mirroring of what is free,
obscured by us. Or that an animal,
a mute creature, looks up camly right through us.
This is fate: being opposite
and nothing but that and always being opposite.

If there were consciousness, such as we have,
in the secure animal that moves towards us
in another direction —, it would drag around us
with it in its progress. But its being is
Unending, not fixed, and without a look
on its state, pure, like its look forward.
And where we see future, it sees there all things
And itself in all things and healed forever.

And yet there is in the warm, alert animal
the heaviness and care of a great sorrow.
For something always clings to it, which
often overwhelms us —, memory,
as though what we urge towards was
once nearer, truer and its connection
with us infinitely tender. Here it is all separation
and there it was breath. After the first home
the second seems not one thing or the other and doubtful.
  O bliss of the *tiny* creature
that always *remains* inside the womb that brought it forth.
O happiness of the gnat that still leaps *within*
even when it procreates; for womb is all.
And look at the half security of the bird,
almost aware of both from its origin,
as though it were the soul of an Etruscan,
of a dead man, enclosed within a space
yet with the figure in repose as a lid.
And how dismayed is the womb-born thing
that has to fly. As though afraid of itself,
it zig-zags the air like when a crack
goes through a cup. So the trace
of the bat flaws the porcelain of the evening sky.

Und wir: Zuschauer, immer, überall,
dem allen zugewandt und nie hinaus!
Uns überfüllts. Wir ordnens. Es zerfällt.
Wir ordnens wieder und zerfallen selbst.

Wer hat uns also umgedreht, daß wir,
was wir auch tun, in jener Haltung sind
von einem, welcher fortgeht? Wie er auf
dem letzten Hügel, der ihm ganz sein Tal
noch einmal zeigt, sich wendet, anhält, weilt —,
so leben wir und nehmen immer Abschied.

DIE NEUNTE ELEGIE

WARUM, wenn es angeht, also die Frist des Daseins
hinzubringen, als Lorbeer, ein wenig dunkler als alles
andere Grün, mit kleinen Wellen an jedem
Blattrand (wie eines Windes Lächeln) —: warum dann
Menschliches müssen — und, Schicksal vermeidend,
sich sehnen nach Schicksal?...

Oh, *nicht*, weil Glück *ist*,
dieser voreilige Vorteil eines nahen Verlusts.
Nicht aus Neugier, oder zur Übung des Herzens,
das auch im Lorbeer *wäre*.....

Aber weil Hiersein viel ist, und weil uns scheinbar
alles das Hiesige braucht, dieses Schwindende, das
seltsam uns angeht. Uns, die Schwindendsten. *Ein* Mal
jedes, nur *ein* Mal. *Ein* Mal und nichtmehr. Und wir auch
ein Mal. Nie wieder. Aber dieses
ein Mal gewesen zu sein, wenn auch nur *ein* Mal:
irdisch gewesen zu sein, scheint nicht widerrufbar.

Und so drängen wir uns und wollen es leisten,
wollens enthalten in unsern einfachen Händen,
im überfüllteren Blick und im sprachlosen Herzen.
Wollen es werden. — Wem es geben? Am liebsten
alles behalten für immer... Ach, in den andern Bezug,
wehe, was nimmt man hinüber? Nicht das Anschaun, das hier
langsam erlernte, und kein hier Ereignetes. Keins.
Also die Schmerzen. Also vor allem das Schwersein,
also der Liebe lange Erfahrung, — also
lauter Unsägliches. Aber später,

And we: Onlookers, always, everywhere,
turned toward all that and never transcending it.
It overwhelms us. We order it. It disintegrates.
We order it again and disintegrate ourselves.

Who has turned us around like this, so that,
do what we may, we are in the stance
of someone who is leaving? Like him, who
on the last hill that shows him all of his valley
once more, turns, halts, tarries —,
so we live, forever taking our leave.

THE NINTH ELEGY

WHY, when this brief interval of being might be spent
as a laurel, slightly darker than all
other greens, with tiny waves on the edge
of each leaf (like the smile of a breeze) —: why then
have to be human and, shrinking from Fate,
still yearn for it too?...

Oh, *not* because happiness *is*,
its premature profit the prelude to imminent loss.
Not out of curiosity, nor just to exercise the heart,
which would also be there in the laurel.....

But because being here means much, and because all
that is here, all that is fleeting, seems to need us,
and concerns us strangely. Us, the most fleeting of all. *Once*
for each thing, only *once*. *Once* and no more. And the same for us,
only *once*. Never again. But having been
this *once*, though only *once*:
having been *earthly*, seems irrevocable.

And so we urge ourselves on, trying to accomplish it,
seeking to contain it in our simple hands,
in our overcrowded gaze and in our speechless heart.

Trying to become it. To give it to whom? We'd rather
hold on to it all for ever... Ah, but — alas — what can we take
over into the other relation? Not the art of seeing,
which was learned so slowly here, and no event of the world. Not one.
Take then the pain, above all else, the huge weight of being
and the long experience of love, — take what is truly
unsayable. But later, under the stars,

unter den Sternen, was solls: *die* sind *besser* unsäglich.
Bringt doch der Wanderer auch vom Hange des Bergrands
nicht eine Hand voll Erde ins Tal, die Allen unsägliche, sondern
ein erworbenes Wort, reines, den gelben und blaun
Enzian. Sind wir vielleicht *hier*, um zu sagen: Haus,
Brücke, Brunnen, Tor, Krug, Obstbaum, Fenster, —
höchstens: Säule, Turm.... aber zu *sagen*, verstehs,
oh zu sagen *so*, wie selber die Dinge niemals
innig meinten zu sein. Ist nicht die heimliche List
dieser verschwiegenen Erde, wenn sie die Liebenden drängt,
daß sich in ihrem Gefühl jedes und jedes entzückt?
Schwelle: was ists für zwei
Liebende, daß sie die eigne ältere Schwelle der Tür
ein wenig verbrauchen, auch sie, nach den vielen vorher
und vor den Künftigen...., leicht.

Hier ist des *Säglichen* Zeit, *hier* seine Heimat.
Sprich und bekenn. Mehr als je
fallen die Dinge dahin, die erlebbaren, denn,
was sie verdrängend ersetzt, ist ein Tun ohne Bild.
Tun unter Krusten, die willig zerspringen, sobald
innen das Handeln entwächst und sich anders begrenzt.
Zwischen den Hämmern besteht
unser Herz, wie die Zunge
zwischen den Zähnen, die doch,
dennoch, die preisende bleibt.

Preise dem Engel die Welt, nicht die unsägliche, *ihm*
kannst du nicht großtun mit herrlich Erfühltem; im Weltall,
wo er fühlender fühlt, bist du ein Neuling. Drum zeig
ihm das Einfache, das, von Geschlecht zu Geschlechtern gestaltet,
als ein Unsriges lebt, neben der Hand und im Blick.
Sag ihm die Dinge. Er wird staunender stehn; wie du standest
bei dem Seiler im Rom, oder beim Töpfer am Nil.
Zeig ihm, wie glücklich ein Ding sein kann, wie schuldlos und unser,
wie selbst das klagende Leid rein zur Gestalt sich entschließt,
dient als ein Ding, oder stirbt in ein Ding —, und jenseits
selig der Geige entgeht.— Und diese, von Hingang
lebenden Dinge verstehn, daß du sie rühmst; vergänglich,
traun sie ein Rettendes uns, den Vergänglichsten, zu.
Wollen, wir sollen sie ganz im unsichtbarn Herzen verwandeln
in — o unendlich — in uns! Wer wir am Ende auch seien.

Erde, ist es nicht dies, was du willst: *unsichtbar*
in uns erstehn? — Ist es dein Traum nicht,

what's the use. *They* are *better* unsayable.
For the traveller does not return from the mountain to the valley
with a handful of earth, unsayable to others, but instead
a word, hard-won, pure, the yellow and blue
gentian. Are we perhaps *here* to say: House,
Bridge, Fountain, Gate, Jug, Fruit-tree, Window, —
at most, Column, Tower.... but to *say* them — you understand —
oh to say them more intensely than the things themselves
ever dreamed they could be? Is it not the secret purpose
of this sly earth when she urges the lovers on,
that all things should delight in the feelings they feel.
Threshold: what is it for two lovers,
that they too should wear away the ancient
threshold of their door a little, after so many before them
and before so many to come...., lightly.

Here is the time for the *sayable*; *here* is its home.
Speak and bear witness! More than ever before
the things we experience are falling away, for
crowding them out is an act without image.
An act encased in a shell, which readily splits open when
the act inside outgrows it and seeks new limits.
Between the hammers our heart,
endures, like the tongue
between the teeth, which still,
even so, continues to praise.

Praise this world to the Angel, not the unsayable. *He*
cannot be impressed with the world of splendid sensation; in the universe
where he feels more feelingly, you are a novice. So show
him a simple thing, fashioned from generation to generation,
so that it lives on as ours — near the hand, in the gaze.
Tell him of things. He will stand more amazed; just as you stood
by the rope-maker in Rome, by the potter on the banks of the Nile.
Show him how happy a thing can be, how guiltless and ours,
how even the lamentations of grief might purely settle on a form,
serve as a thing, or die into a thing — and escape, blissfully,
beyond the violin. And these things that live
from decline understand that you praise them; transient
they look to us for salvation, us the most transient of all.
They want us to change them completely, in our invisible heart,
into — o infinitely — into ourselves! Whatever we may be in the end.

Earth, is it not this that you want — to arise
invisibly within us. Is it not your dream

einmal unsichtbar zu sein? — Erde! unsichtbar!
Was, wenn Verwandlung nicht, ist dein drängender Auftrag?
Erde, du liebe, ich will. Oh glaub, es bedürfte
nicht deiner Frühlinge mehr, mich dir zu gewinnen —, *einer,*
ach, ein einziger ist schon dem Blute zu viel.
Namenlos bin ich zu dir entschlossen, von weit her.
Immer warst du im Recht, und dein heiliger Einfall
ist der vertrauliche Tod.

Siehe, ich lebe. Woraus? Weder Kindheit noch Zukunft
werden weniger..... Überzähliges Dasein
entspringt mir im Herzen.

DIE ZEHNTE ELEGIE

DASS ich dereinst, an dem Ausgang der grimmigen Einsicht,
Jubel und Ruhm aufsinge zustimmenden Engeln.
Daß von den klar geschlagenen Hämmern des Herzens
keiner versage an weichen, zweifelnden oder
reißenden Saiten. Daß mich mein strömendes Antlitz
glänzender mache; daß das unscheinbare Weinen
blühe. O wie werdet ihr dann, Nächte, mir lieb sein,
gehärmte. Daß ich euch knieender nicht, untröstliche Schwestern,
hinnahm, nicht in euer gelöstes
Haar mich gelöster ergab. Wir, Vergeuder der Schmerzen.
Wie wir sie absehn voraus, in die traurige Dauer,
ob sie nicht enden vielleicht. Sie aber sind ja
unser winterwähriges Laub, unser dunkeles Sinngrün,
eine der Zeiten des heimlichen Jahres —, nicht nur
Zeit —, sind Stelle, Siedelung, Lager, Boden, Wohnort.

Freilich, wehe, wie fremd sind die Gassen der Leid-Stadt,
wo in der falschen, aus Übertönung gemachten
Stille, stark, aus der Gußform des Leeren der Ausguß
prahlt: der vergoldete Lärm, das platzende Denkmal.
O, wie spurlos zerträte ein Engel ihnen den Trostmarkt,
den die Kirche begrenzt, ihre fertig gekaufte:
reinlich und zu und enttäuscht wie ein Postamt am Sonntag.
Draußen aber kräuseln sich immer die Ränder von Jahrmarkt.
Schaukeln der Freiheit! Taucher und Gaukler des Eifers!
Und des behübschten Glücks figürliche Schießstatt,
wo es zappelt von Ziel und sich blechern benimmt,
wenn ein Geschickterer trifft. Von Beifall zu Zufall
taumelt er weiter; denn Buden jeglicher Neugier
werben, trommeln und plärrn. Für Erwachsene aber

to be one day invisible? Earth! invisible!
What is your urgent command, if not transformation?
Earth, my dearest, I will. Oh, believe me, your
springtimes are no longer needed to win me; *one*
— ah even a single one — is too much for my blood.
Before all naming I was yours — from the first.
You were always right, and your holy inspiration
is our intimate, Death.

Behold, I am living. On what? Neither childhood nor future
diminish ..... Being without number
springs up in my heart.

THE TENTH ELEGY

MAY the time come when, my stern seeing over,
I raise up my song of praise and delight to the voice of the angels.
And may the clear blows from the heart's hammers
not strike dully on strings that are soft, doubting
or brittle. And may my tear-streaming cheeks
shine all the more brightly; and the weeping in secret
bloom. Oh how dear you will be to me then, you nights
of sorrow. Would I had knelt even lower, to accept you, disconsolate sisters,
given more of myself in touching
your hair that was untied in mourning. We, who are wastrels of sorrows.
We see them approach, into the endless sadness,
hoping perhaps they will end. But they are
our leaves through the winter, our dark green of remembrance,
one of the times of the inward year — not merely
time —, are our place, settlement, encampment, ground, habitation.

But, alas, how alien the streets of Grief City,
where in the counterfeit silence, made of a surfeit of noise,
blatantly struts the form that is cast in the mould
of emptiness: the tinselly din, the statue burst open.
O, how an angel would trample to nothing their Cure-All Fair,
with the church hard by, the one bought to order:
tidy and shut and forlorn like the Post on a Sunday.
But outside curl around still the amusement park's edges.
Swings of Freedom! Acrobats of Enthusiasm!
And prettified happiness' shooting gallery, befigured,
all jostling for aim, each jangling the other,
when a good marksman scores. From claps to chance-taking
on his way then he lurches; for sideshows are there for the curious,
their barkers hailing and drumming. Adults Only!

ist noch besonders zu sehn, wie das Geld sich vermehrt, anatomisch,
nicht zur Belustigung nur: der Geschlechtsteil des Gelds,
alles, das Ganze, der Vorgang —, das unterrichtet und macht
fruchtbar.........
....Oh aber gleich darüber hinaus,
hinter der letzten Planke, beklebt mit Plakaten des »Todlos«,
jenes bitteren Biers, das den Trinkenden süß scheint,
wenn sie immer dazu frische Zerstreuungen kaun...,
gleich im Rücken der Planke, gleich dahinter, ists *wirklich*.
Kinder spielen, und Liebende halten einander, — abseits,
ernst, im ärmlichen Gras, und Hunde haben Natur.
Weiter noch zieht es den Jüngling; vielleicht, daß er eine junge
Klage liebt..... Hinter ihr her kommt er in Wiesen. Sie sagt:
— Weit. Wir wohnen dort draußen....
Wo? Und der Jüngling
folgt. Ihn rührt ihre Haltung. Die Schulter, der Hals —, vielleicht
ist sie von herrlicher Herkunft. Aber er läßt sie, kehrt um,
wendet sich, winkt... Was solls? Sie ist eine Klage.

Nur die jungen Toten, im ersten Zustand
zeitlosen Gleichmuts, dem der Entwöhnung,
folgen ihr liebend. Mädchen
wartet sie ab und befreundet sie. Zeigt ihnen leise,
was sie an sich hat. Perlen des Leids und die feinen
Schleier der Duldung. — Mit Jünglingen geht sie
schweigend.

Aber dort, wo sie wohnen, im Tal, der Älteren eine, der Klagen,
nimmt sich des Jünglinges an, wenn er fragt: — Wir waren,
sagt sie, ein Großes Geschlecht, einmal, wir Klagen. Die Väter
trieben den Bergbau dort in dem großen Gebirg; bei Menschen
findest du manchmal ein Stück geschliffenes Ur-Leid
oder, aus altem Vulkan, schlackig versteinerten Zorn.
Ja, das stammte von dort. Einst waren wir reich. —

Und sie leitet ihn leicht durch die weite Landschaft der Klagen,
zeigt ihm die Säulen der Tempel oder die Trümmer
jener Burgen, von wo Klage-Fürsten das Land
einstens weise beherrscht. Zeigt ihm die hohen
Tränenbäume und Felder blühender Wehmut,
(Lebendige kennen sie nur als sanftes Blattwerk);
zeigt ihm die Tiere der Trauer, weidend, — und manchmal
schreckt ein Vogel und zieht, flach ihnen fliegend durchs Aufschaun,
weithin das schriftliche Bild seines vereinsamten Schreis. —
Abends führt sie ihn hin zu den Gräbern der Alten

Special attraction! The reproduction of money (anatomical details),
not just for amusement: money's organs of gender,
the whole lot, nothing left out —, what they get up to — a lesson and
brings you results........
.... O but further beyond,
past the last billboards, stuck over with posters for 'Deathless',
that bitter beer that seems sweet to the drinkers
only as long as they chew fresh distractions to go with it....
Past the boards, just beyond, there, things are real.
Children are playing, lovers embracing, — away from the others,
pensive, on a few blades of grass, and dogs — do as dogs do.
The boy is drawn further on; perhaps he's in love with a young
Lament. And he follows after her over the meadows. She says:
— Far. We live away out there....
Where? And the boy
follows, touched by her walk, her shoulder, her neck —, perhaps
she's of noble descent. But he leaves her, turns round,
about once again, waves... What's the point? She's a Lament,

Only the young dead, unheeding,
untouched by time, taking slow leave of life,
follow her, loving. The girls
she waits for and offers them friendship. Shows them gently
what she is wearing. Pearls of Sorrow and the fine–woven
veils of Forbearance. — With boys she walks
in silence alongside them.

But there, where they live, in the valley, one of the older Laments
answers kindly the boy as he asks: — We were,
she says, a Mighty Nation, once, we Laments. Our fathers
dug out the mines there in the high range of mountains; men
sometimes will show you an ancient fragment of Suffering, polished,
or, out of a crater, Wrath, molten, rock-hardened.
Yes, we took it from there. Once we were rich. —

And with ease she guides him through the Laments' wide expanses,
shows him the columns of temples or the ruins of
fortresses, where the Laments' princes
once held wise sway. Shows him the tall
tear-trees and fields of Doleful in blossom
(known to the living only when it's still in first leaf);
shows him the creatures of sadness, grazing — sometimes
a bird starts, and unfolds, flying low as they gaze upwards,
the pattern of letters made by her cry in the loneness. —
At evening she leads him to the tombs of the patriarchs

aus dem Klage-Geschlecht, den Sibyllen und Warn-Herrn.
Naht aber Nacht, so wandeln sie leiser, und bald
mondets empor, das über Alles
wachende Grab-Mal. Brüderlich jenem am Nil,
der erhabene Sphinx —: der verschwiegenen Kammer
Antlitz.
Und sie staunen dem krönlichen Haupt, das für immer,
schweigend, der Menschen Gesicht
auf die Waage der Sterne gelegt.

Nicht erfaßt es sein Blick, im Frühtod
schwindelnd. Aber ihr Schaun,
hinter dem Pschent-Rand hervor, scheucht es die Eule. Und sie,
streifend im langsamen Abstrich die Wange entlang,
jene der reifesten Rundung,
zeichnet weich in das neue
Totengehör, über ein doppelt
aufgeschlagenes Blatt, den unbeschreiblichen Umriß.

Und höher, die Sterne. Neue. Die Sterne des Leidlands.
Langsam nennt sie die Klage: — Hier,
siehe: den *Reiter*, den *Stab*, und das vollere Sternbild
nennen sie: *Fruchtkranz*. Dann, weiter, dem Pol zu:
Wiege; *Weg; Das brennende Buch*; *Puppe*; *Fenster*.
Aber im südlichen Himmel, rein wie im Innern
einer gesegneten Hand, das klar erglänzende »*M*«,
das die Mütter bedeutet......—

Doch der Tote muß fort, und schweigend bringt ihn die ältere
Klage bis an die Talschlucht,
wo es schimmert im Mondschein:
die Quelle der Freude. In Ehrfurcht
nennt sie sie, sagt: — Bei den Menschen
ist sie ein tragender Strom.—

Stehn am Fuß des Gebirgs.
Und da umarmt sie ihn, weinend.

Einsam steigt er dahin, in die Berge des Ur-Leids.
Und nicht einmal sein Schritt klingt aus dem tonlosen Los.

*

Aber erweckten sie uns, die unendlich Toten, ein Gleichnis,
siehe, sie zeigten vielleicht auf die Kätzchen der leeren

of the race of Laments, the sybils and sages.
At nightfall their footstep is softer, and shortly,
bright as the moonlight, looms up
the tomb standing watch over all,
brother to that on the Nile, the lofty Sphinx:
face of the chamber hidden in silence.
And they take in with wonder the regal-crowned head, that forever,
not speaking, laid the face of man
on the scales of the stars.

His gaze cannot grasp it, so early dead,
unsteady. But their beholding,
over the top of the diadem, scares out the owl. It,
slow in its flying, barely touching the cheek,
where it rounds at its fullest,
softly it draws into the new
dead's hearing, on both halves of the paper,
folded in two, the outline that hand cannot trace.

And higher, the stars. New ones. The stars of the Land of Suffering.
The Lament names them slowly: — Here,
behold: the *Rider*, the *Staff*, and the cluster of stars
they call *Garland of Fruits.* Then further on, nearer the Pole:
Cradle; *Path*; *The Burning Book*; *Puppet; Window*.
But in the southern skies, pure like the palm of a
hand that is blessed, '*M*' burning clearly and brightly,
standing for Mothers......—

But the dead boy must depart, and in silence the older
Lament brings him as far as the gorge of the valley,
where there gleams in the moonlight
the spring of joy. In hushed tone
she names it and says: — Among men
it is a mighty river. —

They halt at the foot of the mountains.
And there she embraces him, weeping.

Alone he makes his way up into the mountains of Once-Suffering.
Not even the ring of his steps is heard, his lot is silence.

*

But were they to waken for us, the endlessly dead, a symbol,
behold, they would point to the catkins on the bare

Hasel, die hängenden, oder
meinten den Regen, der fällt auf dunkles Erdreich im Frühjahr. —

Und wir, die an *steigendes* Glück
denken, empfänden die Rührung,
die uns beinah bestürzt,
wenn ein Glückliches *fällt*.

hazel, hanging downwards, or
have us believe in the rain that falls on the dark soil in springtime.—

And we, who think of happiness
rising, our hearts would be moved
more than perhaps we could bear,
when a happy thing falls.